# ROCK AND ROLL

# DEL BROMHAM

# SURVIVOR

# ROCK AND ROLL
# DEL BROMHAM
# SURVIVOR

## WP
## WYMER
PUBLISHING
Bedford, England

First published in Great Britain in 2022
by Wymer Publishing
www.wymerpublishing.co.uk
Tel: 01234 326691
Wymer Publishing is a trading name of Wymer (UK) Ltd

**ISBN: 978-1-915246-33-2**
(also available in eBook)

Edited by Jerry Bloom

Typeset by Andy Bishop / 1016 Sarpsborg
Printed by CMP, Dorset, England.

A catalogue record for this book is available from the British Library.

Cover design: 1016 Sarpsborg
Front cover image © Lee Scriven

# Contents

# Forewords

How did it happen that in the late sixties a drab little country like Britain spawned so many of that era's fabulous guitar heroes? I mean... even Jimi Hendrix had to come to London to get famous.

But not for me the Claptons, Becks or Blackmores... no, for me it was the likes of Rory Gallagher, Tony McPhee and Del Bromham whose bands shows in Croydon I never missed. Even when skint I'd manage to find a way in... through the fire escape... via the kitchens... even "can I help you in with the gear mate" worked occasionally.

It was a magical time for rock 'n' roll with many memorable acts on the road, but it helped if all band members were pulling in the same direction — which Stray's did supremely well not only in their frenetic live shows, but also managed to capture on disc.

Strays first album is perfection from start to finish... it stayed on my turntable for a year or so... in fact until I wore the bloomin' thing out. My ears tuned into the variety of tones Del got out of his guitar which I discovered (by plonking myself right in front of the stage at their South London shows) was by gratuitous use of the volume & tone knobs... the kind of dexterity that sadly went out of fashion when punk arrived on the scene. (⌐͟ J ͟⌐) Oops...

Del also mastered the use of the wah-wah pedal like no other... you have to laugh when you see these modern guitarists with pedal boards crammed with talent boosters... Del's gear was simply wah-wah and amp, that's all he needed to get his sound... which, along with maybe a couple of 'borrowed' riffs along the way was something else those early Stray shows taught me.

*Captain Sensible*

**S**tray should have been a big band. When I say big band I mean Black Sabbath or Deep Purple big.

At the time those bands had broken out successfully I had the first four Stray albums: *Stray*, *Suicide*, *Saturday Morning Pictures* and *Mudanzas* and I thought that their songs, mostly written by Del Bromham were consistently as good as most things that were coming out from that early seventies era. *Mudanzas* broke into the UK top 30 chart and I remember being really pleased for them and thinking that this was it and that they would deservedly go on to bigger and better things too.

I had seen them many times over in the early years at venues near to me in East London, such as the Red Lion Leytonstone, The Standard in Walthamstow and the Fox in Croydon (which was alien territory and a long way for me back then with no transport!).

They were certainly an influence and Maiden even did a cover of their first album song 'All In Your Mind' as a B–side. Also, my daughter Lauren did a cover of 'Come On Over' from *Mudanzas* on her album which I played on, as I used to play rock stuff in the car driving my kids to school!

I got to know Del as a friend a few years later and asked Stray to support Maiden on a European tour where they went down great with our fans.

I'm still friends with him to this day, he is a vibrant character with a great sense of humour. He still has the same enthusiasm and energy for recording and playing live as ever, he has never given up, which is a great credit to him as he's been through some tough times over the years and that just shows his dedication and genuine love of what he does. I now look forward to reading his own account of his long and eventful career just as much as you do!

*Steve Harris – Iron Maiden*
*Croatia May 2022.*

# Preface

Growing old was something I had never thought much about. I suppose that it is because I have always been busy getting on with life and planning the next thing I was going to do. However, when the Covid-19 pandemic hit and began to change our world in March 2020, it gave me time to sit and reflect on my life, past and present.

I think the initial realisation of getting older came to me around my 64th birthday. I remember looking back to when I was about 15 years of age and had The Beatles' *Sgt Pepper's Lonely Hearts Club Band* album. The song 'When I'm Sixty-Four', seemed for me to be light years away and although I'm sure I would have imagined what life would be like when I was 64, I never realised it would come around so quickly.

From time to time people have suggested that I write a book, but I have always hesitated because I didn't think people would be that interested.

Just before my recent birthday I was telling my good lady Annie a story and when I 'd finished she said, "I didn't know that? I'd not heard that one before?" She said, "You should definitely write a book". To which I replied, "No I don't think anyone would be interested". "You might not think that no-one would be interested, but your grandchildren would probably love to hear what their grandad got up to" came Annie's firm reply.

That changed my mind about writing this. I have been telling some of my stories in my live shows and people often say to me, "You should write a book". I don't wish to be morbid but part of the realisation of growing old is that we are not immortal, so I thought I'd better get a move on before the sands of time on the old egg timer run out!

I have some stories that I have been reluctant to share as some might feel they are works of fiction, but what I am about to write, to the best of my memory, really happened.

In life you do not get a rehearsal, so there is no point in looking back wondering what might have been. We make our choices, we take a turning in the road and follow it.

This is my story, predominately about my musical career. It is not in strict chronological order as I often relay specific events rather than an accurate timeline. I appreciate I might shatter the illusions that some have about what it is like playing in a rock band. However, I don't think my life has been a lot different to a lot of other musicians around, but you only really hear about the glamorous side of things.

I can't deny that for most of my life it has been a battle and hasn't turned out exactly as I expected.

Given the chance of would I do it all again? The answer is, yes and knowing me I

would probably make the same mistakes all over again.
Accept what you have and make the best of it.
"Life's alright, it's only what you make it".
(A line from a song of the same title from the first Stray album)

# 1.
# The Early Years

I was born, coming up to lunchtime, on the 25th November 1951, in my mum and dad's bedroom at number 56, Hilary Road, East Acton, West London. The reason I mention lunchtime, is because you could set your clock by the times my mum served up dinner and tea. About 12:30pm for dinner (lunchtime) and 6pm for teatime.

I was my mum's fourth child, the last of four boys. Mum always said that there was nothing to giving birth. It's just like "shucking peas" she used to say. Apparently, she gave birth to me and then got up and made my dad's dinner.

I think my birth was something of a mistake. My mum was coming up to forty years of age and my dad was forty-one. My next youngest brother was Allan who was about twelve years old when I was born. Then there was Raymond and eldest brother Norman.

It was Norman who apparently suggested my name to mum because if I was going to be a girl my name would be Christine and if I was a boy it was to be Christopher. Norman had just returned from doing National Service in the army and you can imagine his surprise when he came home to find his middle-aged mum pregnant!

Anyway when I was actually born, Norman asked what my name was going to be? He said, "No, don't call him Christopher. I went to the Shepherd's Bush Empire last night and saw a funny comedian called Derek Roy. Why don't you call him that? So that ladies and gentlemen is how I got my name. Named after a comedian. I suppose it could have been worse. He could have gone to see Max Wall, George Formby or Issy Bonn, all variety stars of that that era.

There was always music being played in the house. My dad belonged to a record club and used to have deliveries of a couple of EPs every few weeks. I don't know why he ordered these artists as they were pretty random. For example, he might have ordered Robin Richmond at the Blackpool Tower organ along with Perry Como (*We Get Letters*, which I still have) and a soundtrack from a musical. Then of course I had three brothers, Allan, Ray and Norman who were listening to Rock 'n' Roll and Skiffle, which was becoming the music of the youth of that time.

Dad always had the best Radiograms, something he was always proud of. He'd tell you the mark of a good Radiogram is if you can pick up the police on VHF! We could listen to the police attending a robbery in Shepherd's Bush for example, or an ambulance on the way to somewhere or other?

Before I'd started infant school I think I could read pretty well and that was due initially from being able to recognise the names and titles on our big record collection. These were the days when council houses used to have their own painters and decorators in to decorate the houses and I recall my mum asking the painters to ask me to pick a record out and how impressed they were when I could pick out 'The Deadwood Stage'/'Secret Love' by Doris Day, 'In A Persian Market' by Sammy Davis, 'Charmaine' by Mantovani and his orchestra, or one of my favourites 'Zambesi' by the Lou Bush Orchestra. I think they were impressed.

Apparently before I could speak, one of the first noises that came out of my mouth was my word for records which was 'Ooh baba tars'. I think it must have been something to do with the sounds of the records, crossed with the word guitars, who knows? I recognised the labels on the records. Yellow MGM, Blue Philips, Pink Pye. However, the label I was most impressed with was a picture label depicting the vocal harmony group 'The Inkspots', but funnily enough I can't remember what record label it was on? Possibly RCA Victor label but it was the photograph of the band that fascinated me. Oh, and I believe the song was called 'I'll Never Smile Again'.

Mum never got my hair cut until I went to school and I had very blond, almost white curly hair. People used to stop her in the street and comment what lovely hair her daughter had!

I was supposed to start school in September, but my mum forgot to take me (she really did) and in those days you had what was called 'The School Board Man'. He knocked on our door one day and told my mum that I should be at school. I don't recall the visit but I'm sure he wouldn't have got away with telling her what to do without at least a comment of "mind your own business". Nevertheless I did start school, even though it was a few weeks late! I'm sure she never purposely kept me off school, she just never got around to taking me!

Later on, if I was playing up saying that I didn't want to go to school that day, mum would threaten me that 'The School Board Man' would be around to get me. I wonder if the musical character 'The Child Catcher' was based on him?

Believe it or not, I remember my first day at school and mum dragging me... Yes dragging me screaming! Because I was quite happy at home and didn't want to go. Fear of the unknown I suppose because I'd never been with children of my own age for my first five years.

I remember the small bottle of milk and a small cod liver oil tablet all the children got at that time. I didn't know what a cod liver oil tablet was. I thought it was a sweet, it looked like a small jelly, so I bit it. Yugh! I didn't do that again.

Actually infant school wasn't too bad. My first teacher was a lovely lady Mrs Calshaw. In retrospect she reminded me of the comedy actress Joyce Grenfell. I also had a Mrs Readman, who used to like reading us poetry, some of which I can still remember to this day and also a Mrs Lumsden who was a bit scarier than the other two.

Here's a verse from a poem that Miss Readman used to read us. Funny how I've never forgotten it.

New shoes, blue shoes
Red and pink and blue shoes.
Stomp along like that shoes.
They're the shoes to buy.

And here's another:

Moses supposes his tosies are rosies
But Moses supposes erroneously
For nobody's tosies are posies of rosies
Like Moses supposes his tosies to be.

Junior school was good and in retrospect possibly carved out a path for me. This was Old Oak Primary School, right opposite Wormwood Scrubs Prison. If you played out on the Scrubs playing fields, the prisoners would often call out of their cell windows to you.

Anyway back to school and my teacher throughout Junior school was Miss Maple. What a lovely lady and I so wish I had kept in touch with her. She was like Julie Andrews, in fact I remember when the *Sound of Music* was released she sang and played some of the songs on the piano. She played piano every morning for school assembly, and I suppose it was the first time I had heard a piano played live. It's now in later life I realise what an influence Miss Maple had on me. Not only with music, but she also read us stories and got me interested in books and the written word. These days I get so frustrated when I see the use of a wrong word or incorrect punctuation (okay, so you start correcting my text, I know) or slang and American words cropping up in the English language.

I discovered I had a knack for humour and loved making people laugh. One kid at school whose name was Stephen Jowers was a real foil for my humour and was often told off by Miss Maple because I made him laugh so much in class. Miss Maple used to like putting on shows and I remember taking part in a couple of them. My first performance was due to be in the school nativity where I was a shepherd about to give the baby Jesus a gift with the line, "I have an orange", but I was off sick the day of the performance. I was very upset and envious of my friend Frankie Hackett who spoke my lines, but more about Frankie in a later chapter. Another time I was in "A frog he would a wooing go" and my mum and nan made me a great little outfit. I looked more like a Cavalier than a frog. I played in that outfit for ages after that performance, usually imagining I was D'Artagnan from The Three Musketeers.

One performance was with my school friend David Keighley and we sang the Bernard Cribbins song 'Hole In The Ground'. Another song I performed was with a very tall girl called Louise Wroxsley. We sang 'There's A Hole In The Bucket' recorded by Harry Belafonte and Odetta. I remember that one went very well although I don't know how Louise and I got paired up. I suppose it was because we were in the same class. Maybe that was Miss Maple's intuition, I will never know? I was quite small in comparison with other kids of my age and Louise was very tall. I would have had to stand on a chair to give her kiss, but in those days, boys didn't kiss girls unless you got involved in 'kiss chase' in the playground!

On the subject of girls, I had my first taste of being accused of something I didn't do when I was about ten years old. A new girl arrived in class and sat at the desk next to mine but in the opposite aisle. Her name was Delores Hall and I thought she was beautiful. If this was a film she would probably arrive on the set in slow motion through a hazy lens, you know the kind of thing?

I don't know if it was jealousy or because I was popular or someone being downright nasty, but I was pulled out of the classroom and was told that I had been saying that Delores smelled of wee! I know that might sound funny now, but to two 10-year-olds, especially a new girl in a new school, the accusation was cruel and heartless. I was mortified and even now I still think about it occasionally. Fortunately, our teacher and more importantly Delores believed I was innocent and remained friends until I left the following year for Secondary School. I often wonder how life turned out for her?

# 2.
# Family

I think that's enough about me for the moment. I 'd like to tell you about my mum and dad which I suppose is relevant because without them, I certainly wouldn't be here.

Mum was born Clara Lillian Jewell, London, 4th February 1912. Dad John was born in Somerset, 9th December 1911. Dad moved to London when he was a small child and met my mum when she was 17 years old and he was 18. I believe at that time he was working in a green grocers' shop in Shepherd's Bush and mum was working in the Walls factory in Acton. I don't know where or how they met. They got married a couple of years later and were married for over seventy years!

Funny thing was that all through her life, mum would never buy any product made by Walls, you know, bacon or sausages for example, because she used to say she saw how they were made!

I am currently researching my family tree and dad's side of the family is intriguing. I still haven't got to the bottom of it all as there are so many names to research. The story I am sure, once completely researched would be a great television costume drama similar to *Downtown Abbey*.

I never met my grandad — dad's dad as he died soon after I was born. At the turn of the century, he met and married Edith Fry (my grandmother) one of the daughters from the wealthy Fry family in Curry Rival, Somerset. Grandmother died soon after giving birth to dad. He was the youngest of about nine children that I am aware of. Grandad decided to move back to London and soon after met another lady, who according to dad, was a wicked woman and used to hit him with a leather belt. Like a lot of things, dad never spoke much about his early life or his time in the army during World War 2, but I'll come to that.

Apparently the Fry family heard that grandad continued to see this woman (whose name I never knew) and warned him if he continued to see her, they would cut him and the rest of his family off from the family fortune. Quite clearly grandad was stubborn, a characteristic that dad had inherited and he continued seeing the lady. Consequently as warned, the Fry family severed any connection with him. However, it transpired when the children (dad and his siblings) reached a certain age, twenty-one I think? They all received some form of inheritance.

My other grandad — mum's dad went off to serve in the First World War. While on active service he was injured and suffered severe shell shock, but unlike many others he was sent home to the UK and spent the rest of his life, until his death in 1968, in St Bernard's Mental Hospital, Southall Middlesex.

Around 2008/2009 I was doing some research on soldiers who were injured in battle and was shocked to find how many suffered shell shock like my grandad but were executed having being charged with cowardice. I wrote a song which featured on the Stray 2009 album *Valhalla* titled 'Harry Farr'. The story of a soldier. Like my grandad he was clearly suffering from shell shock and was executed at dawn.

Mum's mum consequently found herself alone with four children. She never remarried and throughout her life lived with mum and eventually with mum, dad and me until she died at the age of ninety-eight in 1984.

Nan's eyesight was never very good. She had a lazy eye and you weren't sure whether she was looking at you or not. She always did what she called 'her jobs' around the house. She always reported to mum, what she had done. Although mum's name was Clara, everyone called her Cis. I think her brothers used to call her that when she was a child so it stuck. Anyway, when nan had done 'her jobs' she would call out "I've done the dusting" or "I've done the veg".

She liked her sweets but wasn't too keen on sharing them. She would sit in her chair with a bag of sweets tucked down the side of the chair beside her. Then while sitting there, she would slide her hand down the side of the chair pick one out of the bag and pop it in her mouth. If dad saw her do it, he'd make a point of letting her know that we saw what she had just done.

She was also partial to Rennies and Victory V lozenges. She did have the habit of falling asleep while sucking one and then her mouth opened and her tongue would pop out revealing the lozenge. All very amusing.

Mum had a sister, my Aunt May. She was mum's younger sister and she became like a second mum to me. She and my Uncle Ted had no children. They had a daughter who passed away a couple of months after birth. This would have been around the same time that I was born, so I think May in particular was fond of me for that reason.

May used to come and visit every other Thursday afternoon after she had finished work. Even when she retired she still used to come and see us on the same days. She also came around about one Sunday in four where she used to take nan to see grandad at the mental hospital. They used to take him tins of colouring pencils and paper. Sometimes nan would come home with childlike drawings he had done for her. All very sad actually. As time went on May seemed to become closer to mum.

May was good at knitting and quite often made my mum little knitted waistcoats or cardigans. She would buy mum skirts and blouses, coincidentally the same as hers and in time they would be dressed almost the same. Mum and May would sit on the settee, neither of whom were the biggest conversationalists unless they were talking about someone, which could be quite amusing as they would do that thing where one would talk while the other kind of mouthed what the other was saying. Then invariably end the last word of the sentence together, arms folded and quickly looking away to see if anyone was listening. If you have ever seen the comedians Les Dawson and Roy Barraclough with their characters portraying Cissy and Ada, then you'll get the idea. We used to call them 'the bookends' the way they sat at opposite ends of the settee.

Mum never appeared to have many friends outside of the family. In her own words she liked to "keep herself to herself". She was very direct and I'm sure she could quite easily offend. I'm sure she didn't always appreciate how her comments were received. Having said that, she had a great sense of humour, something that I am sure my brothers and I all inherited. When she really laughed, it was a sight to behold. She would shake, but little sound would come out. Maybe what I can only describe as a donkey eeeaaw sound while at the same times her eyes crossed a little. I called her Ben Turpin. He was the cross-eyed silent movie star for you younger readers!

Dad could be equally verbally abrasive without, I am sure, realising how much he could offend somebody. In his words "I call a spade a spade". This form of straight talking did appear to be the way that people of their generation conversed. I suppose their lives were so much different back then it must have influenced their views of life and relationships.

The second world war began in 1939 and I believe he was called up to do his duty the following year. He was in the First Army attached to The Eighth Army under General Montgomery, or Monty as he called him, just like he was his best mate!

He never spoke much about his time in the army. I so wish that I had talked more to him before his death at the age of ninety-three in 2003. He told me a couple of stories. I suppose the most important story he told was that he was with a team of fellas working the Anti-Aircraft Guns (or the Ak-Ak guns as he called them). Now I don't know what he did, but one day he said that he'd been a 'naughty boy' and was taken off of the gun crew, and as he put it, "Put on spud bashing". So apparently, while he was in the NAAFI peeling potatoes, the gun he was supposed to be operating, backfired and killed all the crew!

Just a thought reader. Had he been a 'good boy' he would have been on the crew, been killed like the rest of the crew and I wouldn't be here to write about it. Funny how things happen in life which can change the lives of others. As I've got older this is something I have thought about a lot recently. Getting up day to day, deciding which direction to take in life.

Dad never went back on the big guns; he stayed working preparing food for the troops. Funnily enough, after he died, I was clearing the house and I found some army paperwork with some instructions and directions to set up camp somewhere in Italy.

Speaking of Italy, he was at the famous Battle of Monte Casino. The way he always described it, he made it sound like it was a walk in the park. As a child I always pictured dad, the war hero, brandishing a machine gun, kicking doors in and as he put it "Chasing old Gerry out". I still have some of his spoils of war. A couple of German medals and a pair of binoculars, apparently left behind after "Gerry did a runner". Oh yes, he also had a pair of very long scissors which apparently came from the German hospital. He used them when he was decorating to cut the wallpaper. If only old Gerry knew? Imagine, one day Hans was probably cutting bandages at Monte Casino with them and a few years later old John Bromham was hanging wallpaper with them in East Acton. Certainly is a funny old world innit?

It wasn't until some years later when I read a book about the Battle of Monte Casino, what horrendous conditions he must have experienced. I believe it was the worst weather on record for Italy and the whole operation took about six months to complete.

When war finished and he came back home in 1945, things were very different for him. Mum, nan and my three brothers had been bombed out twice and were now living in the house in Hilary Road. My brother Allan was so young when dad went off to war that he didn't recall him. Apparently one day he turned around and said, "You can't tell me what to do. Only my mum can tell me what to do".

Back in 'Civvy Street' He returned to working at Howell Brothers, Grocer's Shop, Shepherd Bush until the late sixties when I think it was my brother Norman who persuaded him to work where he was working — at CAV Acton. More money and less responsibility. He said he wished he'd done it years before.

A couple of years before he died, I went to visit him and asked him if he had seen the television programme on a couple of nights before about "The Goons" the legendary comedians.

He said he had not watched it. I said to him that they talked about renting a room above a greengrocer's shop in Shepherd's Bush where they worked on their scripts for *The Goon Shows*.

"Oh yeh" he said nonchalantly "They sometimes used to pop down and I'd give them a couple of apples a couple of bananas or a couple of pears."

"What? You never told me that!" I said.

There were legends like Spike Milligan, Harry Secombe and Peter Sellers above my dad's shop and he never mentioned it! It was like me having John, Paul, George and Ringo in my mum and dad's little room rehearsing.

I remember when I was growing up, sometimes in the evening he would jump up off of his armchair and ask if anyone fancied any chips? He made the best chips, peeled potatoes and fry them in an old chip pan. Something else he did was, particularly on Sundays when mum made the dinner, he would go out to the kitchen and peel the potatoes and prepare the vegetables. He'd always report back to mum to tell her, "I've done the spuds and put salt in the water". This is something I do these days and find as I'm getting older I am getting like my dad.

Maybe it's a generation 'thing? The comedian, Micky Flanagan said that his dad used to report to his mum what he'd just done. For example, "I've shut the cupboard door for you". Dad did that and I have to confess, so do I. I am my dad's son, that's for sure.

Both mum and dad often got their words wrong or mixed up. I mentioned before that he loved his radiograms. One I remember in particular was a Blaupunkt Stereo Radiogram. Blaupunkt was a well-known German company, quite ironic knowing what dad said about the Germans, having been at war with them for 5 years. As he considered himself to be multi-lingual, he referred to the radiogram as a 'Blue Spot', rather than a Blaupunkt, a British name and translation you see.

He often got advice from a chap he knew who was an electrical repair man with the coincidental name of Mr Coil — probably spelt Coyle. But it had an electrical connection so to speak, I thought the radiogram was wonderful. To me it looked massive and reminded me of either a Hammond or a Lowrey Organ. It was a beautiful piece of furniture. It had two sliding doors at the front at the top. Slide one to the left and it revealed the radio in all its technicolour glory, with a row of press buttons where you could select, MW, SW, LW and the latest FM to hear all the sounds in stereo. Slide the door the other way and you could actually pull out the turntable to play the records, it had to be a Garrard turntable of course. Below, double doors revealed a gold silk quilted cocktail cabinet with lights and mirrors. If that wasn't enough he bought a matching separate speaker to put on the other side of the room, to get the full effect. He played everything loud, that's another thing I've probably inherited from dad.

Some years later, when I had my own home, I went to visit him and by this time he had yet another up to date stereo radiogram. This one was made by Decca and it had a Perspex or glass lid. In fact it looked like disco equipment. He'd had this one a little while, so when I went to visit him one day, he said very proudly, "Come in the front room and see what I've done with my stereo". He put on a record and turned up the volume and in a loud voice said, "What do you think of that then son?". "Yes" I said. "It sounds good. What have you done to it then?"

"Well" he said. "I went out and bought a new diamond syphilis".

Well I nearly choked myself laughing, but I knew what he meant.

Mum was as bad. One time I remember, we were sitting discussing the merits of comedians, comic duos to be precise. She said that she didn't care much for that "Mark and Bernie Windows (Mike and Bernie Winters), I like, oh what's their name... you know the short one with the hairy legs and the tall one who wears those horn rimmed testicles". She meant Morecombe and Wise of course.

Mum and dad were not particularly strict with me but in their own way they did teach me right from wrong and to be polite and have manners, the latter which I feel is sadly lacking in today's society. It seems like a lot of people are selfish and just out for themselves.

I think, being a bit 'old school', dad pretty much left bringing up children as a woman's job and left that down to mum. I never actually thought I was a child who misbehaved very often but that doesn't mean to say that every once in a while I wouldn't get a good slap 'round the back of the legs from mum. She'd grab me by the arm and give me several slaps, all in time with each word she said. I'm sure that's what helped give me a good sense of rhythm! Speaking of which when I was in school, maths was never a thing I was particularly good at, but for some reason I could recite all the times tables. In junior school we were given cards which had the times tables on and it's only in recent years that I think I learned all the maths because I'd recite them in beat. You know like, once two is two, two twos are four, three twos are six and so on.

Dad never once hit me, but he did have something about him that I thought, I didn't want to take a chance getting a slap from him. I think this was further ingrained in my mind at the times mum would threaten, "You wait 'til your father comes home". That worked because I'd listen for his key to come in the front door and try and prepare myself what was about to unfold. Of course nothing ever happened but sometimes the power of words can be a warning or a message not to be ignored.

One time myself and a couple of other boys were hauled up before the headmaster at Christopher Wren School. I think it was a Mr Hooton. I remember waiting outside his office waiting to get a couple of strokes of the cane, made even worse when the kid in front of you leaves his office in tears clutching his sore hand!

When it was my turn he gave me a couple of strokes on my right hand. It bloody hurt, but I was determined I was not going to cry because what was more upsetting was the fact that I was innocent of whatever it was I was supposed to have done. Even today I cannot remember what I was accused of or who the other boys were? I remember thinking to myself that when I get home I'm going to tell mum and dad and they are going to go up to the school and sort them out. No such luck. Mum seemed to take it all as a matter of fact, just an everyday occurrence in school. I thought, okay, so dad will go and sort it out. No luck there either. I can't remember his exact words but he was telling me that it was a lesson in life and you'll probably have far worse things happen to you and "Keep your head down". I suppose that's something he might have learned being in the army with those German bullets flying over his head!

They taught me to fend for myself. From an early age, if I used to get any pocket money or birthday present money, I would put it in a Post Office savings account that they opened up for me when I was very young, 10 or 11 years old maybe? I remember with little bits of money, like if someone gave me sixpence or a shilling you could go to the Post Office and buy stamps for the equivalent and stick them in a little book. When I was a little older and started to earn money from playing in a band, dad got me to open a Trustee Bank savings account. This served me well and probably saved them money as I was able to buy records, guitars amplifiers and music related stuff while I was still at school.

By the time I was twenty years old I put a healthy deposit down and bought my first property in London. Not bad for a youngster.

Mum and Dad always took me on holiday every year. The last week in July and the first week in August. We'd get up on the Saturday morning of our holiday, have a bath and put on our best clothes and go to Shepherd's Bush Green where we would wait outside the Odeon Cinema where the coach would pick us up. He always insisted on travelling with Valiant coaches. According to dad this was the best company to go with, painted Grey and Red with nice clean upholstery. For some reason he disliked Garners Coaches which were like a brown and mustard colour. He just thought they were inferior to Valiant Coaches.

We had good holidays to places like Great Yarmouth, Bournemouth, and Clacton. The weather always seemed to be pretty good as I remember. One of the highlights of the holiday was to go to see a show or normally two shows if there was one on the pier and one in a theatre.

As a small child I remember seeing Adam Faith and Emile Ford. George Formby, who we loved as we had his records at home. Ken Dodd, who was hilarious and picked out my dad in the front row because dad was laughing so much I thought he might explode! Eric Delaney playing lots of different drums. We had his hit record called 'Oranges and Lemons'. There was a harmonica player whose name I think was Ronald Chesney and he gave the kids in the audience a tiny harmonica each at the end of his act. It must have cost him loads of money! He probably wouldn't be allowed to give them out these days due to 'Health and Safety regulations'. I bet there were kids who swallowed those little harmonicas. I now have a mental picture of a kid who had swallowed one, letting out a fart and blowing a tune on the harmonica. We saw so many acts it's hard to remember them all.

A couple of hotels we stayed at had the dinner gong which was sounded when dinner was served. We stayed at one particular hotel in Great Yarmouth a couple of times and the landlady let me bang the gong. For a minute or two I was the muscle man who used to bang the gong at the start of films made by *Top Rank Pictures*.

Bournemouth was another place we stayed at a couple of times, at a beautiful big hotel called Bodorgan Firs. It seemed to be surrounded by pine or conifer trees and the grounds had a great aroma of pine. The smell of pine makes me think of Bournemouth and that hotel.

One story I recall goes back to 1958. Dad was a very good darts player. He belonged to The Acton Vale Working Men's Club, in the Acton Vale, Shepherd's Bush. He was that good, as a kid I remember when he practised at home, he'd say to me, "Go on boy, shout out a number" and once I'd given him a number he would throw a dart and hit the number on the board. My dad's a genius I thought.

This particular year he ended up being in the final of the *News Of The World* darts competition held at The Grosvenor Hotel, Park Lane, London. He was runner up and his prize was £10 and a family holiday to Cliftonville. These days the prize money for something like that would be a small fortune.

I remember the weather in Cliftonville that year being awful. Wind and rain. Well it seemed like there was no sun that holiday. They always used to let me choose a toy as a special treat when on holiday. This year I chose a parachute. You ran along the road with it and it opened up. In my mind I was just like one of those soldiers in the war films. One day we were walking along near the seafront running with the parachute along behind me. In my mind I was about to parachute into enemy lines. Well, that's what nearly happened! A huge gust of wind got up and lifted me up in the air. I can remember mum hanging on to me so that I wouldn't fly out to sea or somewhere. After that I put the parachute away and didn't get it out again until I could play with it safely in my back garden.

Despite the bad weather during that holiday in Cliftonville, generally the weather on our holidays was always pretty good. The sun always seemed to be shining so we often went down to the beach. Mum and dad had a deck chair each and I would sit on the sand digging holes and building castles. Mum and dad would sit in the sun in their deck chairs and as old photos will show you, mum usually stayed fully dressed even keeping her stockings on! Dad would just remove his tie and jacket and if he was really daring, he might remove his shoes and socks to have a paddle in the sea with me.

He had bad feet which he said was the result of wearing army boots for all those years during the war and didn't like showing them off in public. However, he did like putting his feet up on mum's lap so that she could tickle them! Mum used to buy me swimming trunks and they were sort of woollen. I had a blue pair and a red pair with white piping down the side. The problem with these trunks were that the water didn't filter out of them very quickly and consequently the weight of the water around the crotch area made it look like I either had large testicles or had shit myself! I've spoken to others of my generation and these swimming trunks were obviously very popular at the time.

Speaking of the sea, another time we were on holiday somewhere and I know I was very small, about six years old maybe? I remember it vividly, walking along from the beach and climbing on to a sloping wall which would have gone from the promenade down to the sea avoiding the beach.

I climbed along like I was about to go mountaineering when I slipped on the wet cobbles which the sloping wall was made of and slid into the sea. I couldn't swim and I remember going under the water several times. I couldn't touch the bottom; I would have drowned had it not been for two young guys who must have seen me and jumped in and pulled me out. Mum and dad couldn't swim. I never knew who the two fellas were but they clearly saved my life.

Following that I was scared of water. When we had swimming lessons at school, I would do everything I could do to get out of going. I'd get my mum to write a note saying I had a cold, or anything to get out of the lesson. The good thing was because all the other kids had gone swimming I used to sit in the school library reading books which fuelled my desire for story telling in one form or another. In my case song writing as I was to discover in years to come.

Many years later, not until the 1980s when I had my two small daughters, like dad, I took them on their first holiday to Spain where they played in the pool all day. I felt so useless because I couldn't swim and join in the fun or even help them if they got into trouble in the water like I had done at a similar age.

When we got home I vowed I would do something about it. So every Tuesday after they had finished school I would take them to the local swimming baths and within a couple of weeks of taking them I'd lost my fear of the water and after all those years, I could swim. One of the best things ever and every year we had holidays with fun in the pool and the sea.

One day I was playing in the back garden. One of my favourite things, was to pretend I was a cowboy running across the roofs and jumping down firing my guns at bad guys or Indians. We had a tall shed (which Ray built) and next to that was a small coal bunker. I would climb onto the bunker then up onto the roof of the shed and open fire. Sometimes I would purposely jump off of the shed and other times I would pretend to fall as if I had been hit! It was quite high up for a short arse like me, but what would a western hero know about fear? One day, and even as a child I thought this was hilarious, mum saw me on the shed roof and banged loudly on the kitchen window (I am not making this up) and shouted, "If you fall and break your leg, don't come running to me". Yes, I remember that and I really am not making it up.

In the summer of 1963 an unexpected holiday happened. Somehow my brother and sister-in-law, Allan and Pat, persuaded mum and dad that we should all go to Spain for our holiday. Dad never liked the thought of flying but we did go and we went by train. This was exciting because nobody I knew back then had ever been out of the UK for a holiday.

We travelled on a train most of the way and we were given carriages with bunk beds in. I had a top bunk and I spent most of the night looking out of the window watching the landscape of France and Spain flash by.

We had two weeks in Tossa De Mar on the Costa Brava. We stayed in a small hotel right in the centre of Tossa De Mar called The Bar Carabella, close to an old church which reminded me of The Alamo.

I loved all those big production, full colour action films like *The Alamo* and we were told that some of the big battle scenes from the film *El Cid* were filmed on the beach along by the big castle along the coast. Whether that was true or not, it didn't matter because this eleven-year-old spent the next two weeks pretending he was Charlton Heston re-enacting some of those battle scenes on the beach. Just a little note here, if you watch *El Cid*, I think there is a scene where if you look closely, a car drives along in the distance on the promenade while there is a battle going on, on the beach.

In the evening and we spent most nights in the hotel bar. We got on well with the family who owned it and as usual dad (being multi-lingual... not) really believed he was having conversations in Spanish with them. Despite the fact they would talk to him in English.

He always told me having served in Italy during the war he could now speak Italian. A perfect example was how he used to say his name, John Edward Bromham, became Giovanni Edwardo Bromhamo. As far as he was concerned that was the same in Spanish. The food was very Spanish as this was really before tourism abroad became popular and they had hadn't cottoned on to English food. You might find chicken and chips if you were lucky. These were the times where some of the ingredients didn't always agree with an English stomach and there was no drinking the water for fear of getting the tummy bug! Consequently, the toilets were getting plenty of use.

There was music in the bar and a popular record in Spain at the time was 'Quando Calienta El Sol' by Hermanos Riguel. Dad bought the single in the record shop and I still have it, as after dad passed away I kept most of his record collection.

The last holiday I had with mum and dad was in 1968 on the Isle of Wight and we stayed at The Spencer Inn in Ryde. I was sixteen years old and like a typical teenager I had other things on my mind and probably no longer found it as interesting trying to be Charlton Heston, Errol Flynn or any other swashbuckler on the beaches or surrounding areas.

There was not a lot happening in the evenings in Ryde, probably more noticeable as the previous years we had been in holiday resorts where there was entertainment literally 'on tap'. High in the pop charts at that time was a record called 'Fire' by The Crazy World of Arthur Brown. I had read that Arthur had a great stage act and I'd seen him on *Top of The Pops* singing his hit with a flaming headdress! I must have seen a poster advertising Arthur Brown playing at The Hotel Ryde Castle. I checked with mum and dad if I could go, saying of course that they could come with me as an incentive, but they declined my offer. I wasn't surprised, because I knew they would say no anyway. I thought it would be good leverage to feel sorry for me and let me go on my own. Going on my own was something of a dilemma as I had not been to what you would call a proper club gig before! Would

I get in if there were any tickets left? Would they let me in? I was only sixteen years old after all and I thought that I looked it. I nervously walked down to The Ryde Castle and approached the door where a big doorman waved me in where I bought my ticket and I was in. No problem at all. I got there early just in case there was a lot of people trying to get in and I didn't want to miss a thing.

Just a note here, it's not beyond the realms of possibility that the fella on the door may well have been my future manager Wilf Pine? He helped run the gigs there and apparently could be found on the door doing 'security'. He would have been the right man for the job that's for sure.

Remember I was still quite small, but I managed to find a good vantage spot not far from the stage and I was determined not to move from that spot for the duration of the evening. I'm not sure my bladder could hold out that long these days. I didn't even move to go to the bar to get a drink, firstly because I didn't want to lose my place and secondly I didn't know if they would serve me even though it would have only been a coke. What did I know? This was my first gig and although I knew what to do on the stage, I realised I knew very little off of the stage!

There was the support band on first who I am sure were called The Halcyon Order. My old school friend Leslie Clarke now lived on the Isle of Wight and he told me that they were a well-known band on the island. As I recall they were quite good and probably played for about forty-five minutes.

It was quite a small stage and the first bands gear was cleared to make way for "Ladies and Gentleman, will you put your hands together for The Crazy World of Arthur Brown. He was crazy alright. He didn't stop moving around the stage from the moment he started until the moment he finished, which of course finished with the hit record 'Fire' complete with the flaming headdress. I was fascinated by his band or the apparent lack of it. Don't get me wrong they sounded great but there were only two of them. Just one guy on drums and another on keys, organ to be precise. Originally he had two now famous names playing drums and organ i.e. Carl Palmer and Vincent Crane but they both had left the band before the Isle of Wight show. It was a great night and I felt a real sense of achievement that I had gone there on my own.

Dad thought of himself as a bit of a 'handy man' and tried to put his hand to anything, although a craftsman he was not! One year, mum and dad decided they were not going to have a holiday. I don't know why as they had never missed a year. I think dad said he was finding it a bit tiring and they were both in their seventies by this time. It may have also been due to the fact that around this time he had discovered the credit card and found that his local bookmaker accepted them.

Dad had always dealt with cash and he fell into that trap that because he didn't see the cash it didn't count... until he got the bill in of course. He did like to put a bet on, but unfortunately it transpired that over the years he gave a lot of money to sick animals, horses in particular!

Anyway, back to the story, my brother Norman had a lovely bungalow across the way from a park in Acton and as he was going away on holiday, he asked mum and dad if they would like to stay there while he was away as he thought it would be a change of scenery for them. They accepted his offer and moved in for a fortnight. Dad became a 'Handy Man' when he got bored. Norman and Audrey had a little front gate with a rock lined border stretching around the side of the bungalow to the garden. The rocks as you know are not cheap to buy. Dad must have had a look around Normans large shed and found a tin of white paint and proceeded to paint every rock white!

When Norman and Audrey arrived back home, they opened the gate and were greeted with a scene which Norman said looked like his garden had been transformed into the M1 motorway with all these white lines. "Looks nice doesn't it?" said dad.

It must have been around the same time I had moved from London to Bletchley in Buckinghamshire. Mum and Dad came to visit. He was getting restless and was staring out of the patio glass doors and decided that my plants needed watering. I had not got around to having an outside water tap and hosepipe fitted at that time, so dad grabbed a bucket and filled it with water. He had walked to the patio door and slid the door open to make it easier for him to walk out with the heavy bucket. Mum was sitting the other side close to the door, arms folded as usual, but she decided to shut the door. Consequently, when Dad returned to go out of the door into the garden, he walked head first into the closed door emptying most of the water down his trousers. "What did you shut the door for?"

"Well, she said, there was a bloody draught!"

Another time when he came to Bletchley, some of my mates used to meet for a pint in the local pub called The Dolphin on a Sunday lunchtime, so I took him there for a pint and to introduce him to the lads. Typically, Dad started chatting to all the lads like he'd known them for years. After a couple of pints, I looked around and he wasn't next to me? I looked over and there he was, sitting on one these sort of half circle settees which the pub had in the Saloon bar.

He was right in the middle of four of my mates probably telling them all of his stories. These were the days when you could smoke inside pubs and the guys were smoking roll ups. Except it wasn't just tobacco in the roll ups, these were small 'joints' and he was surrounded in the aroma if you know what I mean? Well, he was flying by the time we walked home and something had clearly given him an appetite because he devoured the roast dinner with no problem at all and slept the rest of the afternoon.

He told me later that we must go to that pub again because they serve a lovely pint of beer. Little did he know! I wonder if a little additive might be a good suggestion to add to the beer brewed by Charles Wells? Funny thing was, a couple of my mates were asking if dad was coming up again to visit?

Another time, I made the mistake of telling him that at some point I wanted to cut a couple of branches off of a tree that was in the back garden. I must have only left him for a short while, when from the kitchen window I could see that he had climbed the tree, but was standing on the tree branch that he was starting to saw! Just like a character in one of those Looney Tunes cartoons. "What are you doing, come down off of there". I got him down but he couldn't understand what all the fuss was about?

He never liked throwing things away either. One time the local council was doing some work in the road outside mum and dad's house. The workers had just about finished when apparently, he had pointed at some wood and paving slabs and asked if they needed them to which they must have replied, "No you can have them".

Now consider he was in his seventies, he manhandled these big paving slabs into his garden and paved out an area. It transpired he'd given himself a hernia in the process. As for the planks of wood. On his last visit to my new house which I had moved into from Bletchley to Furzton. The previous owners had replaced the skirting boards in the house with tall wooden skirting boards. Dad liked them, but his council house had small skirting made of plaster, not wood. So he got the lengths of wood he had acquired from the council and nailed them to the wall and painted them white. It was er... different!

# 3.
# Hilary Road, W12

I lived at home with mum, dad and nan. Raymond and Norman had pretty much left the family home by the time I was born and by the time I was in primary school Allan had left as well, so that made me sort of like an 'only child'.

Regarding nan's bad eyesight it became worse the older she got but she was so stubborn she never did anything about it. I don't think she ever saw a doctor or an optician in her whole life. I really used to tease her a lot and in retrospect I was an irritating little bugger, well I was to her anyway.

Sometimes when she would go out of the room, I would change the furniture around. She always sat in the same armchair by the fire, so I would move that and the other chair and settee so when she came back she couldn't find her chair to sit down on. Then as she was looking I'd put her chair back in its place and sit down so that she would sit on me.

In the winter when the fire was on, she would sit very close to the fire because she always complained she could feel a draught down one side? She would sit so close sometimes you could smell her skirt getting hot like when you put a hot iron on something.

She also developed what we called 'corned beef legs' where the excessive heat put a weird pattern on her legs. If it wasn't nan on fire, then it would have been Kim our little dog who also sat too close to the fire and you could see her fur smoke. Talk about 'hot dog'. She was a lazy dog.

Nan must have lost her teeth quite early on and for years she had only two teeth. One at the top and one at the bottom. I remember seeing her do that thing you hear about when her lone bottom tooth was giving her 'Jip' (slang for irritation). I watched her tie a piece of string to the lonely prong and then to the doorknob in our front room. She slammed the door shut so that the tooth came flying out. Not a wise thing to do in front of a small child!

Nan also had one long hair that used to grow from the side of her mouth and both Allan and I would tease her by trying to creep up and pull it out, shouting out "Whisker" as we attempted to remove it!

Allan married Pat, the Acton Carnival Queen in 1961. Mum took me to Acton High Street to watch the Carnival procession with Pat sitting on a throne on the back of a flatbed truck. Pat could sing too and used to get up and guest with Allan's group from time to time. They had two children, Justine and Stephen.

Brother Ray was always immaculately dressed. He always looked like he was on the way to a wedding, wearing a dark blue suit, white shirt and tie. I remember him when I was a small kid and he was a young man, I suppose these days you would call him a rockabilly or as it was then a 'Teddy boy'. The story goes that when he was living at home he bought himself a drape suit, popular with the 'Teddy boys'. Mum thought it was shocking and 'lowered the tone' and apparently threw it away while he was out at work!

I remember he arrived one day and he'd bought himself what looked like an American convertible car in two tone brown. He took me, my oldest brother Norman, and sister-in-law Audrey (Norman's wife) out in it for a ride. I don't remember where we went, but the car seemed massive inside and out! It was a convertible so we had the hood down and it felt like you were in one of those American films. I also remember we all ate ice cream cornets while driving along. Funny how it's sometimes the little things you remember.

Ray met a girl named June and went to live in Brassie Avenue, East Acton with her family. They were married, had four children, Gary Tony, Lorraine and Mark and remained married until he passed away on January 19th 1994, unfortunately, the result of his heavy drinking!

Ray was really good with his hands and seemed to be able to turn his hand to anything. He was working for a company who I think were called Adrema in Acton. While he was there he made me a tunnel for my trainset and also made me a metal crown which I wore in one of my school plays. It was really heavy and looked like one of the old medieval crowns. Mum tied some elastic to it to try and keep it on my head.

In later years Ray worked at the BBC in Shepherd's Bush. His ability to make things got him working building sets for various shows. Of all the shows he said that he and the crew always liked working with Shirley Bassey and Bruce Forsyth. I suppose the fact they were generous to the crew was also an incentive.

As I mentioned earlier, Norman is my oldest brother who married Audrey and I was page-boy at their wedding when I was six years old. Together they had two children Karen and Paul. Audrey passed away suddenly on December 14th 2015 following a fall at their home and complications following a broken hip operation. It was such a shock to the family! This was very upsetting, because after all those years she was like a big sister to me.

Like dad, Norman started working in a greengrocer's shop but spent most of his working life until retirement working for CAV in Acton.

# 4.
# Ghosts

## "Is it really real, or just all in your mind"

I am a realistic sort of person at heart and my sensible common-sense head tells me that there are no such things as Ghosts. However, some unexplainable things have happened to me in my lifetime that I swear were not figments of my imagination. Following are a selection of them and make of them what you will.

Nan lived with us in the house in East Acton and I've no idea why but from an early age her bedroom fascinated me. She had the third smallest bedroom in the house which contained a single bed a wardrobe a chest of drawers and a dressing table with a mirror. The furniture was old, that old dark wood which was probably popular during the two world wars and along with her nick-nacks and clothes, that was about all she possessed.

Nobody ever said I couldn't go into nan's bedroom, but it felt that it was out of bounds, so poking my head in or creeping in and loitering with no particular intent seemed risky and dangerous to a small child like me.

Creeping into nan's room was an adventure, almost like entering another time zone, as if I was going back in time somewhere.

One day I was in nan's room when I was looking towards her mirror, when a finger appeared from behind the mirror and was gesturing to me as if to say come here, come towards me. It was like a human forefinger. I remember I froze for a moment and then I was out of that room as fast as I could, and I didn't go back in there for quite some time.

Maybe if I had not have been so scared of being in that room, I may have discovered Narnia had I opened the wardrobe?

In retrospect I wonder if the finger behind the mirror started the thought I had that another world lived in the mirror? A kind of parallel universe existing within the mirror, an *Alice in Wonderland* kind of scenario.

Many years later I wrote and recorded the song 'I Believe It' on the album *Mudanzas* which drew the comparison of another land within the mirror. It is one of my personal favourite songs and has always been popular when I have played it in concert.

When I was about ten, my bed faced the bedroom door and mum used to leave the door open after she had put me to bed. I suppose it made me feel safe so that if I needed her, she was only out of the door and downstairs. To the left was the flight of stairs onto a small landing. Mum and dad's bedroom door was directly in front as you came up the stairs, my room would be to the right.

I have never been a good sleeper and this particular night was no exception. I had been laying there for quite some time, always hoping mum or dad might come up the stairs and pop in to see if I was okay. While I was laying there I saw a vision, or an apparition of two people, a man and a woman, who appeared at the top of the stairs on the landing outside the bedroom. They were dressed in Victorian or Edwardian clothes. He had a black suit, a black hat and a moustache and beard. The lady was wearing a white gown and was slightly taller than the man. It looked as if they were in wedding attire, but often clothing of that era was quite grand! It all happened very quickly. The images were misty, almost transparent and once they had reached the top of the stairs they seemed to hover momentarily and then disappear up towards the loft directly above the landing. That was the only time I had that vision, but I learned of an interesting story some years later which had some relevance. More about that later.

From about eleven to thirteen I often used to get what only can be described as paranormal experiences. Because of various things that kept happening I was not getting much sleep and I know the bags under my eyes were becoming quite noticeable.

Mum didn't take what I was telling her at all seriously. She would tell me I was just imagining things and I should get some sleep. Sleep was exactly what I needed to have but I could not relax enough to sleep. Who could I tell if mum wouldn't believe me?

One day when I was at my friend Leslie Clarke's house. My problem of not sleeping came up in conversation with his mum — maybe because my eyes looked so tired? Leslie's mum was a listener and I suppose I could have looked like I might need some professional mental guidance, but no, Leslie's mum seemed to believe every word I said. I don't know what Leslie's mum said, but one evening she made the excuse to come and collect Leslie from my house which gave her the opportunity to have a conversation with mum about how concerned she was about my well-being. I'm not sure anything she said made much difference, but the fact that an adult actually heard what I had to say and appeared on the surface to believe my stories gave me a huge psychological boost.

I had been hearing gypsy violin music as if it was coming from the loft. Remember the loft door was on the landing outside my bedroom.

Early one evening Leslie and another friend Alan Golding were at my house and we were in the little room. I left the room to go upstairs to the toilet. As I got to the top of the stairs I could hear this music again. The strains of a violin being played! I went back down the stairs and said to Leslie and Alan "Quick, come and hear this music playing which I've been telling you about". So all three of us ran up the stairs and sure enough I was not imagining it. All three of us could hear it, either that or all three of us were imagining it.

As I had my mates with me I was feeling brave, so I got a chair and placed it directly below the loft hatch door and then with another foot on top of the bannister, hoisted myself up (with Leslie and Alan below supporting my feet) and pushed the hatch door open. A musty smell emitted from the loft and the hatch door fell back and at that moment the music stopped! I felt justified at last that I was not the only person who had heard this. I don't think I ever heard that music again, but that was not the last of the strange occurrences in 56 Hilary Road.

Sometime after this happened mum was telling me that apparently soon after the house was built in the early 1900s a family who lived in the house were believed to be some kind of Russian dignitaries. Many Russians escaped Russia at the turn of the century during the revolution and the murder of the Russian Royal Family has been well documented. The startling thing that mum told me was, the story of a man who had committed suicide in the house by hanging himself from the loft!

Remember the images and the music I had heard? Coincidence or what?

Alan and I were walking back to my house early one evening when Alan looked up at my bedroom window and said there was a face behind the curtain. I looked up and I could see it too. I had net curtains hanging in the window but we could see the silhouette of someone with grey wavy hair. I said "Oh that, must be my Auntie Vi, she comes over to visit, every other Monday when she finishes work". I didn't realise it immediately but this was a Thursday. Anyway we went indoors and into the front room and said to mum and dad, "Oh, I see Auntie Vi is here then?"

"Auntie Vi?" they replied "No, she's not here". I said "She must be. We've just seen her up at my bedroom window". Well you may have gathered by now mum just disregarded our apparition as purely a figment of our imagination... both of us? That was mum, if you can't explain it, you must be imagining it.

When I went to bed, I was woken up by how cold the room felt. I could feel a presence in the room and a feeling as if someone was sitting at the foot of my bed. I was scared and hid my head under the bedcovers. After a while I moved the covers slightly over my head just so that one eye was looking out from underneath the covers and I could see a grey misty figure with the same shock of grey hair sitting on the bed looking towards the window. It wasn't human because the image was virtually transparent and there was no significant weight on the bed as if it were a human being!

I laid there for ages, too scared to move, too scared to shout for help. I can't explain it but after a while it seemed the temperature in the room had risen to perhaps how it should be and I became brave enough to poke my head out of the covers. Nothing there now, the room was back to normal.

I never mentioned what happened because I know I would have only been told that I had been imagining it again.

As time went on things in the house went back to normal and I don't recall any other strange things happening.

One evening I was talking to mum and dad about the family. Both sides of our family had interesting stories and we had boxes of photographs of family members past and present.

I never knew either of my Grandads. As mentioned, mum's dad spent his life in a mental institution and dad's dad died shortly after I was born. Apparently he fell off of the back of a 105 bus. The buses used to have a platform on the back with a pole handle to assist you getting on and off. It seems that he probably slipped or missed the handle, fell back off of the bus and hit his head as he fell. He never recovered from the fall and died shortly after and soon after I was born. He would have seen me but I never was aware of seeing him. Although the description of him with grey wavy hair and a photograph I saw looked very much like the vision in my bedroom that night. Was it grandad who came back to pay me a visit?

# 5.

# Big School

September 1963 and the time had approached when I was due to start at St Christopher Wren Secondary Modern School, Shepherd's Bush, London W12.

I was leaving the comfort of Old Oak Primary — all my friends and the lovely Miss Maple, for what I gathered might be some kind of torture chamber!

I was scared stiff. Fortunately one of my neighbours, Barry Towns, a tall lad and a couple of years older than me. He knew the ropes and went with me to 'big school' on my first day.

Us new kids really stood out with our brand new, pressed and clean uniforms. Fodder for the waiting lions to swallow us up. This was a tough school in a tough area and I was aware I had to try and keep my head down to avoid trouble. There were the usual rumours, like they get the new kids and take them in the toilets and flush their heads down the lavatory pan. Or take them in the toilets and 'debag' them which meant ripping the clothes off, or worse (use your imagination please). Or chalk on your blazer or slashing your blazer with a razor blade! If I went home like that, what would mum say? I'd probably get a whack from her as well!

Names were called out in the first assembly and I found myself in class 1A1 and in Clarendon House.

Clarendon was one of four houses which were basically competitive groups which I never thought had much use but to increase more rivalry within the pupils. Clarendon, Newton, Gibbons and Dryden were the four houses.

I've never thought as to why, as it was a local school — particularly as I found I was the only pupil in my class that came from my primary school — but I soon made friends. Some have remained lifelong friends.

Like in my primary school, I discovered I had the ability to make people laugh and also to do impersonations of well-known TV personalities, as well as some of the teachers at Christopher Wren. I found that being funny or popular, however you want to describe it, can have its benefits.

All schools throughout history are known for the 'school bully'. The problem was that Christopher Wren had dozens of them and a little fella like me had nowhere to hide.

One day, I was sitting in class, when I felt an almighty stab in my back... with a ruler, not a knife! I am and have never been a violent person, but I stood up sharply, instinctively, turned around and gave the perpetrator behind me a hard slap around the face. In retrospect it was probably a girlie slap but nevertheless it was a slap!

You've all heard the saying "I wanted the ground to open up and swallow me!" Well that's how I felt at that moment. The kid I slapped was Kevin Foran, who shall we say had something of a reputation.

"Right you, outside Bryony Gates after school"! Oh shit! I was in big trouble. I think I must have been walking around all day in a daze wondering how I could get out of being beaten to a pulp!

3:30pm arrived. There was Kevin waiting and there was I outside the school to teach this little short arse a lesson. I know it was hardly Clint Eastwood facing Lee Van Cleef, but it was serious stuff.

Kev walked up to me and grabbed the lapels of my jacket, looked me square in the eyes for a moment (although it seemed like hours), loosened his grip and started to laugh. He said something like "You're alright Bromham" and let me go. It transpired that no-one, especially a little squirt like me had ever had the 'bollocks' to give him a slap. He was my mate and bodyguard throughout my years at school.

Proof of his bodyguard work occurred one day when a group of friends and myself were standing chatting in a doorway, in the old part of the school, in the Bryony Road playground. Quite a few kids had money on them for school dinners and some with their bus fares. As I lived in walking distance from the school, I went home lunchtimes and consequently, like royalty, I never carried any money on me. A group of lads surrounded us and started demanding money. You know the sort of thing "Oi, lend us sixpence", with no intention of paying it back of course. I thought, oh no, here we go again, more trouble. When out of nowhere the crowd parted and Kevin Foran was there, shouting "Oi, leave Bromham alone." Kev, my saviour!. Hearing his words, the gang departed and I can honestly say I don't ever recall being bothered by anyone again.

# 6.
# East Acton:
# The New Neighbours

I was about 14 years old when new neighbours moved in. There appeared to be lots of them initially, but there were lots of friends and family visiting at the time of them moving in. There was a mum and dad and five children. Four girls and one boy. They were the Collins family. Dad Bill was a coach driver for the well-known local company Fox's Coaches. They had a smart looking fleet of buses painted in blue and yellow. One of their buses featured in The Beatles film *Magical Mystery Tour*. He kept it parked in Norbroke Street outside their house and opposite my house in Hilary Road.

Some Sundays all of the family were out helping their dad clean the bus. As it turned out Bill didn't like me very much even though I had never spoken to him. As far as he was concerned, I was that "long haired git who lived next door" and he especially didn't like his girls talking to me. His girls were Pauline, Jackie, Deborah and the youngest Tina.

The only time that Bill spoke to me was when they thought little Tina had gone missing and I volunteered to help the search for her. Fortunately, she was found in the house in bed. How they didn't see her there in the first place I'll never know! Mum Jean worked at Lime Grove swimming baths and then later for the BBC at the Television Centre, Shepherd's Bush. Jean was really proud to work for 'The Beeb'.

After a while I started to talk to all of them, except for Bill, and we all got on well. I particularly got on well with Jackie and sometimes I would talk to Jackie by standing on a large mound of earth in the corner of our garden. A good vantage point to look up at her talking from her bedroom window. The mound of earth I stood on was not really a rockery, more like a mockery, but it gave me enough height to look over the hedges. This vision gave much amusement to my family who enquired if I was doing what became to be known as 'the sermon on the mount'. Ha, ha very funny.

I got to know a few of Jackie's friends. A couple of them I already recognised because they went to my primary school. Gary Giles, came around to my house quite often and he became friendly with one of the friends whose name was Sandie. I must have been sixteen and Jackie was seventeen when we first started going out together, as were Gary and Sandie.

The only boy next door was Peter and I was very fond of him. As I was almost an only child he was like a little brother to me. As he got older, like me he developed an interest in music and when it was time for him to leave school I helped him find his first job. I suggested that perhaps he could learn to be a recording engineer, but warned him he would have to start at the bottom as a tape engineer (aka tape op) and it would be handy if he could make a decent cup of tea or coffee.

I contacted a few people on his behalf. I took him to meet record producer and engineer Martin Birch who I had worked with on the *Saturday Morning Pictures* album. Martin showed us around the new De Lane Lea studios in Wembley. I had also contacted George Peckham who mastered some of the best albums at that time (including the early Stray albums).

I went to meet him at The Apple Studios in Saville Row and consequently George put a good word in on my behalf and Peter got the job working for Apple Studios which was owned by The Beatles. In time Peter got to know all of The Beatles individually and to his credit he was known as a hard worker and I think it was George Harrison who nick-named him 'Little Beaver'. He often found himself driving a 'Beatle' around in the company Volvo car. One day he stopped off to see me as he had just dropped George off at Heathrow Airport. I have to say I was a wee bit envious of Pete now working closely with my heroes.

When Apple closed down, he went into partnership with a guy named Patrick and became involved in record distribution eventually forming their own record label, Arawak Records. It was primarily a Reggae label and their biggest chart hit was with Janet Kaye with her number 1 single 'Silly Games'.

Peter and Patrick had some kind of business falling out so Peter did a couple of jobs and eventually decided to become a Black Cab driver and later an executive chauffeur mainly working with people in the film industry including stars like Tom Cruise, Julie Andrews and Bob Hoskins to name but a few. Pete sadly and unexpectedly passed away on 21st December 2016 from a brain haemorrhage. He was still young and had much too live for. Life can be cruel sometimes. Very sad indeed.

# 7.
# First Bands

**W**hen I started at Christopher Wren I was just getting into playing guitar. My best friend at that time who lived around the corner on The Westway (Western Avenue A40), was Frankie Hackett. From an Irish family, he had two older brothers John and Alfie, along with his mum and dad. His Dad was the manager of The Western pub.

Frank was also learning to play the guitar. We used to get together and try and learn the songs of the time. I always thought Frank wanted to be Graham Nash, we both loved The Hollies. Back in school a kid in my class whose name was Alan Dennis played the drums. It's funny how you meet people in life but some you remember more than others. I remembered Alan because I played in my Old Oak School football team and we had a match against neighbouring Ellerslie Road School. Alan, as I remembered, was the goalkeeper. A real character as I recall, shouting instructions from the goal line. He was no bigger than me which made it even more entertaining.

He had just got a Ringo Starr snare drum and cymbal for Christmas. I invited him around to my house where I had a small bass drum and pedal left over from my brothers Skiffle group days. I thought he could link that up with his Ringo items.

Meanwhile back in school, Stephen Gadd was another kid in my class who I always thought looked good and was always singing. I got to know him better and duly invited him to my house for a band practice. To us it sounded great, very promising. We've got a band, but what shall we call ourselves? I think it was Steve's mum who suggested The Fads. Frank, Alan, Del, Steve, get it? Well it was a bit short lived. I think Frank lost interest, partly I think because he discovered girls!

Around this time, I had become friendly with another classmate, Gary Giles. It turns out he had learned a few of The Shadows tunes. I had no desire to be Hank Marvin or any other lead guitarist at that time, so I invited him around to my house. He had a Vox Shadow electric guitar, with a tremolo arm on it, just like a Fender Stratocaster that Hank played. I accompanied him on my Hofner Senator and he played tunes like 'Wonderful Land' and 'Apache'. Mum and dad listening in the in the living room, thought it was wonderful (no pun intended).

I had started writing songs. I wrote my first song when I was about eleven or twelve called 'Someone'. Anyway Gary and I got on really well, but I felt we needed a bass player. To be honest, I was considering playing bass myself, particularly as I loved what Paul McCartney was doing.

Where I lived in East Acton, there was a little shop who sold mainly second-hand stuff, radios and electronic items. One day I walked past the shop and there was a second hand Hofner Congress bass guitar in the window. I mentioned it to

Gary and next day he came to my house with his dad. I took them to the shop and they bought it. Result, I had a bass player!

I was discussing this recently with Gary, trying to work out why Gary decided to change from guitar to bass guitar. It seemed a smooth transition but neither of us can remember how or why. Needless to say it was a superb move as he became a renowned bass guitarist and an influence to many.

I then got a solid body Hohner Zambesi electric guitar and a Fenton Weil amplifier. Alan Dennis had persuaded his dad to buy him a full Olympic drum kit in blue sparkle. Alan, Gary and myself started to learn various songs. Old blues, R&B, pop tunes of the time by The Beatles, The Stones, etc.

My sister-in-law Audrey and Norman were going to have a party for their daughter Karen and asked if my new group would play at their house. A big old Victorian terrace house in Overstone Road, Hammersmith with lots of kids friends and neighbours in attendance — it was a lot of fun.

I seem to recall we played one other show which I believe was at St Katherines Hall in East Acton. That was big time for us as a local up and coming group. I had recently seen The Vectors play in the same hall. They were good and they were loud! We had to think of a name for our new group which was The Detours. It was also one of the original names for The Who. Unlike The Who, The Detours didn't last very long. I think like Frank in The Fads, Alan discovered girls too.

Mum and dad had taken me on a couple of holidays to Butlins holiday camps, which were loads of fun especially for a kid of my age.

One year, I think it may have been the summer of 1965 and always the last week in July and the first week of August we went to Butlins, Clacton. Gary Giles knew I was going so he persuaded his dad to take him there and they met up with us on the second week.

I couldn't wait to take him to one of the small ballrooms there to watch a live band called The Committee. They were great. As they had a residency, we used to go and see them every time they played which was possibly lunchtime to early afternoon and again in the evening. Musically they really hit the spot with Gary and myself. They were a four-piece group: Two guitars, bass and drums, and they all sang. We could see live what a group could really do.

We had been listening to Tamla Motown for example which had brass and orchestra backing, but The Committee seemed to be able to reproduce the songs in their own way without it sounding like there was something missing. They picked good songs which is the main key to any performance, but it was the arrangements which really fascinated us.

I remember the rhythm guitarist, who looked a bit like Russ Ballard of Argent and if I remember correctly, played an electric Burns Double 6, 12 string guitar. I think the guitarist had a Stratocaster and the bass player had a Fender bass. I think Gary and I decided there and then if we were to form another band we would try and be like The Committee. Sure enough about a year later we formed The Stray and our set list featured songs like 'Baby I Need Your Lovin', 'I Can't Help Myself', 'Ain't Too Proud To Beg' and so on.

How The Stray, who simply became Stray evolved into what was known as a hard rock band is a mystery to me. Regardless of what ever category you want to put Stray into, the emphasis has always been on the song, regardless of the style. If there was one criticism of Stray, it would be that when we made albums the music was perhaps too diverse in style.

People generally like to put music in a category. As far as I was concerned, an album of songs regardless of their genre was irrelevant. I believed it gave us individuality. I mean, The Beatles used to make albums like that. What ever happened to them?

The Traders was the name of my brother Allan's group which I played in for a while, but before I tell you about that, allow me to tell you about Allan — his influence and how music quite possibly fuelled my desire to be like him and be involved with the music business.

As I said previously, there was always music in the family home and Allan was probably like most teenagers of the late 50s early 60s, buying records and really getting interested in music. As I recall his first attempt at forming a band was a Skiffle group. Made popular in the 50s, particularly with artists like Lonnie Donegan. There was quite a well-known Skiffle group in the West London area called The Vagabonds and they used to drive around in an old London taxi, part of it painted with yellow stripes on. Another skiffle group who were local to West London were The Vipers. Wally Whyton sang and played guitar and banjo with The Vipers but went on to achieve fame on television, hosting a programme called the *Five O' Clock Club* where his partners were two puppets, an Owl called Olli Beak and a dog called Fred Barker.

As Allan's Skiffle group developed, they changed to electric guitars and played some rock 'n' roll music. I think Allan was playing rhythm guitar at the time and the lead singer was a fella named Duffy Power. Duffy was a young, good-looking guy with a big blond quiff. He was signed up by the well-known impresario Larry Parnes. He joined others on Larry's roster such as Joe Brown, Marty Wilde, Billy Fury and Georgie Fame to name but a few. Duffy later got into the Blues scene and notably made an album with Jack Bruce. Coincidentally he was signed to Transatlantic Records, the same record label I would eventually be signed to.

Around this time someone Allan knew had a kitten who needed a home. It was a very pretty little kitten, basically a tabby cat. We had an old cat in the house when I was born which had long since passed away. I think in those days cats were there to catch mice as much as just being the family pet. However, the little kitten was very pretty. I was allowed to keep it and Allan and Pat suggested I call it Duffy (after Duffy Power).

Allan had met a guitarist named Brian Freeney who could play all The Shadows hits and could sing harmony with Allan. They got another guitarist in called Tony Cummings who also had a good voice. He sounded a bit like Cliff Richard. This now meant that Allan was the main vocalist. This particular line up also had Fred Hindhaugh on drums and Charlie Rawlings on bass guitar, and for a while a young guitarist called Peter Dyer.

\*\*\*\*

Our house in East Acton was a council house and made of stronger stuff than the houses of today. Downstairs there was a kitchen, although they called it the scullery. Two other rooms, which they called the front room (where the TV and three-piece-suite was) and the little room, which was the dining room but also became the music room.

The little room was where the music was. Allan's group used to come around once a week and practice in there. It's hard to believe that a band could practice in one room and mum and dad could still hear the TV in the front room next door. That's how solid those old houses were. Trying to drill a hole in the wall and stick a rawl plug in, was a mammoth task in those days.

There was a sideboard in the room and I used to sit on the sideboard and listen and watch. In terms of Health and Safety, I'm surprised I was allowed to enter the room, for as the evening wore on it became filled with cigarette smoke and I've no doubt there was the odd swear word thrown in as well, but I was far too fascinated with the music to notice the language.

Brian and Charlie often left their guitars at the house and unknown to them I used to get them out and just stare at them. Brian's guitar in particular was absolutely gorgeous. It was a German make called Hagstrom. The body was gold sparkle and the entire neck was Mother of Pearl. It had a small square insert with press buttons which changed the tone. A stunning looking guitar and I always wanted it.

It was Brian who introduced me to other music, by very kindly leaving some of his records for us to listen to. The one artist that sticks in my mind was Carl Perkins, so by the time The Beatles came along and recorded songs like 'Honey Don't', I was ahead of the game. I might have still only been a kid but I knew these tunes.

Moving on it must have been sometime in 1965, I was thirteen coming up to fourteen years of age, I had been playing guitar then for a couple of years and aside from a couple of gigs with my school bands, I had never played what you might call a proper gig (e.g. clubs and you get paid ha ha).

Tony the rhythm guitarist left The Traders, I'm not sure why, but he had a heart problem, which unfortunately lead to his death some years later. They had regular gigs and a couple coming up the following week. They wondered how they could fulfil the first couple of gigs at least.

I have to hand it to Allan, because as I understand it, he turned around and said to the rest of the band something like "Well 'D' knows all the songs". These were all guys in their mid to late twenties and what would they think about having a kid in the band?

Well, whatever the initial thoughts were, I had I think, maybe one practice (two at the very most) and played my first paid gig at The Co-Op Hall Acton. Brian drove over in his car to take me. It's really funny how I can remember that it was a small black Renault Dauphine and the number plate was SPF 111.

It was either a wedding reception or a 21st birthday party, I can't remember exactly. Mum had already been out and got me a smart grey suit and a pair of desert boots and I felt really grown up. I used my Hofner Senator guitar which had one pick up on it and my little Fenton Weil amp. I was aware during the gig that a lot of the adults in the audience were looking at this kid on stage, but I also remember all the kids at the party all congregated to the front of the stage where I was standing.

Well, I must have done something right because I stayed playing with The Traders for a couple of years until the shows began to conflict with my own band, The Stray, but more about that later.

I think it was generally decided that I needed a solid electric guitar now as I was playing regular semi-professional gigs. So I went to Marshalls in Hanwell and bought a Hohner Zambesi solid body electric guitar. Marshall Music was owned by Jim Marshall, now world famous for creating Marshall amplification. Along with his friend Ken Brand they began making amplifiers in their garage around this time. I met him many times and visited him at his factory which he opened in Bletchley, Milton Keynes where I moved to in the late 70s.

I wish I could remember how much I paid for the guitar back then, about £29 I think, but without trying to sound flash, money had not become a problem. Imagine this, most kids at school, if they got a paper round or did part time shop work, were lucky if they got paid 17s 6d or £1! Work it out for yourselves, the band probably got paid an average of about £25 per gig, split that between 5 people and that's £5 each and for two nights £10. The average wage in the early sixties wasn't much more than that unless you were lucky.

The band needed a new bass player. Terry Cullane, a kid a year older than me at school was the bass player in another friends band. I suggested him to Allan, he went along, played and fitted in perfectly. Later, Terry also deputised on bass a few times for the Edgar Broughton Band.

About 1965 we went into R G Jones Studios in Morden, Surrey and recorded an album (not for public resale) of various hits of the time. I was really excited about making a record and Brian allowed me to play lead on a couple of songs: The Hollies 'Look Through Any Window' which has a tricky guitar intro and break, and also the lead solo by The Yardbirds 'Evil Hearted You'. As time went on I found I was playing the lead breaks in the then, up to date songs, while Brian stayed with the earlier sixties Hank Marvin style which he did so well.

As I mentioned earlier The Stray was beginning to interest me more and very soon I had to make one of the biggest decisions of my life. I left The Traders to concentrate solely on The Stray.

****

Fast forward: It is now Tuesday 2nd December 2020 and I have received a telephone call earlier today at 12:30pm from Allan's son, Steve, to tell me that Allan had passed away only a half an hour before in Spain, 12:00pm UK time (13:00 pm Spanish time). I knew he had been in hospital but I had spoken to Allan's wife Pat on Saturday and it sounded like he was getting better. I was going to phone Pat today to see how he was and to be honest I was expecting him to be home. I had thought of so much more I wanted to talk to him about. I cannot take it in at the moment what has happened particularly at this time as I am writing about him. I so wanted him to read this and understand what a huge influence he had on me and music.

If there is an after-life, then I know he will be singing his head off! Although he retired from singing with the band some years ago, like an old trooper he was still getting up in the bars close to where he lived in Spain and giving them a song or three.

Rest in peace bruv... I love you.

# 8.
# The Stray

I know this might sound like I'm a bit of a big head, but the truth is I don't actually remember learning to play the guitar. I just picked it up and found I could play. I knew instinctively where to put my fingers.

I was about 11 when Allan handed me a battered up old acoustic guitar, which I still have. It looks a bit like the one you see in those old photographs of the blues artist Robert Johnson.

Apparently Allan came out of the flat where he was living at the time in Acton and noticed the neck of a guitar sticking out of his dustbin of all places!

Question is would I have ever started playing guitar at that time if this mysterious person had not decided to dump it in my brother's bin?

I suppose because I had spent so much time watching Allan's group practice up close in our little room, playing the guitar became second nature?

I got on well with this old guitar. I didn't know how to tune it properly and I spent some time playing it in what is known as the open E tuning. Many of the old blues players used this tuning for bottleneck or slide guitar playing. It sounded right to me. I think it was some while after that Brian Freeney showed me how to tune it properly. He showed me a few chords and I learned some more from a book by Ivor Moirantz.

To my surprise, less than a year later Allan had persuaded mum and dad to buy me a decent guitar. One day Allan came to the house and along with mum and dad handed me a Hofner Senator guitar which he had bought (with mum and dad's money of course) from King Street Music in Hammersmith. I think it might have cost about £26 back then which in today's money would have been a couple of weeks' wages for the average man.

I loved that guitar and took it everywhere with me, my favourite place being the toilet! The acoustics were great in there although a bit cramped I had to hold the neck upwards, much like Bill Wyman of The Rolling Stones used to hold his bass guitar. I still have that guitar and would never think of selling it. As a matter of fact, I still have my first guitar from Allan's dustbin!

It was a sunny day early 1966 and I seem to remember sitting in the art class in school alongside Steve Gadd, Gary Giles and Steve Crutchley. Quite possibly the subject of forming a new band had come up prior to this in the playground or somewhere at this time, but I'm quite sure it was this particular day that the band was officially formed. Little did I realise it would become almost a lifetimes work!

Our first choice of drummers had been Alan Dennis, but for whatever reason he wasn't interested. Steve Crutchley said he played drums although none of us had heard him, but he was a mate so we went with it. That's what mates did. As it turned out he was a good drummer and had a good ear for vocal harmony.

Recently I was speaking to Gary and in the mists of time we both seem to have different thoughts as to where the name Stray originated? Gary seems to think that he thought of it while we were walking through Acton Park, deciding on band names. I thought that it was Steve Crutchley's mum while trying to think of a name, made some random remark like "You lot are like a bunch of strays" or something like that? I guess we may never know and does it really matter?

We got a set together really quickly. Playing all sorts of stuff, pop, R&B, even some new songs which I had written. If my memory serves me correctly, we only played a couple of gigs with Steve Crutchley.

His mum was going out with a fella who had a Trad Jazz band, getting paid money and most importantly were about to appear on *Opportunity Knocks*, the famous talent show hosted by Hughie Green.

It was like we'd stopped before we barely got started and Alan Dennis still wasn't interested in playing drums. Steve Gadd had a Saturday job working in a butchers' shop in Acton Vale. He said that Richard, the other kid in the shop played drums and was rehearsing with his band in St Katherines Hall East Acton, close to where I lived, suggesting that I should pop along and see if he was any good?

So I went to the hall and hung around outside for a bit until I heard them fire up. I crept in and stood for a while at the back of the hall and witnessed what I thought was the best drummer I had ever seen! This kid was on fire! He had all the moves. A real showman. It was like witnessing Keith Moon playing right in front of my eyes! If I remember rightly he had this old battered kit but cleverly disguised with an old Union Jack across the top of the kit. I couldn't wait to report my piece of talent spotting to Steve and Gary.

Steve and Richard then came over to my house where we set up and played as usual in the little room. We went through various songs and it all knitted together perfectly, but his style of drumming brought something else out in all of us. It was loud and powerful. So loud in fact that for the first time ever, my mum came in to tell us to "turn it down!"

I really don't know how it happened but we started to get gigs almost straight away. We were all only about 15 years old so none of us could drive. How do we get to these gigs? Two of the young guys, both 21 or 22 years old Stan and John, worked full time in the shop that Steve and Richard worked in and they volunteered to drive us to the gigs, which at that time were all over London. Richard's dad and Uncles had a family building firm called Cole Bros. They let us use one of their vans, a Bedford Dormobile to go to gigs.

A favourite gig at the time which may have been booked by Stan was The Old Actonians Sports Club. It became a regular gig for us and we always had them up dancing to our mixture of pop, soul, Tamla and R&B as it stated on our publicity cards which we had printed.

Don't forget bands like The Who were playing similar styles of music at that time, so although it might seem odd now, knowing how Stray ended up sounding later, it was quite normal then.

I think it might have been Stan who knew someone who had something to do with the legendary Goldhawk Club in Shepherd's Bush and somehow he managed to persuade them to put us on one evening. They had lots of big names who played there. The Who played there a few times and they were doing Motown songs in their set at that time, so I thought we would be okay playing there.

It seemed quite an achievement so early in our career to play such a top venue, particularly when we were so young. I am not sure what I was expecting but the club was not as grand as I expected it to be. The Club was actually in the Goldhawk Road Shepherd's Bush in what was once probably the home of someone of wealth. Many of the houses were similar to these Victorian 3 or 4 storey houses with basements. The rooms on the ground floor must have been knocked into one to make quite a sizeable room and dance floor with a high wooden stage at one end.

I have a ticket which I kept and it says something like 'The Goldhawk Club presents 'The Stray' plus DJ Jacko Ortis'. It turned out to be so disappointing as on the night the room was almost empty. I was expecting too much maybe, or maybe they just put us on, on a night when usually they didn't have many people in anyway so they didn't have to pay any money to the band as such. Who knows, but on one of our first outings it taught us that the road ahead might be a tough one. As it transpired, for me it has been a tough and long road.

As I mentioned, The Who, were also local lads from Acton and Ealing although a few years older than us. We had the same line up guitar, bass, drums and lead vocalist.

I have often thought that Pete Townsend and I approached the guitar in a similar vein in as much as being the only lead instrument in the band we had to compensate with the type of chord structures we played and something which I felt I began to develop once I wrote more songs.

I've never considered myself to be a great guitarist although I'm honoured to have had some wonderful comments about my playing. I just consider myself to be a writer first and use the guitar as the way to interpret the music as such.

****

It was June 1967 and we decided it would be a good idea to make a demo recording and try and get a record deal. So I asked Allan to book us into R G Jones Studios for a day's recording where I'd recorded with his band The Traders. We recorded two songs. One was a song I'd written entitled 'Love In Her Heart' which was a catchy Motown influenced number we'd been playing at gigs and had always gone down well. The other song we recorded was 'Loving You Is Sweeter Than Ever' originally recorded by The Four Tops and written by Stevie Wonder.

In recent years I have been playing "Loving You" in my solo set and also recorded an acoustic version, on an expanded edition of my first solo album *Devils Highway* as it is one of my favourite songs.

With our first acetate recording, Steve, Gary, Ritchie and myself got on the train to Central London. Times were much different then and most of the record companies and music publishers were based either in Denmark Street or in the central London Soho area. So we decided to go knocking on doors to play these companies our latest recording and of course as far as we were concerned they were going to love it, sign us up and in no time we were going to be as big as The Beatles. Well that's what we thought.

I think we got to play it to one or two people but quite clearly there were no takers on what we assumed would be a golden opportunity for them. Oh well, we thought. Their loss. However, the best thing about that day as far as I was concerned was that as we were walking down a street, probably off of Oxford Street somewhere, when who should walk out of a restaurant, but John Lennon! We could not believe it. It must be an omen or a sign. We called out "Hiya John", to which he replied quite simply, "Good morning". I think we were so 'gobsmacked', but none of us pursued him and left it at that, watching him walk off to a waiting car. Many years later I wrote and recorded a song on the Stray album *10* where I mention this scene within the song 'Years'.

As we walked around the streets of London we walked past what looked like an old school and we could hear music playing from inside. Like four kids we sneaked into the building (which was open by the way) and found a band playing in a large room. They looked like a proper band, like we'd seen on the television. They looked good, wore fashionable clothes of the time and sounded really good.

They saw us lurking by the door and one of them gestured to us to come in, which we did and sat at the back for a little while. I remember they were rehearsing an old song which I was familiar with called 'Our Day Will Come'. We didn't want to outstay our welcome and besides we had a record deal to get before we went home for tea. We crept out pretty much as we had crept in and talked about what we had seen. The band were called Rupert's People, a band that were having a fair amount of success at the time but never went on to reach the fame and fortune they deserved (sounds familiar to me). We decided to try and learn 'Our Day Will Come'. I bought, or pinched from mum's wardrobe, chiffon scarves like Rupert's People were wearing and back combed our hair. Oh yeah, we were a proper group now.

It was becoming apparent that The Stray had become very important to me and I knew at some point there would be a clash of dates with The Traders and should this happen what could I do? How could I tell The Traders that I couldn't play the gig and more important how could I tell Allan?

Well the clash of dates arrived and was soon approaching. I told Allan that I wouldn't be able to play on this particular date because The Stray had got through to the final of a talent competition over in Romford. Allan told me The Traders had a gig the same night at Ealing Town Hall. He suggested I change my date, but how could I change a date for a talent competition and anyway The Stray were now the most important thing in my life.

I told Allan on numerous occasions that it was a talent contest and I couldn't change the date, but I honestly don't think he or the band thought I would not play The Traders show. The day came and there I stood dressed in my Kaftan and chiffon scarf telling The Traders that I was not playing with them that night as I had been saying for some weeks. They were clearly not happy with my decision, but in my defence I had been telling them for weeks that I could not play that show. I don't recall saying I was leaving and I don't recall being fired. I just never played with The Traders again.

The next few weeks were awkward as Allan and his wife Pat used to come to the house. Sitting opposite Allan at the dinner table trying to make small talk as if nothing had happened was taxing to say the least! I think in his heart Allan appreciated that my band was as precious to me as his band were to him and in time we were brothers again and everything was okay as before. I didn't lose my brother, but I did lose regular good pocket money from his band!

About the talent contest over in Romford, it was sponsored by the local Gas Board and we came second to a band playing Shadows covers. We were playing music which was current for the time and looking up to date as well, but we knew we wouldn't win, because the judges looked like sixties throwbacks and I believe the winning band were friends of one or more of the judges, local Essex boys. What chance would four West London pop stars in Romford have?

Anyway, like I said we came second, which is not a bad thing and we won a big silver cup which despite coming second, we were very proud of. It was agreed that as there was only one cup and four band members, we would share the cup on a weekly rotor basis. Richard took the cup home and nobody has ever seen it since! It probably spent its lifetime on his dad's or his Aunt Marge's sideboard.

****

The thing at the time was to contact the various music agents that advertised in the back pages of the music press. Well known papers like the *Melody Maker*. The agents (if you were lucky) invited you along for an audition, which more often than not, were open to the public. The agent could put on several bands, charge admission fees and not have to pay the bands because it was an audition. In retrospect it was a big 'con', but it got the bands seen to an audience.

After one such audition we were approached by a fella named Bob Pemberton, an odd looking chap who said he was managing The Grass, who were going to be big and he thought he could get us plenty of work. Well, we did get plenty of work but mainly all the pubs in and around East London.

In 1968 a band called The Love Affair had scored a hit with 'Everlasting Love'. They were getting a lot of press at the time because they were reportedly only 17 years old. That was nothing. We were 16 years old! We had caught the attention of the local paper *The Acton Gazette* and they ran an article about this up and coming young local band. The heading was "Love Affair for The Strays?"

Two guys who saw this article were Peter Amott and Ivan Mant. Peter had been the drummer with various bands, but notably with The Footprints who coincidentally had played shows with The Who. Peter had decided he wanted to stop playing the drums and go into management. So along with Ivan, the two of them got in touch with us. They came to see us play at a dance organised coincidentally by The Old Actonians Club. This time not at their club house in Gunnersbury Lane but at The Woodlands Hall, Acton.

The following week we met up with Peter and Ivan and although I don't think they approved of all the material we played, they obviously saw something there that was worth working on and developing. We began rehearsing... Yes "rehearsing"... it's a word I always associate with Peter as he always corrected us when we said practice, because he said, "No, you practice at home. You rehearse together".

They suggested that until we had enough of our own original material, we do our own arrangements of cover versions as some of the "Underground" acts were doing at this time. We also developed what we called "The Act" incorporating sound effects via a reel-to-reel tape recorder. Our own light show, stroboscopes, fluorescent light tubes which lit up the stars on the amplifiers and speakers. Ivan had painted my Fender Duo Sonic in fluorescent paint so that it lit up!

Like I said we started doing arrangements of other peoples' songs and one such song we ended the set with was The Beatles' 'I Am The Walrus'. Steve would come out wearing a white sheet that glowed in the dark. He also wore a tin foil mask. Towards the end of the song, Gary stopped playing, ripped of Steve's mask to reveal his face covered in fluorescent multi coloured dots. Then Gary would grab this large wooden spear (harpoon) and pretend to stab Steve. Meanwhile Ritchie and I would be making a right musical racket in the background.

I can't remember which came first, but there were two recording events which must have happened at almost the same time. I mentioned The Love Affair earlier. Well, Pye Records were looking for a new Love Affair and somehow record producer John Schroeder got in contact. Peter and Ivan invited John to a show. In walks the record producer, quite sixties style trendy, back combed hair and the blonde bird on his arm. He obviously liked what he'd seen and heard. We soon found ourselves in Pye Recording Studios where we recorded, at their suggestion, 'In The Night' a song recorded by Dominic Grant, later a member of Guys 'n Dolls, along with 'The Man Who Paints The Pictures', a song by an American band Fever Tree. This song was in our set at the time.

Well, we didn't pass the audition. I think even though we were the kind of age they wanted, our music and image was a bit too edgy for them.

We also went to Regent Sound Studios in Denmark Street London and recorded two songs. One I wrote called 'Outcast' and another written with Gary entitled 'Always In My Heart'.

You can see by these early recordings how the music had changed by the time we got to record our first album for Transatlantic Records in 1970.

Our first taste of what it might feel like being in a successful pop group happened one night at The Silver Blades ice rink in London. It was an odd place to play. People would be on the ice, skating. Then there would be a break in the middle where a band would play.

We did our act and I was aware there were a lot of girls in the audience. As we left the stage, the group of girls got bigger and bigger and before we knew it, we were being chased down this sort of corridor to the nearby dressing room by what seemed like hundreds of screaming girls! We got inside the dressing room, shut the door and they were outside pounding on the door and screaming like wailing Banshees! I admit I was scared. I'd never witnessed anything like that in my life, well except with watching The Beatles in the film *Hard Day's Night*. Furthermore, if they'd broken the door down, we had nowhere to go. No fire exits and no windows!

After some time, the hubbub outside the dressing room door subsided and I believe it took some hefty bouncers to disperse them. God know what would have happened to us if they'd all got in. In the future we weren't so worried about letting the girls in the dressing room, but that's for another time. Nudge nudge, wink wink, say no more Squire!

If we ever had any gigs on the other side of London we would come back home via Oxford Street in Central London. In those days, the late 60s and early 70s you could drive and even park up in Oxford Street. We would always aim for The Golden Egg restaurant. I use the word restaurant loosely as it was not the greatest eatery in the world. It was situated towards the end of Oxford Street near to Marble Arch. We would park our van up in the middle of the road outside The Golden Egg actually on Oxford Street. It seems unbelievable now, parking up in the middle of Oxford Street, but it's true.

We would eat things like a hamburger (no bun) with egg and chips. If you were still hungry you would pick a Rum Baba, which always tasted stale as it had probably been sitting in the warm glass case all day. Why did we do it? I don't know. It was almost like some kind of ritual or a marker to indicate we had done a gig and we were nearly home. In some ways, later on, The Watford Gap service station better known as The Blue Boar on the M1 motorway had a similar appeal, although the food was marginally better and gave the opportunity for star spotting or seeing other bands as they made their way home from shows up and down the motorway stopping off for a break in their journey.

# 9.

# Swinging Sixties

## (As They Were Known)

**A**s people get older you often hear them talk of "The good old days" and wonder if they really were? Occasionally I have doubted myself regarding nostalgia, but whatever my memories of that era are they are really happy ones.

Most people would want to be young again and probably I am no exception although I think a lot of it is your state of mind and how you live your life. I personally do not feel a lot different now than I did when I was twenty, although I do confess to look a lot different these days. I have got mirrors in my house you know!

I feel I am really lucky to have been born in the fifties and growing up in my teenage years during the sixties. There was an atmosphere around, you could almost smell it or sense it in the air, but I'm sorry, you young ones out there, but you really had to be there.

So much was happening and seemingly quite fast. When the second world war finished in 1945, Great Britain was putting itself back together again financially and socially. When I was very young there was still that feeling of comradeship and neighbours stopping in the street or knocking to see if you and the family are okay. I don't think that happens so much these days. Everything is rush, rush and people don't seem to have a lot of time for anyone else other than themselves.

From an early age I was aware of music and it was always an important part of the Bromham household. Of all the music that played in my house, one record that sticks in my mind is 'Heartbreak Hotel' by Elvis Presley. According to records this was released 27th January 1956 which means I would have only been 4 with my 5th birthday in the November. Even so at that young age I remember being totally fascinated with the sound of the production. The sparse instrumentation and the reverb on the recording. Even by today's standards, I believe it is still a classic recording.

However, when The Beatles came along, that changed everything for me. I wanted to be a Beatle. I wanted to make music like The Beatles. I wanted to form a group and be as big as The Beatles and for many years that was my serious ambition. It seemed that after The Fab Four other bands and producers were upping their game and some great original music was coming out. Although I have to say that my attention was also being drawn to the music going on in the USA. Tamla Motown, Stax, Sun Records, so much good music. For a kid like me I could quite easily overdose on this musical drug.

The more I think about it, music for me was becoming like an addiction. It completely took me over. I was like human blotting paper soaking up as much music as I could. I had very little interest in anything else and spent most of my time at home, playing guitar, writing songs, experimenting with my tape recorder. I never went out much except for playing with the band which obviously meant I never had much time for girls unlike other teenagers.

I recently read Dave Grohl's autobiography (Nirvana/Foo Fighters) and he commented on the same thing that music can become an addiction! So it wasn't just me after all!

Nan bought me a Fidelity tape recorder for my 13th birthday and on a Thursday at 7:30pm, I would sit down in front of the television, set up my tape recorder with the microphone in front of the TV speaker and proceed to record the songs I liked, which were in the charts and screened on *Top Of The Pops*. I hoped there was nothing I wanted to record at 7:45pm because dad had a cuckoo clock hanging on the wall directly above the TV and the bloody thing used to go 'cuckoo, cuckoo' incessantly for what seemed liked minutes!

I also used to record my earliest group rehearsals in mums' little room. I know there are some recordings of when I first started playing guitar and I used to persuade nan to sing some of the old time musical songs. Our favourite was 'Sweet Rosie O'Grady'. Dad, as well as thinking he was multilingual, had an accordion and a harmonica. The reality was he couldn't play either of them, but that didn't stop him getting them out. I probably have recordings of him playing harmonica to my guitar accompaniment. Truth is he was such a suck and blow merchant, I think mum's *Hoover* vacuum cleaner was more melodic.

My old Fidelity was either a two or four track recorder with a selector button so that you could record two lots of recording on the same side. Kind of splitting the tape in half. Music was really taking over my life.

A big influence were the times that Gary Giles and I used to go over to Alan Golding's house. Alan had an older brother who went to work, earned money and was buying albums. We probably weren't supposed to, but we used to get his brother's albums out and play them. Alan's mum obviously didn't mind because I remember she loved the music and would often pop in to the room to check if we were okay although I think it was an excuse to be in with the lads and have a little dance and sing along. She was a lovely lady.

The three albums I remember most of all which were influential to me were The Rolling Stones' *Aftermath*, The Pretty Things' first album and The Yardbirds' *Five Live Yardbirds*. We played them every time we went to Alan's house. I'm surprised we didn't wear them out! I developed a fascination with The Yardbirds, but more so after Eric Clapton left the band (he was on the *Five Live Yardbirds* album). Jeff Beck joined and I was fascinated by the sounds he was producing from the guitar. I bought all the singles and looked forward to hearing what was on the B-sides. The Yardbirds, like The Beatles put good tracks on the B-sides and not throw away tracks as some other artists tended to do. Later on I will tell you a couple of stories of when I met Jeff Beck and Phil May from The Pretty things, but where was I? Oh yes.

During my last year at secondary school I was thinking ahead as to what I wanted to do at the end of the summer term. I didn't like school that much anyway so the prospect of staying on another year to the upper sixth didn't appeal. A few of us, Steve Gadd, Gary Giles and a couple of others, decided we should go to art college. Not only that, it sounded cool to say you were going to art college. After all, one of our local heroes Pete Townsend went to art college as did quite a few other guys in bands in the sixties.

My grades were pretty good at the end of term so I thought I would get into college with no problem. What I never did consider was that the art teacher, a little Scottish fella, whose name I cannot remember, clearly took a dislike to me. It probably didn't help because I was getting a bit overconfident by coming out with smart remarks in class (not so smart perhaps?).

I remember one incident where he was about to say something and midway through the sentence he started to say, "My hand is itching to..." but before he got a chance to finish the sentence, I said in a loud voice, "Well scratch it then". It received laughter from the class, but I think I had to stand outside the classroom for the remainder of the lesson! I'm going to blame Allan for this because I think where I 'd been playing the clubs with his group at that time, I was learning how to deal with 'the heckler'. So this incident with the teacher was like he'd handed me a line which I couldn't help but pull in. I reckon I'm still pretty good even now on stage with my one liners.

I was really upset when I discovered I had not been selected to go to Hammersmith Art College but Steve and Gary were. Particularly when I discovered a couple of others who got lower grades than me were going to college. It transpires that the art teacher himself had made the decision who was going and who wasn't. It all made sense now. I went home and told mum. She was going to the school open evening. I thought, great she'll give him a piece of her mind and come September I'll be in art college with my mates. I waited for the good news — heard the key go in the front door followed by mum entering the front room.

"Well, how did you get on, what did he say?" I asked.

"He said he didn't like you, so you won't be going to college", she replied.

"Great" I said, and what did you say to him?" I asked.

"Nothing" she said "It wasn't worth it... I'm not stooping down to his level, ignorant sod. You'll just have to go and get yourself a job".

When I told you the story of the headmaster and the cane incident, here then were two examples of what I meant when I said in their way, my parents sort of taught me to fend for myself.

In an odd way it reminded me of something else as I explained earlier on in my primary school days when I told the story about being accused of something I didn't do. Well it happened again in Christopher Wren School and I 'm sure it's jealousy which makes people say or do things to others.

It was at a time when Steve Gadd and I were really becoming good friends. I used to love going around to where Steve and his family were living at that time in a flat in Emlyn Gardens, Shepherd's Bush. Steve had just got a white Rosetti Lucky 7 acoustic guitar.

I truly loved Steve's mum. She, unlike my mum, seemed full of fun and had a good sense of humour and always made me feel welcome in their home. I really had to fight to get the clothes I wanted to wear probably because mum was older, whereas Steve's mum was much younger and more fashion conscious.

One day at school Steve came up to me and was really angry because apparently I had been saying some very unkind things about his mum. I was mortified because I loved her and nothing could be further from the truth. I think it took a little while but fortunately Steve believed me and our friendship continued. Always amazes me these people who start viscous rumours often become invisible when you try and find out where malicious gossip originates! Jealous shallow people... get a life will ya!

As a teenager I was becoming quite fashion conscious and I was growing out of going to Saturday Morning Pictures. My friend Allan Dennis suggested that we could go to the Hammersmith Palais as they were opening Saturday morning until lunchtime for the teenagers. We went for a little while and I must confess I was too self-conscious to be a dancer but it did enable me to watch everybody dancing chatting and listening to the chart music being played by the DJs. I think I've always been a people watcher and that's probably why I'm not bad at doing impressions of people.

Dad was concerned that my hair was getting too long (not by today's standards) and that people were looking at me walking down the street and thinking I was a girl (he obviously made that bit up — or did he?).

My hair was obviously causing a problem in the household so a compromise was struck. I agreed to have a little bit cut off and maybe have it styled. I could go to the hairdressers where Allan went. If it was okay for Allan then it must be alright.

So I reluctantly got on two buses which took me to a hairdresser on the Boston Manor Road, Hanwell — next door to McLenning Bookmakers where Allan was working at the time. I can't remember what the hairdresser was called now but it might just as well have been Dewhurst's the butchers shop by the time they had finished.

I could see in the mirror my lovely locks coming off. I was getting nervous but I thought well it's okay he must know what he's doing and Allan comes here.

When he finished I could cry. The hair looked ridiculous as far as I was concerned. It was worse than those photos you used to see in the windows of barber shops at that time. I had so much lacquer on my head you could have used it as a bread board. He had also given me this giant hair wave on top which made me feel seasick just looking at it. As my mum used to say, "Ooh, one more wave and you'll be overboard".

Now, I had to get not one but two buses to get home to East Acton. I thought, one look at me and people will think the circus has come to town. Anyway I got home, mum thought I looked lovely, but her eyes were not that good anyway. I was so upset, I ran upstairs and shut myself in the bedroom for ages. Then, there was a knock on the front door and my mate Frankie Hackett came around to see what my hair looked like, having just come back from the 'Stylist'. I locked myself in the bathroom and wouldn't come out. I decided I'd have to do something about this bird's nest perched on my head. So I got a hammer and chisel... no I didn't, but with all that lacquer on it, it felt like that's what it needed. I gave it a good wash and miraculously turned it into something a bit more normal. Actually, it didn't look too bad so at least I could go out in public without people wondering if I was wearing a warped Frisbee on my head!

My future hair dressing expeditions were of my choosing. I used to go to Dimitri in Hammersmith right opposite the Palais because Frank's brothers went there and they were mods. His brother Alfie even had a Vespa Sportigue with silver bubbles, chrome headlamps and a long ariel on the back.

I later started to go to The Grampians in Shepherd's Bush. Some of the lads at school went there and there was a fella called Jerry who worked there and had a good reputation. He was a mod and had great sideburns (or sideboards as my mum used to say). When it was your turn, you would jump up in the chair, he put a big white sheet around your neck and when he asked you what you want, you'd say. "Give me a half centre parting and Boston off the back". Jerry knew what you meant and when it was finished you walked out of the shop with the knowledge that a hair dressing local legend had done your hair and you'd gained a bit of street cred' as well.

So now as it transpired I wasn't going to college, it was time to find a job because there was no way I was going back to school. Thinking back, certainly in

1968, it was comparatively easy to find a job, so I bought the local papers, *The Acton Gazette*, the *West London Gazette* and of course the *Evening Standard* and searched the 'Vacancies and Jobs' pages for employment. The big question was "What am I going to do?"

I wrote after a couple of jobs and I attended a couple of interviews, two I recall which were sort of art/advertising studio kind of jobs. Office junior and work my way up to be Managing Director, that sort of thing. Actually, no, I had already made my mind up by then that I was going to be a musician and a job would just be a temporary thing until the band took off.

I don't think I really knew what a Telex Operator was, but I think I saw an advert in the *Evening Standard*, applied for the job, got and interview and almost immediately I was offered the job to start right away. I was to be a Trainee Telex Operator for Foster Wheeler Ltd and I think the salary was £8 per week. They were a very big engineering firm (also Foster Wheeler, John Brown Boilers) and the office was actually a very tall office block right above Marks & Spencer next to Edgware Road Station on the corner of Edgware Road and Praed Street right in the centre of London.

I was recently visiting BMG Records in nearby Paddington and the office block and Marks and Spencer is still there. Let me explain about the Telex Machine. I suppose it was the forerunner of the email. You sat at what I can only describe as an electric typewriter with attachments. You were given a message to type and the message came out of the side like a coded 'tic a tape'. You then fed the tape into the attachment which also featured a telephone dial. Every company which had a telex machine had their own individual phone number and company code name which came up once you were connected. Once connected you'd press the 'send' button and the coded tape would start and the message you'd typed was received and printed at their end. I remember our Foster Wheeler code name was REWOP LONDON (that spells POWER backwards... get it?).

Like I said all companies had their own identifiable call sign but my favourite was one which always made me chuckle when it came up once I'd contacted the company Siemens who were based in Staines, Middlesex. Have you guessed it yet? Their answer back code was SIEMENS STAINES! Immature maybe, but it made me laugh!

There were four of us in the office. Two young ladies in their early twenties, Pam and Barbara. Also my boss, my supervisor, Feliciana Martinez, known to us as Feli. She was a lovely lady and I think she was very fond of me and was always interested in me and my music. I had quieter moments in the office where she let me practice my typing skills and most of the time, if I'd written a song, I typed my new song out on the telex machine but keep the typed document and take it home.

I was recently reminded of the smell of that office fifty odd years on as it smelled of the paper and presumably as the telex machines got warm the carbonated paper gave off an odour. As I moved house recently, I found a box which had some of my old song lyrics in and there in the box were some of my lyrics typed out on the aforementioned telex paper and the smell is still there.

I found Feli to be an interesting lady. She was Spanish and it seems her family literally escaped from Spain during the Franco revolution. She lived close to Portobello Road and I mentioned one day that I intended to go to Portobello Market on the Saturday. She said that I must go to her house and stop by for coffee, which I did. While I was there, her brother arrived. I can't remember his name but he was an interesting guy and he spoke a lot about politics which I had never really taken an interest in to be honest.

However, something came out of the conversation a line of which I used in one of my songs many years later. Her brother was questioning the rights and wrongs of politicians and that they should be working for the people not against them. The point I was about to make was that he said this line which stuck in my head which was, 'but what is politics if it is not people'. I eventually used that line in a song I wrote titled 'Somebody Called You' which featured on the *Move It* album.

Occasionally I used to grab some lunch at a little Italian café along from the office in Edgware Road called Capitellis which was a vibrant but noisy place and I think it was Mama Capitelli, a real friendly lady who would be calling out the orders to the others cooking and serving. I liked their coffee and cappuccino which was quite new to me as we had tea at home.

I used to have to go downstairs to the post room to drop off the internal mail from our office. The post guys in there all looked like they were middle aged, probably ex-servicemen, not unlike my dad and I could imagine anyone of them being one of my dad's mates. They were a funny bunch and occasionally a couple of them would tell me a rude or slightly risqué joke which I'm sure was told to try and shock me. As time went on and fashions changed my hair got a little longer and my clothes to them, I imagine looked a little more flamboyant. Certainly in comparison to what they were wearing that's for sure. So I endured the wolf whistles and inferences about being a girl with good humour, because I could give it back to them in equal measure and once again I think it was my other apprenticeship playing in the working men's clubs and pubs which enabled me to respond.

A guy about a couple of years older than me started working in the post room. He seemed to be the odd job guy and runner, back and forth to the smaller office further up Edgware Road towards Marble Arch. He wore some really hip fashionable clothes and looked like he should be in a band. He was always keen to share with me any musical or up to date news or rumours.

One day he told me that he had heard the shop which was owned by The Beatles, called The Fool, was closing down and they were giving all the stock away. My lunch break was an hour from 1-2pm and I ran as fast as I could up the road towards Baker Street, only to find that everything had gone!

Another time he told me that The Beatles were playing on the roof of The Apple Records studios in Saville Row. By the time I'd finished work at 5:30pm, I'd missed that as well.

Finishing work at 5:30 pm also presented another problem playing with the band in the evening, when there was a mid-week show. This is where Feli was really understanding and I never had a problem getting off early to get home or be picked up to go and play a gig. I sometimes worked though my lunch break and other times she would just let me go early and make some excuse to her bosses, something like I was doing some work related errand.

As time went by Barbara and Pam left and we had a succession of temp workers until permanent staff were found. One day a new young girl started and was totally different to Barbara and Pam but funnily enough more in common with Feli and me. She was a bit of a 'Hippy chick' and wore clothes that she probably bought in the Portobello Market or the Kensington Antique market (where I used to get some of my clothes) — Lennon style national health round glasses, very short skirts and coloured tights. Purple, blue, pink all the colours of the rainbow. Her name was Maria and I really felt that we had something in common and at last I had an ally in the office. Maria was living with a guy named Bob who happened to be a bass guitarist playing with a couple of different blues artists, so we had other stuff to talk about aside from what goes on in the office.

I eventually left Foster Wheeler in 1969 to go professional with Stray. It was soon after Maria started there. I had lost contact with her but we managed to find each other recently on Facebook. She remarried and is now living in Kuwait, but we hope to meet up someday soon.

Incidentally on a fashion note, my friend Alan Dennis had a sister named Susan. He told me she was selling a white silk Kaftan. Very Hippy, Indian styled which was very fashionable at that time. I think I gave her ten shillings for it and I came out of her house in Primula Street and put it on to walk back to my house. Mum had been looking out of the bathroom window and had watched me walk up Norbroke Street. She opened the door and greeted me with "What on earth do you look like?" I could see nothing wrong with what I looked like. However, having heard her response I was waiting for the "Wait 'til your father gets home" and actually what he would he say when he got home. He didn't say anything and clearly mum didn't tell him either. I made sure if I wore it, I put it on after I got out of the front door. I wore this lovely Kaftan playing with the band and I have some photos of me in a very early 'The Stray' photo shoot wearing it. I have to say I looked quite angelic, not really a Hippy like I thought I was supposed to look like. Dad would have said "He looks like a bloody girl!"

Saturdays, I would jump on the train to High Street Kensington or Chelsea to look at or buy clothes at the antique markets or go to Portobello Road Market. I seem to remember that Freddie Mercury and Roger Taylor from Queen may have a had a stall in Kensington Market for a while. As you went in, there was a flight of stairs in front of you and their stall was right at the top of the stairs in front as you left the staircase. Oops Freddie wouldn't want it to be called a stall, more like a boutique I reckon? I think I bought some velvet trousers there and some tops. I got my starry t shirt in the market which I wore on stage and is on the inside cover of the first Stray album. You could also buy second hand ex-army clothing. A favourite with our lads were the sailor trousers which you could buy dyed in various colours. We used to call them 'Willie trousers' because they had no fly buttons or zips, just a large flap done up with buttons so consequently it revealed a bit of a bulge in the front area!

I won't tell the full story, but Danny Baker has written some fascinating books about his life and in one book he tells a story about Queen going into the record shop he was working in when he was 17 years old. He said he liked what he heard of Queen's music on their first album and it reminded him a bit of Stray (one of his favourite bands). Clearly Freddie didn't like the comparison, because according to Freddie "Stray, they are just a fucking pub band!" Oh dear, you can't win 'em all.

By 1969 we could sense that Stray were starting to become very popular on the live gig scene despite the fact that we still didn't have a record out... something which was soon to change.

I realised when I used to go out shopping or somewhere, I could hear people saying or whispering quite loudly "That's Del Bromham" or "Stray" or "That's the guitarist in Stray" stuff like that.

Strange at first although I have to confess I rather liked being recognised. When the first album was released in 1970, the whispers changed to face to face confrontations in public by people actually wanting signed autographs. I could sense older bystanders looking over as if to say, "Who the hell does he think he is". I've always been up to signing stuff for people because the fans are very important to me. Without the fans one would not have a career. Thank you folks, xx.

# 10.
# Music Biz/Learning The Trade

**O**ur managers, Peter and Ivan were working hard to get us into gigs which carried some credibility to raise the profile. As far as I am aware we were the youngest band to play the Roundhouse, Chalk Farm at that time. The Roundhouse was an old engine shed and held about 2,000 people. This was nothing like The Old Actonians Club.

The aroma in The Roundhouse was a mixture of incense sticks, patchouli oil, cannabis and if it had been raining, damp Afghan coats. The place was dark and the liquid light show was projected on the walls with moving images. I recall two stages in the early days. One band played while the other set up.

The bill on our first appearance there was The Byrds, Deep Purple, Love Sculpture, The Gun and Stray. The Byrds didn't appear. As I understand it was something to do with them having some problems arriving from the USA.

Deep Purple had recently had a hit single with a song called 'Hush', which funnily enough we had featured in our set for a while. Love Sculpture, with Dave Edmunds on guitar had the instrumental hit 'The Sabre Dance'. The Gun had a hit with 'Race with the Devil' and I think we might have even played that for a while. I've never thought of it before but although it was supposed to be an 'Underground' alternative venue, all these bands had hit records and would have been on TV! This line-up of Deep Purple had Rod Evans on vocals and Nicky Simper on bass, before Ian Gillan and Roger Glover.

Fairly recently I was at a party for my friend and Sax player Terry Marshall celebrating his birthday. Nicky Simper and I were sat at the same table and had a good old chat about those times.

I think we played first and we were all nervous because it felt we had a lot at stake to go down well at a venue like that. We were wearing the latest gear bought from Kensington Market. We had white satin shirts and we all had different colour crushed velvet trousers.

We played our set and there were a few of what they called 'idiot dancers' gyrating around. We couldn't really tell if we went down well or not, because the audience applause was quite lukewarm. But maybe because it wasn't cool to look too excited or maybe most of them were too stoned to organise clapping their hands together? However, we must have done something right, because we were invited back to play a couple of months later — the next time with Spooky Tooth and Family.

This show was a 'lightbulb' moment for me. Family sounded like nothing I'd heard before. I went out and bought their album *Music In A Doll's House* soon after the show.

I remember seeing Spooky Tooth arrive at the venue and they looked really cool before they even got on stage. They played a couple of cover versions in their set with their own arrangements. Their type of arrangements were exactly like what Peter and Ivan were trying to explain to us to do. If we were going to play a cover then make it your own. I went and bought their album *Spooky Two*, still a great album over fifty years on.

****

Another venue which we really enjoyed playing was the California Ballroom in Dunstable, Bedfordshire. Once again two stages, the big one where the main band played and the smaller one at the other end. There were often three bands on, so the bands alternated from one end to the other. One band finished and the other band started.

The manager of 'The Cali' as we called it was a little chap named Dennis. He was a lovely fella and he liked us too I am pleased to say, because we played there lots of times in a relatively short space of time, supporting some of the big bands of that era. I think because Dennis liked us, our managers had no trouble persuading him to let us play the big stage with the headliner. I think we only ever played on the little stage once.

Here are some of the bands we played with at The California Ballroom. Dave Dee Dozy Beaky Mick and Titch, White Plains, Grapefruit, Cupids Inspiration, Status Quo, Traffic, O.C.Smith and possibly Dave Berry and Crispian St Peter.

O.C.Smith was high in the charts when we supported him. I was looking forward to seeing him as I liked his hit song 'Hickory Hollers Tramp' and I liked soul singers. Unfortunately to our surprise there was a very small audience turn out and his set didn't go down very well, primarily because he was singing with a jazz trio, piano, double bass and drums with O.C. singing. Nothing was mic'd up and it was an acoustic piano and double bass so it sounded so quiet you could hear people talking above them playing. Ideal probably for a jazz club... "mmm nice".

Status Quo were on their second hit single 'Black Veils of Melancholy' following the success of 'Pictures Of Matchstick Men'.

We always got to gigs early and when Quo arrived we were in the dressing room, which actually was a big kitchen at the back of the building. When their road manager arrived, he was shouting that he needed to have a good wash because he'd been up all night. I couldn't possibly say what he said he'd been doing all night!

I was chatting to Francis Rossi and he was showing me his Grimshaw guitar, which was a copy of a Gibson Les Paul. If you see the old *Top of The Pops* with Quo performing 'Pictures Of Matchstick Men', you will see the Grimshaw guitar I am explaining to you. Francis told me the guitar he really wanted was a real Gibson Les Paul. Funny really because throughout his career I've never seen him use a Gibson Les Paul. He's better known for the Fender Telecaster. They were a good pop band and just like us playing cover versions in their set.

To be perfectly honest, I think every act we played with at The Cali were good. I think that is because these were all acts who had learned their trade on the road playing night after night.

Without a doubt, the biggest thrill of all was when we were about to play at

The Cali with Traffic, but I must give you some background on why this show was so important to me personally.

At this point I have to wind the clock back to about 1964 or '65. The Savoy Cinema, my local had been turned into a bowling alley so a walk up the road to Saturday Morning Pictures was now out of the question. There were other cinemas of course doing the morning matinees, but they were all a bus ride away. One day I decided to try the ABC in Hammersmith. Unlike the Savoy, on this particular day they showed a documentary on up and coming beat groups. What really hit home was a piece about a band from Birmingham called The Spencer Davis Group featuring the 15-year-old Stevie Winwood.

I loved the way he looked, he had a nice, checked shirt on (funnily enough I've just noticed I'm wearing one now as I am writing this piece) and I like the way he was holding the guitar and of course that voice! To think he was only a couple of years older than me really made me believe that I could make it too. I had to find out more about The Spencer Davis Group and I did somehow manage to find an LP which had various R&B and blues style songs on it. But their version of Hoagy Carmichael's 'Georgia On My Mind' based on Ray Charles hit version was and still is outstanding. And sung by a 15-year-old? Unbelievable!

The following year they had their first chart hit record with 'Keep on Running' and a hit album titled *Autumn 66* a great album and it's still one of my all- time favourite albums. I was really sad to hear that the following year he had left The Spencer Davis Group but Stevie's next band Traffic were ground breaking for the time and sounded like no-one else.

So fast forward to Stray opening for Traffic at The California Ballroom, Dunstable. I was beyond excited at the prospect of just seeing the band yet alone meeting my hero. As usual we arrived at the venue first and waited for Traffic to arrive. When they did they were all in a Ford Transit parcel van, painted purple with their own symbol painted on the side.

When the back of the van was opened it was packed with equipment and I think there were two Hammond Organs piled one on top of the other. Steve is known these days for using the B3 model, but I think the two in their van were M100s. People who know me will know that I am not usually stuck for words, but when I met Stevie Winwood, I just could not speak. I had so much to say and so many questions. I was so in awe of this guy that I probably sounded like a blubbering idiot. This was the original line up of Traffic with Stevie on guitar and organ, Jim Capaldi on drums, Chris Wood on Saxophone, Flute, organ and congas and Dave Mason on guitar and bass guitar.

Surprisingly enough the gig was not packed with people, so during their set I watched them from various vantage points in the ballroom, but I spent a fair bit of time side stage next to Stevie while he played Hammond and bass pedals with his feet while singing at the same time.

He also played guitar which was a non-reverse model Gibson Firebird VII, a two pickup model in Kerry green. I had never seen or heard a guitar sound or played like it. To say I was blown away was an understatement. Sometimes meeting and seeing your heroes can be a disappointment, but my goodness he nor Traffic were a disappointment. I am still a huge fan to this day and if I had one ambition in life it would to play a song with Steve.

Traffic played their set and their equipment was hastily removed from the stage because we were due to finish the night off with our set. For some reason, although Steve Gadd was our lead singer, we played in our set a version of Traffic's 'Dear Mr Fantasy' which I sang. This song featured the ultraviolet lights coming on and I had dots on a pair of granny style sunglasses which had ultra-violet dots on them. Ivan had painted my Fender Duo Sonic with ultraviolet paint. The speaker cabs had ultraviolet stars and Steve Gadd twirled sticks around which had ultraviolet ribbons tied to them.

Naturally, just seeing the real thing playing 'Dear Mr Fantasy', I didn't think we would be playing that one tonight, especially right after they played it. However, our managers, particularly Ivan, insisted that we keep it in our set (it was the second song from the end) as it was part of 'the act'! We played it, I sang it, but I was really self-conscious of that fact and wished we hadn't done.

Not long after playing that show we had our van broken into and a lot of our equipment stolen including my beloved Fender Duo Sonic guitar. I began to look around for a new guitar. There were no Duo Sonics around at that time as they were not a popular guitar and that one was a 50s model anyway. Stratocasters, Telecasters, Les Pauls, SGs and Rickenbackers were the ones being used by all the well knowns so they were the ones of choice.

Denmark Street in central London has always been the street lined with music shops, so one day I decided to have a look there. I walked into Top Gear, a shop well known for stocking good guitars and getting good advice. I recognised a guy in there who turned out to be the manager at that time. His name was Sid Bishop who I had previously seen at The Roundhouse when he was playing guitar for The Social Deviants, later called The Deviants, lead by a now legendary singer/poet/journalist, Mick Farren.

I was telling Sid what had happened and just having a general chit chat, when I noticed hanging on the wall a three pick-up non reverse Gibson Firebird VII similar to Stevie Winwood's one. This model had three black plastic coated P90 pickups and the colour was Pelham blue so it was not identical to Stevie Winwood's but it was similar and it was a Firebird and there was no others around at that time which I had seen. It was £175, quite a lot of money for those times but I had to have it. Over the years I have bought several of them and over the years I have found my name appears to be synonymous with the Firebird style guitar.

One of our regular gigs was at The Farx Club, in Potters Bar. One night in particular around 1970, who should walk into the dressing room but Spencer Davis! He seemed a really nice fella and during the conversation he asked if he could get up and jam on a couple of songs with us. Well we had never jammed with anybody. Nobody got into our little circle, but hey this was Spencer Davis! And he might discover me as the new Stevie Winwood. I can't remember what we played exactly. It was a couple of 12 bar blues numbers and I don't know if we were any good as his backing band or not but we played, it went down well, but he'd gone home by the time we finished our set so we never heard from him again. It looks like he hadn't discovered the new Stevie Winwood after all.

# 11.

# PFAIM International

Things were starting to move very fast for Stray and important decisions were having to be made by all of us, Steve, Gary, Ritchie and me. Also so were our managers Peter and Ivan. We were getting many offers and it was getting almost impossible to do a day job and go to play a show as well. It wasn't such a problem for Steve and Gary who were at college but the rest of us were getting paid from our day jobs. Up until now we had been taking very little money out for ourselves and investing in the band. Ritchie was working for the civil service. Peter and Ivan had comparatively good jobs, so for us four it was a bigger gamble going professional. For me personally playing music for a living is what I always wanted to do anyway, so my decision making wasn't going to be so difficult.

I vaguely remember Peter Amott and Ivan Mant, coming around to see dad, explaining to him what they planned to do for us, now we were about to turn professional. Mum and dad never discouraged me from playing music in the band but I guess they had concerns — their son giving up a proper job with a regular wage. After a while with dad having listened to what Peter and Ivan had to say he just had to ask the question about how much did they think that I would earn? I think I am right in saying that the intention was to start by paying us £20 per week. That was probably double what I was earning as an office boy and about £2 more than dad was earning. It's hard for me to describe his reaction to this but he kind of coughed and sat up and said, "Well yes that seems good, is there anything I have to sign?"

On 6th January 1970 we went to the offices of Transatlantic Records and signed our first recording contract. It was a standard three-year deal with two one-year options, which sound okay but bear in mind the options where stacked in the record company's favour.

Transatlantic had been primarily a folk music label but they decided to branch out to try and get in on the up and coming Progressive Rock scene. Other bands like Jody Grind and Little Free Rock were also on the label at that time.

Soon after we went into Sound Techniques Studios in Chelsea with engineer Jerry Boys and producer Hugh Murphy (who went on to have hit records with Gerry Rafferty). Our days were like going to work hours, normally 10am to 6pm. We had lots of songs so I don't remember why we chose the ones we did for the recording session. We basically played live in the studio, just like we were on stage to get the backing tracks down. Then we overdubbed other instrumentation and vocals. The album was recorded and finished in a week. We were well rehearsed so that made things easier and virtually every song was put down with the first couple of takes.

I suppose because like many bands, we were well rehearsed and with the exception of one song 'Around The World In 80 Days', all the other songs we had played in our live set.

I was having a conversation with Steve Gadd a while ago and I mentioned some of the songs we had at that time but never recorded. One of the first songs Steve wrote was called 'Nowhere To Go', a really good song which for a while we opened the show with. There were some other songs I recall, 'I'm Flying', 'In Search,' 'See How High You Fly' and 'Life' to name but a few.

I recorded 'Life' some fifty years later and you will hear it on my solo album *White Feather*. I tried to keep it just like I used to play it with the band back then and it does have that kind of late sixties psychedelic vibe to it.

The opening track to this, our first album release was 'All In Your Mind' which is over nine minutes long. By any standard, recording a track for that length, yet alone starting the album with it, was quite a bold move. You are always advised to make a record that is only a few minutes long and get the hook in early as possible as many radio stations won't play it. I am sure we never took any of that into consideration. We were young, playing out music and that's how it is, take it or leave it. Neither Steve nor I can figure out why we chose the ones we did, but I think we chose the right ones.

We never had any issues with Hugh Murphy or Jerry Boys while recording the album, they seemed to get what we were doing and made our first recorded album an exciting and a satisfying process. In fact, Hugh Murphy worked with us for our second album *Suicide*. There was always fresh coffee on the go and to this day when I smell coffee it does remind me of Sound Techniques Studio.

It occurred to me while writing this and the songs which we had for that first album, that we were still playing covers of other peoples' songs in the live set prior to the recording. I think it's very possible that from the moment we started playing shows promoting that first album is probably the start of us playing totally original songs in our set list.

I mentioned earlier about bands like Family and Spooky tooth at The Roundhouse. Well having bought their albums we had introduced into our set 'Better By You, Better Than Me' and 'Society's Child', both recorded by Spooky Tooth and 'Peace Of Mind' by Family.

Peter and Ivan set up their management company called PFAIM International, which were the initials of their combined names, Peter Frederick Amott and Ivan Mant. Fame eh? Clever don't you think?

They shared an office in central London with The John Sherry Agency. John Sherry's agency were booking many of the bands working on the scene at that time so it was a great move being right there on the front line. Quite a few of the agents who worked in those offices went on to have successful careers in the music industry.

The first Stray album received mixed reviews but overall quite good ones. However, there was always this reoccurring backhanded comment about being good for their age, or they are very young rather than acknowledging or actually reviewing the record for its merits.

Fortunately, we were quickly gathering a loyal fan base and we were playing to pretty full houses almost everywhere we went. And we went everywhere, the length and breadth of Great Britain and quite a bit of time abroad, particularly in Holland France and Germany.

Our shows were loud and energetic. I believe it captured our youth and consequently our fan base was all about the same age as us. We always seemed to play the songs fast, much faster than the records. Why that was I don't know, but it seemed natural at the time. Maybe it was youth and enthusiasm, who knows? Because of this we were also getting known as a 'Speed freak' band, but at that time we barely touched an aspirin yet alone amphetamines! We were different to other bands on the scene at the time. Yes, we were young but we moved around a bit on stage as well, which I think at that time wasn't cool. You were expected to stand still and look miserable. How could we possibly look miserable? We were out there, playing our music and doing what we wanted to do for a living, thoroughly enjoying life.

Ivan in particular, really helped to develop the stage show visually. We carried the whole show everywhere we went. PA, lighting and pyrotechnics, smoke bombs, explosions strobe and ultra violet lighting — everything but the kitchen sink. We replaced the kitchen sink for a dustbin actually. We could often be found backstage before a performance tearing up small pieces of paper which were put onto a larger paper skin covering the top of the dustbin (almost like a drum skin). An explosive charge was wired up and placed in the bottom of the dustbin and at a given point, which was normally in the start of the second half of our final song 'All In Your Mind', the bomb in the dustbin exploded taking with it the pile of torn up paper pieces, so it looked like snow or something falling to the ground. It certainly used to surprise the audiences.

To be honest it still surprised me even though I knew it was coming! Even years after when we stopped using the dustbin and bomb, I still used to tense up at approximately the point in the song where the bomb would go off! It was bloody dangerous actually. Sometimes the bomb went off with so much force it would rip the side of the dustbin out with it. One time a piece of shrapnel hit Ritchie and another time a big lump flew off and hit Gary in the back and he still has the scar to prove it. He was taken to hospital after that show to get checked out and when the doctor asked him how he got the injury he replied something to the effect of "Well, I was on stage and we have a bomb that goes off and..." Well you can probably guess the rest.

One time in Europe, we played a big festival in Belgium and we went on stage before Yes. We had already played a couple of shows here and there with them in the UK so we kind of knew them and what they were all about.

As usual towards the end of 'All In Your Mind', the bomb went off and blew a big hole in the stage. Yes refused to go on until it was fixed. They did play so we must have got the stage fixed but I wonder if they were aware the band with the bomb were on before them? The first time we played with Yes was at a college somewhere in London.

We could have got quite stroppy with them as a result of what happened. I was backstage which was being used as a communal dressing room. The singer Jon Anderson was in panic mode dragging one of his road crew in with him and shouting in his high voice, "I can't find my belt, I can't find my belt"! Then he started opening our personal bags and when he got to my bag I called over to him, "Oi, what are you doing?" to which he replied "I can't find my belt!" "Well you won't find it in there. I am not a thief you know!". "I'm just checking, I need to find my belt", said Jon. To be honest I had to bite my lip. With my warped sense of humour and the fact that Jon did have a high voice, which reminded me of Jimmy Clitheroe , the old radio comedian known as 'The Clitheroe Kid'. I've seen old photos of Jon Anderson around that time wearing the wide leather belt with a big buckle on it worn over his shirt. Oh yes I believe he found the belt eventually.

I have seen music film footage of Yes on location in Belgium which I recognised, because this film is almost identical to a film which the same film crew shot of Stray.

I have never seen the Stray film and I often wonder if it still exists somewhere. Some old footage of us filmed in Germany was found recently and I remember filming this piece. We were in the countryside miming to the song Jericho so this must have been 1971. I remember Bob our roadie arguing with Ritchie because the drum kit was wobbly because the ground wasn't level. Funny how you remember these things.

Another time in Germany, and I think it was in Dortmund, we had a night off and went to a Bier Keller where there was an 'Oompah band' playing. All lederhosen, tubas and stuff like that. The place was packed and in full swing. Despite it being packed we managed to find a long wooden table — four band members, roadies Phil and Bob and I think Peter Amott was with us as well. Bob went to the bar and like a typical Englishman he attempted to order the drinks by doing the shouting and pointing thing which some people, particularly the British, find the best way to translate.

The bar staff must have understood the two magic words "beer" and "band" and soon the waiters and waitresses were bringing the beers over to us, again and again and again. Stein after stein, which as some of you know are bigger than pints. At the end of the night we began to think that this is going to be a big bill and as we walked over to the bar they couldn't understand that we were asking for the bill, instead they were smiling and waving and wishing us "Aufwiedersehen and goodnight". Ah, of course, the words beer and band made sense now. They thought we were with the 'Ooompah band' and the drinks were on their tab. You know how much I love an 'Oompah band'.

We used to do some odd things and one time I remember in Belgium or Germany Phil our road manager, Steve and I were walking along a street and we passed a pet shop — in the window was a tortoise. We stood there looking and one of us came up with something like, "He looks like a good old boy", so we went into the shop and bought the tortoise. What were we going to do with a tortoise? He could be our band pet or mascot? We must have been mad, just as well it wasn't a puppy or a kitten. What shall we call it? "Good old boy" of course. Good old boy was probably the only tortoise in history to go on tour with a band. He travelled in a cardboard box in the van with us. When we got home we decided to take it in turns to look after Good old boy until the next gig. To be honest I think the novelty wore off after a while and we felt it was better for him to stay in the comfort of a warm home. If I'm not mistaken Gary took it back to Sandies house? Good old boy got a mention in one of our press releases and I made the joke that Stray now had a tortoise so that Del Bromham could make his own personalised tortoise shell plectrums! Yes, silly I know, but not as silly as buying a touring tortoise!

In the early days, one of our road crew, and I won't mention his name got us into big trouble while we were playing in Switzerland. There was a support band who happened to be a friends of the promoter. The band had a guitarist who was blind but pardon the pun, the rest of the band didn't keep an eye on him. At several times during their equipment set up, the poor chap was wandering around the stage, tripping over cables and at one point knocked over an expensive microphone and stand. Not totally his fault, understandably, but his band mates should have been looking after him in that environment.

They played their set and because had their own friends, they were not in any hurry to move their equipment off of the stage so that we could begin. In those early days we only had two regular road managers, along with Ivan. One for stage and one for PA and sound. Our man on stage (who will remain nameless) had something of a reputation for having a short temper. So on this occasion the support band were asked on several occasions to politely move their equipment so that we could begin.

It would appear that being polite was not going to work, but that was when our man threatened to throw their gear off of the stage if they didn't move it and quick! Well our man duly proceeded to throw one of their speaker cabinets off of the stage followed by something else. Then all hell broke loose! The band jumped back on stage to try and stop him removing any more of their equipment. There was shouting and people threatening to exchange blows and in the middle of all this the blind guitarist was wandering around the stage trying to do, I'm not quite sure what? I only wish there had been a camera to film it. A scene like that in a rock documentary would never be believed. It would look like it had all been staged purely for effect.

I think the promoter managed to calm things down and we played our set. However, it didn't end there. After the show, the police arrived and we were escorted back to our hotel. We were under house arrest! When we awoke in the morning, we had breakfast and the police informed us no charges would be brought against us, but we were to be escorted out of town. I don't know what they expected us to do if we stayed in the town, I mean we had another show to get to. What did they expect, that we were going to perform a scene like in the film *Blazing Saddles* where we would "Go riding into town, raping the horses and shooting the women!".

Over the years I have got to know Bernie Marsden a fine guitarist and songwriter who is most famous for playing in *Whitesnake*. I would have to make a correction to a story he wrote in his autobiography. He said that a band he was in once supported Stray and said that our drummer, which would have been Ritchie, was not co-operative and would not move his drum kit, and said that later when Bernie was playing with Cozy Powell and Stray opened for them, our drums had to be moved, so Ritchie had learned his lesson when he was supporting (what comes around goes around kind of thing), or something like that, I hope that made sense?

The point is that Ritchie would never had been like that and furthermore he never touched his drums, in fact we rarely arrived early to do a sound check as Phil our sound engineer at the time and later Dave, knew our sound requirements inside out. All that was necessary for the band were line checks which the crew carried out. The person who may have had the drum altercation with Bernie's band would have been our man the equipment tosser! Ritchie Cole is innocent, honest guv.

1971 saw us record and release our second album *Suicide*. We had achieved a lot in 1970 with the release of our first album and played so many shows I've lost count. We were over in Europe quite a lot and were picking up a following particularly in Belgium, Holland and Germany. We played quite a few festivals. One of the top rock bands in Belgium was Ghengis Khan. They attempted to sing some of their songs in English, even though they were in their own country. Towards the end of their set they played a song where they would try and get the audience singing along... in English! One time I remember we were all standing side stage and they started shouting from the stage "C'mon everybody, sing with us". When we heard what they were singing in English us mischievous lads could do nothing more (apart from laugh) and join in with great enthusiasm of course. We all sang at the top of our voices the words "What do I got". It sounds funnier when you sing it out loud in a group of a couple of thousand people.

I remember we played in Dortmund a couple of times. Quite a few people in the audience were English and were the sons, daughters or even the servicemen themselves of a nearby army camp. I think that is quite probably where we got the taste of on the road partying! We always liked Dortmund.

In 1971 we started recording the *Suicide* album at Olympic Studios, Barnes, London. It was quite a feeling to be in these studios where so many great artistes and so much history had been made. It was a real buzz to know that, one of The Beatles had just been in or Keith Richard was next door. You wanted to take deep breaths to try and lap up some of their talent. One day we were in the big studio 1. There was a Hammond C3 organ set up and it had two or three Leslie cabinets set up in a sort of half circle. I loved Hammond organs but I'd never really played one at that point. It was like viewing the Holy Grail of keyboards sitting there in all its glory. It turned out that it belonged to Stephen Stills who was in there the night before.

All through the day during our recording session, I kept checking the studio door in the hope that Stephen himself might walk in and introduce himself. Just think if he had come in, he might have even played on our album. That would have been a real name dropping boost for us. However, we never had guests with us and we had never really played with anyone else. We were a little family, a tight unit and we seemed to exist quite happily in our own bubble. There were other bands whose line ups were changing from time to time, but playing with anyone else other than each other never entered our heads. Remember we had now been playing together for four years and we were still only 18 and 19 years old! We were tight as a unit, that was band, management and crew and musically tight when we got in the studio. What could possibly go wrong? Don't go away my dear readers, there is much more to come.

I played more keyboards on this album although the album was basically recorded the same way as the first album. Gary, Ritchie and myself played the backing tracks live and we overdubbed the vocals additional guitars and keyboards afterwards. I remember when we started to record the title song 'Suicide', in order to get the right sound, I had to be put in a small sound booth on my own with my 100 watt Laney stack, that's an amplifier and two 4x12 speaker cabinets, so that my sound didn't overspill into the microphones on the drum kit. The amp was up at full volume and in that small booth it's a wonder I am not deaf? Eh? What did you say?

In studio 1, there was a beautiful black Steinway Piano, a Baldwin electric harpsichord and a Mellotron. I used all of these keyboards on the recordings. The Mellotron was a fascinating instrument. I had only ever heard them on recordings by other artists but I had never played one. I was told that this one was possibly the one that The Beatles had used, so naturally I had to turn it on to the Flutes setting and play the intro of 'Strawberry Fields Forever'. Yes, that sounded just like it to me.

I used the Mellotron in its strings (orchestra) setting for the songs:' Son Of The Father' and 'Dearest Eloise'. I know particularly at that time the purists would say that it didn't sound like a real orchestra but the Mellotron had it's own character. You know when it's a Mellotron. Thinking back the first two records I heard with a Mellotron on would have been 'Nights In White Satin' by The Moody Blues and 'Space Oddity' by David Bowie. I went to see King Crimson at The Marquee Club in London when their first album came out and heard one being played live.

The music press at that time used to print a chart of best guitarists, drummers, bass players, keyboard players as voted for by the public. I was nominated in the category of best guitarists one time. Modesty prevents me from telling you where I was in the list, but it was good to be mentioned along with some very big names. Stray were playing everywhere at that time and it's obvious that we would have been the musicians that the voters would be seeing at the time of vote casting, so you have to get it into perspective and not get carried away with how great you are.

What really made me chuckle was I got nominated in the keyboard category as one of the best Mellotron players. Funny thing was except for my few days in Olympic studios tinkering with one, I had never owned a Mellotron in my life! The keyboard I was using on stage at this time was a Farfisa Compact Duo, plugged into a Watkins Copycat (tape echo machine) and with the strings setting on the Farfisa, it did sound a bit like a Mellotron. Later it looked more like a Mellotron because the casing got smashed and was fitted into a large black wooden case. How did it get smashed you might ask? Well that in itself is quite a funny story.

We were playing a show at The Mayfair Ballroom in The Bullring, in Birmingham which was part of the Mecca Ballrooms chain of venues. There was quite a big stage and was very high up as I recall. During one of our songs there must have been a long instrumental break so consequently on this occasion Steve wandered over to my side of the stage and leaned nonchalantly on the Farfisa Organ which was standing sideways to the front of stage. When Steve leaned on it there was nothing to stop him and the organ falling off of the side of the stage. I didn't actually see it because I was probably in full flight during one of my solos, but from what I gather happened was, Steve and my beloved Farfisa went off of the side of the stage and landed with a crash (it was still plugged in, by the way). From what I was told it probably looked something like that famous scene in the sitcom *Only Fools And Horses*, where Delboy falls through the hatch in the pub!

The Farfisa Organ had a plastic casing and didn't survive the fall, although surprisingly it still worked! One of our roadies, Marty Haynes had a friend who was a carpenter so he gave it to him and he built a smart black case to house the organ in. A black case which made it look like a Mellotron. I've only realised in recent times that I have no idea what happened to that Farfisa Organ.

We continued touring and it was as busy as the year before. We could really feel there was a 'buzz' going on in the business and I am aware that there were those who were saying Stray were going to be the next big thing like Led Zeppelin, Free or Black Sabbath. It was decided we should get into the studio and record another album.

We were booked into De Lane Lea Studios, Kingsway, Central London with up and coming engineer Martin Birch. This studio although smaller than Olympic had many great artistes and recordings made within these walls. After two reasonably successful albums we were raring to go and were feeling more relaxed and experienced about recording the next album. I had plenty of songs written and the songs, not unlike my previous songs, were little stories. Songs like 'Queen Of The Sea', about the old Whaling ships and 'Sister Mary' about a young lady jilted at the alter and joins a convent. Steve Gadd had written a song called 'Mr Hobo' which was slightly different to what we had done before. Sort of funky but with a country blues feel. The opening song was 'Our Song' which we all wrote together while we rehearsed in Wendell Park School, Shepherd's Bush which was just around the corner from where Steve and Ritchie lived.

Funnily enough I moved house recently and I found an old exercise book where Steve was writing down lyrics. He came out with a couple of lines and I suggested that maybe the song should be about the days of prohibition when there was little or no work for people in the USA in the early 1900s.

I was then and always have been into the old musical films of the thirties, forties and fifties and dad had a lot of these records I used to love listening to. I must have seen the film *Easter Parade* with Judy Garland and Fred Astaire and their duet of 'We're A Couple Of Swells' must have stayed in my subconscious, because I did a little play on words with the line in the song which Steve sings, "I'd like to buy a ticket for the station but I haven't got the money yet to pay". This was my influence from the 'Trolley Bus' song in the film where one of the lines they sing is "We could ride on the trolley bus but we haven't got the fare". You see what I mean? I suppose I was using the comparison of people who had nothing like Fred and Judy in the film.

On this particular day in the large rehearsal room, I became aware I was the only person in the room who wasn't on the same planet that the other three were on. I remember spending a fair bit of time waiting for the others while they rolled items along the wooden school floor getting enthused about the sounds they were hearing. Needless to say I hadn't swallowed the same brand of paracetamol that they had, so I didn't have a clue what they were talking about. However, 'Our Song' was written on this particular day and I have to say it's one of my favourites and became a live favourite with band and audience alike.

I think I am right in saying that I noticed Steve was becoming very aware of his voice and how to portray a song rather than just singing the note. Like an actor would do, which is something I started doing but a long time after Steve. He 'got it', long before I did.

He wanted an earthier sound to his vocal in 'Our Song' and wasn't happy with what he was doing. So he started smoking one cigarette after another until his voice became quite croaky. I wouldn't have tried that myself but his vocal on 'Our Song' is exactly what the song needed and is arguably one of his best vocal performances. As a comparison, well I don't know about Tom Waits, more like ten weights! That was for the mature reader!

Gary Giles was and still is a great bass player. I know very few people who can play as fast as he can. He used to exercise his fingers all the time. When we would drive to a gig, he would be sitting there clicking his fingers one by one on his lap. Dad would have thought he had a problem, but fortunately dad never travelled with the band so Gary was safe from criticism.

I don't remember why, but for some reason I played bass on Steve's song 'Mr Hobo'. In any case it was very gracious of Gary for allowing me to do that. I used his Fender Jazz (this was his spare as he always used a Rickenbacker) and being a fan of American soul music the feel of this was right up my street.

During the sessions Martin Birch suggested it would be great to have, as he put it 'Chick singers' doing backing vocals on 'Our Song' and 'Mr Hobo'. He made a couple of telephone calls and the following day three ladies arrived, all well-known ladies on the scene, Lisa Strike, Vicki Brown (the wife of Joe Brown) and P.P. Arnold. What! P.P. Arnold who a couple of years earlier had the hit record 'The First Cut Is The Deepest' and sung with The Small Faces on their song 'Tin Soldier'! She is singing on our album! When they started singing together on 'Our Song' it was one of those goose pimples on the skin moments. We had never had anyone else play with us and then the cream of vocalists arrive to sing on our sessions.

There is a line in the chorus where we all sing "Life gets harder every day. Poor man's got to find a way". We were all in the control booth listening to the girls singing the chorus and when the track stopped a voice with an American accent asked, "Excuse me, the singer, are you singing Poor or Paw?" We did find that amusing, but she was dead serious because she/they wanted to get the phrasing right. I suppose that's what you get when you try and sing in an American slang accent to an American.

P.P. or Pat to her friends... Cough cough, was at the time going out with a well-known bass player named Fuzzy Samuel (Calvin 'Fuzzy' Samuel). I saw him play with Stephen Stills and Chris Hillman in their band Manassass. He arrived at the session with Pat looking like he did on stage. He was a black guy who always wore a bowler hat. He stood leaning against the wall jigging up and down when the girls were working on 'Mr Hobo'. He said 'Yeh, nice bass man. Who's the bass player?". Gary gestured that he was the bass player. Fuzzy complimented him on the bass part on 'Mr Hobo'.

Well that's the best bass playing compliment I never got.

There was a young 'tape op' working with Martin whose name was Chris. One day we were in the studio working on 'Our Song'. We decided we'd like to hear some weird backward orchestra strings in the background behind the solo towards the end of the song.

What we did was, we gave Chris a couple of pounds to go down to the nearest record shop, then to go to the classical music section and pull out the first album he came too. This Chris did and he came back with *The Surprise Symphony* by Haydn. A coincidence, as this choice really was a surprise! Martin recorded a section from the symphony and then ran the tape backwards and mixed it into our track. We all thought it sounded great. We did a couple of mixes of the track. One with the backward strings and one without as well as an edited single length version, as this song was going to be the next single.

We found out at this point that we were not totally in control of our destiny, because the powers that be at Transatlantic Records thought that it was too 'far out and freaky' for the general public's consumption. I personally was really annoyed that they were interfering with our music, our art. I recall I had an angry exchange with the record label A&R man John Cooper, but he presumably was only obeying instructions from above and we lost that decision. As far as I was concerned, we make the music you, the record label, sell it. I never found out what happened to the version with the backward strings.

The VCS3 synthesiser had not long been on the market and it was suggested (possibly by Martin) that we get one in and have a go of it to see if we can get some interesting sounds from it. Just like the backward recorded strings, Martin Birch was really on the same page as us and it felt like for the first time we had a fifth member in the band. When the VCS3 arrived, it reminded by of a small telephone exchange with a small piano keyboard at the base. Nobody knew how to operate it so it was given to me to try and work some sounds out. I ended up using it on two songs, 'Sister Mary' and 'Our Song'. I'm surprised I never got a nomination for best synthesiser player of the year.

One of the guitars I used on this album (and on stage at this time) was a 12-string Danelectro, Belzouki. It sounded a bit like the Rickenbacker 12 string used by The Beatles and The Byrds.

Despite having various types of echo and reverb on the studio desk, Martin found a place in the building which had a great echo. It was at the top of a flight of stairs on a landing which was all concrete. These were the days before radio guitar transmitters were invented, so I played along with the track and had a really long guitar lead going down the stairs and into the control room. The sound is there to be heard on 'Queen Of The Sea'. The guitar sound was then transferred to a Leslie cabinet, a rotary speaker cabinet designed for organs.

We recorded a song called 'How Could I Forget You' and we used a couple of unusual effects on Steve's voice. He recorded two vocal tracks, Martin put one vocal track through a Leslie cabinet. I have used this effect on my guitar several times over the years. The other vocal track, I decided to tap the vocal on the tape with a pencil as it was going around which gave the vocal a slight wobble. It was an idea based on what I had read Paul McCartney and George Martin were doing when they were experimenting with tapes and I think they were referring to John

Lennon's vocal on 'Strawberry Fields Forever'.

I have always enjoyed the recording process and it felt good sitting at the mixing desk for the first time with Martin Birch. In retrospect I wish I had taken the time and trouble to devote more time to music production, as I find, the whole process of recording, the collaborations and developing new ideas inspirational.

I had always loved the musicals on film, like the Busby Berkley big Hollywood productions. Featuring stars such as Fred Astaire and Ginger Rogers, Gene Kelly, Donald Connors, Judy Garland and Doris Day. All those big productions really stirred my imagination. When I wrote 'Queen Of The Sea' I had in mind the old Spencer Tracy film *The Old Man And The Sea*. Although this film was not a musical, I wanted the song to set a scene in your mind. Even to this day when I write a song, it's as if I have the film in my head. The films of the thirties forties and into the fifties had classic productions which you just don't see anymore. I remember as a kid going to the cinema to see *Ben Hur* starring Charlton Heston. It seemed so big and colourful. At home I always looked forward to seeing films by Errol Flynn, my favourite being *They Died With Their Boots On*, about General Custer and 'The battle of Little Big Horn'.

I remember there were a few titles which were thrown into the hat as album titles. I will probably receive phone calls following this, but I am pretty sure I thought of the title "Saturday Morning Pictures" as going to the Saturday Matinees at The Savoy, East Acton were an important part of my childhood.

Transatlantic Records employed the up and coming design studio Hipgnosis to design the album cover with the then up and coming designers Storm Thorgerson and Aubrey Powell, otherwise known as Poe.

Transatlantic agreed to have a gatefold sleeve, which for Transatlantic Records was quite something as they had always been very careful with expenditure. The final front sleeve design was a combination of the big tiered cake featured in the Busby Berkley film *Top Hat* while in the foreground was Carole Lombard with the MGM Lions either side of her.

The inner sleeve was a collage of our personal photographs of us as children. The finished album sleeve looked really impressive and received an award on Thames Television for album design.

The album was titled *Saturday Morning Pictures* and we were all expecting it to be 'the hit' album and we would break the band into the big time.

Peter and Ivan met with Transatlantic Records to discuss the promotion of the album. What must be a first was that it was decided we were to play a Saturday Morning matinee at the famous Rainbow Theatre, Finsbury Park, London on 27th November 1971.

It was a hell of a gamble as we didn't know if people would come out to see a gig at 10 o'clock in the morning. We need not have worried, by 9:30am people were queuing around the block. We showcased the songs from the new album plus a few of the older songs. It went really well, it was great publicity and I don't think anyone has ever done it since.

When you went to Saturday Morning Pictures you always could get your SMP badge to show you were in that special club. We had our own badges printed and handed out on that day and they now appear to be worth money these days on sites like eBay.

The album received good reviews. John Peel had been a great supporter and had always played our music on his shows, but this time our single 'Our Song' was played on the Radio 1 afternoon show hosted by Noel Edmunds, where some of that week's new releases were reviewed by a guest panel. I can't remember who the panel were but I remember someone on there saying they thought it was a good record but the singer was trying to sound like Rod Stewart! Well I bet Rod never smoked as many cigarettes as our Steve to sing a song like that! Bloody cheek, hurrumph!

1971 went into 1972 and it seemed that our success was continuing with sell out venues all over the place. What could possibly go wrong?

1972 was yet again a busy year with shows at home and abroad, however there was a feeling beginning to grow that Transatlantic Records were definitely not the label for us. We had all so believed in the *Saturday Morning Pictures* album and we were sure this would elevate us to the next level. But we found that we were still playing the same places and other acts who were on the same level as us were starting to break it to that next level. The feeling was that all our contemporaries had better record labels and bigger management companies.

While writing this, it is like forming a big jigsaw puzzle and in retrospect it can give you a better understanding of why things happen. I was discussing this funnily enough only today over the telephone with Gary Giles.

We were billed to play the Reading Festival in 1971. The band seemed to be going places and to be on this festival was quite an achievement. You have to remember that playing Reading was big, it was like Glastonbury is today (although not televised). We had a great time slot mid-afternoon on Sunday 27th June. All of our equipment was on the stage (and we had quite a lot of it) and we were ready to walk on when the unexpected and unbelievable thing happened! We were told we could not perform because there was not enough time.

This was crazy because all of our equipment was set and ready to go. It appears that they wanted to pull us off to make way for another act which by some strange coincidence was managed by the management of the festival. In retrospect we should have just gone on and played, but we submitted and consequently never played. To say this was disappointing would be an understatement and I cannot imagine it happened very often if at all and I've never been aware of it happening to any other act. In retrospect I believe that this may have been the point that the feeling within the band was that our management was perhaps not strong enough or influential to have prevented something like that happening — being pulled off in favour of a relatively unknown act. Why didn't they pick on another band? It makes no sense at all, but we will never know.

The sweetener was that it'll be okay, you are definitely promised a spot on next year's Festival. Later that year we played at The Weeley Festival another huge event with much had more of a hippy feel to it and I think people wanted it to be the UK's version of Woodstock.

The Weeley Festival was on a site near Clacton-On-Sea, Essex and like Reading all the big and up and coming names of that era were on it. I don't remember much about the day, but I do remember standing side stage watching Van Der Graf Generator who I really enjoyed and sounded like no other band around at that time. The sound of their Hammond organ particularly appealed to me. They were on at 11:30pm on the Saturday night and we were following them at 1.am, early hours of Sunday morning 13th August. The bands played right through the night on this festival and I can't think of any other festival that did that.

We went on played and put on quite a show with a finale of a massive firework display which nobody did back then. It has become fairly common place these days. Our firework finale has become something of a story in rock folklore. Our managers had sent two of our crew out to buy the pyros for the show, one of the crew was a guy named Terry Williams. What probably no-one realised was what they had actually purchased were distress flares and I'm not referring to the type of trousers I was wearing at that time. It seems that our distress flares alerted the Lifeboats in nearby Clacton and they launched boats to look for a ship or boat in distress! Oops! We sent the R.N.L.I a donation by way of an apology.

Also in 1971 we made our first and only appearance on UK television on a programme titled *Disco 2*. This was the forerunner of the now legendary *Old Grey Whistle Test*. We played, or rather we mimed along to two songs from the then current *Suicide* album. I think we performed 'Jericho' and the other to be honest I'm not sure. It may have been the title track 'Suicide' or 'Son Of The Father'. Unfortunately the BBC wiped the tapes, which is not the first time that happened in my career, the next time was some years later, but that's another story which I will get to later.

As I mentioned earlier, we were in Europe quite a bit playing festivals and club shows and on a few occasions we made short films for a couple of TV companies in Germany, Belgium and France. Fairly recently some footage of one of those film shoots surfaced when someone found them accidentally, while doing some research on another topic. One piece is us once again miming to 'Jericho' out in the country somewhere and another is of us playing a cover of John Lennon's 'Cold Turkey'. It was not one of our regular show tunes but we had played it a couple of times as an encore. The cameras caught it and it's not a bad version either.

January 1972 started with some shows in France, but one show was particularly special. We played at the Midem Festival in Cannes. We stayed at a really lovely hotel for about three days and the weather was beautiful. Cannes is a beautiful place but quite clearly it was a place where you would need plenty of money. We all went down to the bar area in our hotel and I think that most of the people who were involved at Midem were staying there. As we walked towards the entrance I could see Roger McGuinn and presumably a couple of other members of the American Band The Byrds, sitting by a window. Roger McGuinn was easily recognisable because I had seen him so many times on television with his little glasses and a 12-string Rickenbacker playing 'Mr. Tambourine Man' and various other hit records. Once again I was thinking back to when I was a 15-year-old and never imagining that one day I would actually meet and play with artists like these.

Okay, I admit I am a bit starstruck when I meet my musical heroes and I tend to go into rewind a bit, stand back and say nothing, unlike some people who are able to go over and easily strike up a conversation.

Gary and I decided to sit at a table. There were a lot of people in the bar area and we were sitting on a table for four. While we were chatting two guys came over and asked if it was okay to sit at the table with us. They both looked like they were in a band. One of them young, good looking with very long dark hair and the other guy had wavy dark hair and a big droopy moustache. He would have looked good in a cowboy film. We said our hellos and it was apparent they were both Americans. We introduced ourselves and they introduced themselves. Well... Maybe I should have known. The guy with the moustache was Gene Parsons, Only the drummer with The Byrds and the other guy said he was Tim, the bass player in Poco.

Tim turned out to be Timothy B Schmit, who a couple of years later became world famous when he joined The Eagles. A waiter came over and asked what we all wanted to drink. "Screwdriver" said Gene. "Screwdriver" said Tim. I looked at Gary, Gary looked at me. I turned to the waiter and said "What's a Screwdriver?" "Vodka and orange juice" he replied. "Okay, we'll have two of them as well please".

I know what you will be thinking; everyone knows what a screwdriver is. Well yes, maybe you do now, but many of these drinks back in 1972 never had names and us youngsters had only recently been weaned off of Coco-Cola. We sat for hours in conversation with Gene and Tim and after quite a few Screwdrivers we were drunk in the process. Gene in particular was trying hard to persuade me to let him take my guitar so he could fit a 'B Bender' to it. A 'B Bender' fits to an electric guitar where the strap fitting sits, pulling the guitar up and in turn pulls the lever which in turn bends the B string. The effect is pretty much the same as you would hear on a pedal steel guitar. Gene and his fellow Byrds' guitarist Clarence White invented this.

Gene asked me what my main guitar was and I told him it was a Gibson Firebird. Consequently, Gene kept dropping into the conversation "Let me put a Bender on your Bird". We talked about lots of things but one thing which really fascinated me was when we got on to talking about PA equipment in particular. "We (The Byrds) want to get a Wemmer" said Gene. When he said a Wemmer he was referring to equipment made by the amplification manufacturer Charlie Watkins actually named WEM. Apart from Marshall Amplification, WEM was the other big name in amplification at this time particularly for PA systems.

"Yeh, when we get to England we are gonna get a Wemmer" he kept saying. We told him we had a WEM PA with not one but two Audiomaster mixing desks, but the irony was we wanted an Electrovoice, JBL or Altec Lancing PA system which the Americans used. I don't know if they ever got their Wemmer.

Both Gene and Tim were very nice guys. Tim invited me to his home in California if and when I get there. I wrote Gene's and Tim's phone numbers down on a piece of paper (actually I think it was on the back of a beer mat!), but by the time I got home to England I had lost it.

I think it was after our session on the Screwdrivers that once Gary and I returned to our hotel room, he became a bit worse for wear. I woke up to find Gary standing at the sink being sick! Except he was about three feet away and was actually being sick on top of the fridge we had in our room. I jumped out of bed and repositioned him to the nearby sink where he continued with the technicolour yawn. Once he finished I helped him back into bed and cleaned up the fridge top and pebble dashed sink.

It must be a thing which comes with youth, because I don't recall any of us ever having bad hangovers the next day following a session. Now I am older I have found it harder to recover. Bloody kids!

We watched The Byrds and Poco who sounded really good, both musically sounding very polished. We probably sounded like The Sex Pistols by comparison, but nevertheless we played our set and it went well. So well in fact that a major French drum manufacturer, ASBA drums endorsed Ritchie and on the way home to the UK, we had to go Paris to pick up a drum kit for him.

We were travelling in two vehicles. Phil and Bob were in the Ford Transit parcel van and we also at this time had a Ford Transit minibus driven by Neil. Phil and Bob went to Paris and picked up the drum kit and boy did they pick up a drum kit!

We had played another show in the south of France after Midem which might have been in Nice, just along the coast? We got into a bit of trouble at this club because as usual we let off our pyros and the exploding bomb and the club owner/promoter went crazy. He was going to call the Police, the National Guard, the Foreign Legion, anyone to help him teach these English types a lesson. If only we had Nat Joseph with us, he might have thought we had the ghost of Napoleon Bonaparte' on our side. A big argument ensued and he would not let us out of the club with our equipment. Phil and Bob had to go back the next morning where the club was opened and they were allowed to reclaim our equipment. I am not sure but I think Peter Amott had to really 'sweet talk' him to get the equipment back.

Phil and Bob were due to pick up the new drum kit at the ASBA factory while Neil was driving us back to the UK and we would all meet up at Calais to get the ferry back to Dover. It was a long drive back through France and as it was getting late we decided to stop off in a small town somewhere to get a night's sleep and make the final leg of the journey in the morning.

I don't remember the name of the town but I think it was somewhere near Lyons. We managed to find a hotel and we decided that we were going to have a quiet night following the partying. We came downstairs to see if we could get something to eat and drink and then get an early night. It was only a small town, it was a small hotel and a small bar, typically French and would not have been out of place in the sitcom 'Allo 'Allo. A quiet night we thought? Maybe not. The place was buzzing, really alive with conversation although we couldn't understand a word of it but nevertheless there was a great atmosphere in there. There seemed to be mainly fellas in the bar, not surprisingly all about the same age as us or thereabouts. Some of them were trying to make conversation with us so we were doing the best we could to communicate, when all of a sudden, quite possibly the only female in the bar, translated what they were saying to us in perfect English. Hardly surprising because it turned out that she was English.

She was a teacher in the local school giving the French children English lessons. Quite clearly she had no pupils in the bar, whether that or she was not a very good English teacher, but whatever, she came in very handy that evening. It seemed like a never ending supply of wine bottles kept coming out and naturally they kept getting emptied. Neil and I had started to get a little rapport going with a few guys down at the other end of the table.

Neil and I had a similar sense of humour and I really believe that humour can communicate the world over. Neil who had some experience in the holiday camps was very much at home with an audience. He and I would often stay awake on the way home from a gig and I would sit in the front and the pair of us would do impersonations, tell silly stories and just be downright stupid, quite possibly, to the annoyance of anyone in the back who hadn't fallen asleep. Anyway these guys suggested we should go with them as they wanted to take us to another bar so we could taste a different wine.

So Neil and I left Steve, Gary, Ritchie and Peter and the English teacher, and set off to this other bar somewhere with our French hosts. I have to admit I do not remember much about the new venue because I think when the fresh air hit us it, it clouded my memory. Neil and I stayed for as long as the bar remained open, we said our goodbyes and attempted to find our way home. I vaguely remember laughing and joking as we walked the empty streets trying to find our way back to the hotel.

Miraculously we got back to the hotel which was now empty as they had closed up for the night and we went up the staircase to the room that I was sharing with the rest of the band. We opened the door and it may well have been quiet downstairs, but there was one hell of a party going on in our room. It was a mad night and we were obviously making one hell of a noise because the hotel owners banged on the door several times and when they finally threatened to "call the Police", it was clearly time to calm it down a bit.

The next morning at breakfast, no-one in the hotel spoke to us and Peter Amott was clearly disgusted with these yobbos he had ended up in the middle of France with! We quietly left the hotel and the town never to be seen again. I wonder what happened to the English teacher?

Ritchie had been using a lovely old Ludwig kit. A standard set up with snare drum bass drum floor tom and tom on top of bass drum. Unknown to us, ASBA had given Ritchie a double kit. Two bass drums, two floor toms two (or maybe four) rack toms plus some small toms on a separate stand, as well as a set of congas. The drum kit itself was all metal in a wonderful chrome finish. It was loud and I mean loud! It was the loudest kit ever made and Ritchie was the man to whack them (remember my mum would confirm that). They looked great under the stage lights too. ASBA were very generous and for some time Ritchie was in all the music and trade papers as an endorsee for ASBA, great publicity for both parties.

August 1972 saw Stray return to The Reading Festival and what do you know folks? We got to play it this time on Sunday 13th August. I had this idea from remembering how the lights rebounded off of the mirror balls which you used to see hanging on the ceiling in dance halls. So I bought a roll of silver vinyl or plastic type of material which I cut into squares and glued to a cotton shirt, some old velvet trousers and a pair of grey platform, souled boots. Although when we initially took the stage it was still light, but as our set went on it became darker and that's when my mirror suit came into its own. I was like a walking ray gun or mirror ball.

It always looked better at venues indoors but with the aid of our lights it looked quite spectacular. I later made another suit this time I used small real glass mirrors. That looked impressive, but one time some of the glass squares on my shoulder cut me to pieces because they were directly under my guitar strap and the weight of the guitar really dug into my skin.

Anyway back to Reading and this was the first time I had worn the mirror suit. So picture this, I was about to climb the steps to the stage when I realised I could not bend my legs. The mirrors had created a kind of splint, so I was like a scarecrow. So with the assistance of two roadies, I was lifted onto the stage. The set went down a storm and we really thought that okay, then 1971 wasn't, but 1972 will be our year. Interesting to note that Status Quo went on before us and Roy Wood's Wizard followed us.

Speaking of Status Quo, when we had previously seen them they were a pop group and were having hits singles like 'Pictures of Matchstick Men'. By now Quo were down to a four-piece band as they no longer had the keyboard player and were playing harder rockier bluesy songs. They were trying to shake off the pop group image and wanted to get to the more rock orientated audiences like we were playing to. It was acknowledged that Stray always pulled a good audience. We were known in some quarters as the 'Peoples band' an accolade I'm prepared to accept. Generally speaking, our audience were the same age as us and we were like them but fortunate enough to be on the stage playing the music.

Quo's management had contacted our management/agency and suggested that Stray and Status Quo could play a show together. They wanted to tap into our kind of audience. There were a couple of new venues opening in the London area with the venue name The Sundown. There was one at Mile End and another in Edmonton.

The show was organised and was packed out. One thing I do remember was that when Status Quo arrived at the they all looked smart but when they got on stage they had changed into t-shirts, jeans and trainers. Probably didn't want to look too different from their audience.

As time went on Status Quo got the hit album and were packing out venues in their own right everywhere. It looks like they had the management and record company. We couldn't help but notice that this was another act that started on the same level as us and like many others were leaving us behind!

# 12.
# Under New Management

**B**efore we get into this chapter let me give you a brief story about Wilf Pine, who became our new manager. Wilf entered the music business working for one of the biggest music managers of the 1960s namely Don Arden. Don had a fearsome reputation and would do literally anything to get his own way, and one of his ways was to use violence or 'strong arm' tactics. Wilf was already known to many in the British underworld and gangland bosses. In fact, he was friends with the Kray twins and Reggie Kray once said that Wilf was the best fighter he had ever seen and was, I quote 'a fucking animal'.

Don would send a couple of guys out, normally Wilf and one other to deliver a stern warning or message to other managers or agents who might be encroaching on his territory. Wilf did tell me once that he often used to go accompanied by a guy he called 'Big Vinnie'.

An example of the type of message Wilf would deliver on behalf of Don Arden, is a story which goes something like this: Don was managing The Small Faces and he got word that another music manager, none other than Robert Stigwood (he went on to manage The Bee Gees) was interested in offering the Small Faces a new management deal. Don decided to take some action and duly told Wilf to go and visit Stigwood in his offices. Wilf never needed an appointment in order to make an entrance to a meeting. I was with him on a couple of meetings which I will explain in some detail, but I will tell you about that later.

This has almost become music business folklore, but apparently Wilf told Stigwood that Don had heard the rumour going around that he wanted to manage The Small Faces and be their new manager, but he should not even think about it. As I understand it Stigwood must of thought who on earth is he telling me what I can and can't do? It became apparent that Stigwood was not going to take any notice of any instructions or threats from Don Arden so he suggested that Wilf should leave and go back and tell Don. Not a good idea, Wilf and his partner grabbed hold of Stigwood and hung him upside-down by his feet out of the balcony of his offices and threatened to drop him on to street below if he continued not to agree with the message (or advice) he had delivered.

Obviously he got the message because Don continued managing The Small Faces up until singer Steve Marriot left to form Humble Pie with Peter Frampton, Greg Ridley and Jerry Shirley. I believe Clifford Davis who was managing Fleetwood Mac at the time had shown an interest in The Move, another of Don Arden's acts and I believe Wilf had to also pay him a visit to deliver a message from Don. However, it didn't require any further danglings from balconies presumably because that had become quite infamous by that time.

By the 1970's Wilf had teamed up with Patrick Meehan, another employee of Don Arden, who set up his own company Worldwide Artistes and in the process they signed Black Sabbath and Wilf was their co manager with Patrick.

By 1973 Wilf was visiting the USA fairly regularly and was becoming involved with the Mafia. He became very close to Joe Pagano part of the Genovese family. Wilf apparently was one of only two Englishman to be allowed into the Mafia.

I could write a book on Wilf, but one has already been written and I would recommend you read it. The book is called *One Of The Family – The Englishman And The Mafia*, by John Pearson.

****

The Groundhogs were a band that appeared to be doing very well at this time. They had been having continued success over a few years with albums such as *Thank Christ For The Bomb*, number 9 in May 1970. *Split*, number 5, March 1971. *Who Will Save The World*, number 8 March 1972 and *Hogwash* which was released November 1972.

We were asked to join The Groundhogs on their UK tour which began on 11th November and finished on 22nd December. We thought what a great opportunity. Many of the shows were at the larger venues we were hoping to play in our own right but never seemed to have the where with all to put us there on our own merits.

The tour was a great success. Opening the shows were Gentle Giant formerly known as Simon Dupree and The Big Sound (they had a hit single a few years earlier with a song called 'Kites'). They were very good, all brilliant musicians and very different to both Stray and The Groundhogs. We probably seemed even more raucous than usual going on stage after Gentle Giant.

I remember them having one road manager who used to have to set up all their equipment on his own and they had quite a lot of equipment which included several keyboards including a Mellotron. You could often hear him cursing the damn thing because Mellotrons don't travel very well on the road and he was always taking it apart and repairing it before they could play their set. They have these big tape cassettes in the casing and they have the tendency to fall out of the housing which attaches somehow to the keys. I'm not 100% sure but I think they also had a Wurlitzer electric piano which are also a bit temperamental travelling on the road and the soldering iron would have come out regularly to keep it in tune.

Speaking of keyboards, I think this was the first tour that Tony had used a Moog synthesiser on stage. It was also the first tour with their new drummer, Clive Brooks who we had seen a few years before with a band called The Egg.

We didn't see very much of Gentle Giant socially as they seemed to keep themselves pretty much to themselves.

Maybe it was because having previous 'pop' chart success they felt a bit uncomfortable with the new audience they were about to play to or maybe they just thought they were too good to be the opening act? Who knows?

We were always guilty of being in our own little bubble so we didn't think too much of it. Like I said earlier, bands on our circuit didn't seem to mix very much at this time.

The Groundhogs and us got on really well and on a couple of venues shared the same dressing room while Gentle Giant had one on their own! Very unusual, but that explains what I meant by The Hogs and Stray getting on well together. Tony

McPhee, in particular was a revelation to me because his stage persona always seemed that of the deadly serious blues guitarist but off stage he had and has a great sense of humour. The tour began a friendship that has remained right up to date and over the years we have played many shows together.

The Groundhogs were signed to one of the biggest music management companies of the time called Worldwide Artists and their personal manager was Wilf Pine.

Wilf had made himself known to us and often used to pop into the dressing room and have a chat to make sure that everything was okay and that we had got everything we needed.

Wilf told us that he had been watching us prior to the tour and thought we were a great new upcoming band, and we could be the next big band like Black Sabbath were at the time who were also signed to Worldwide Artists. He said he asked for Stray to be on the tour so he could see us perform every night. Also we both knew that we would pull an audience, which was a good thing because The Hogs would gain new fans from the Stray fans (or Stray army as they are affectionately known these days) and vice versa. Everyone's a winner!

By the end of the tour, Wilf Pine had made it very clear that he wanted to be our manager and for us to join the ever-growing roster on Worldwide Artists. The offer came at the right time for us but not really the right time for everyone involved with our Stray family. We had a meeting with Wilf and basically 'he made us an offer we couldn't refuse!'

As I said before, we the band and management had all been together a long time and we were more than friends, we had almost become a family. So any decisions to disrupt our little group could not be taken lightly. I cannot speak for everybody, but when we the band were offered a new management deal by Wilf Pine, it took me personally, a while before I could decide what was the best thing to do. I don't normally find writing difficult but trying to explain this is problematic because I want to try and make it as clear as I possibly can with the dilemmas that I felt the band and myself were being faced with.

There were people, friends around the band who like to talk into your ear about what you should be doing and that you won't get anywhere if you carry on with this record label and this management and we know such and such a band and they are doing this and that and you should be doing the same.

We were all disappointed that the previous year and the release of the *Saturday Morning Pictures* album none of which took us to the dizzy heights of fame and fortune, so it could only be down to the management and not the band! I was beginning to think that as I was the main songwriter and that I wrote in many different styles that perhaps part of the lack of success was down to me. On stage we were very much a loud rock band but even I would have to admit our albums were never the same as the live performance as the albums we had recorded which showed a variance in song styles, whether they be acoustic or electric. I know there were those who thought that seemed like a very different band to that which they saw live.

During this year it was something I had discussed with Peter and Ivan and ideally I needed a music publisher who could place some of my songs with other artists because Stray was the only outlet and I had to get my songs out there. The other conversation was for me to make a solo album so that the future Stray albums would be of a specific genre. This is something which over the years has become very apparent. Music critics and people in the business like to put something into a category, a bag or a genre and as I said before I was brought up listening to bands like The Beatles, where the albums were all about songs. The songs for me were the important factor and I had never considered really up until this time how important something like categorising could be.

Part of me wanted to do a solo album, but a bigger part of me wanted to stay loyal to Stray which is what we had all worked together for since we were 15 years old. Remember, we were in our own little bubble and we'd never played with anyone else which I suppose in hindsight was insecurity thinking that someone might prefer to play with someone else, if that makes sense?

Speaking of loyalty, my friendship with Peter and Ivan was a big issue as they had become good friends and business partners and we had been through a lot together. I don't think it helped, childish as it may seem, that Peter and Ivan had taken on a couple of other acts. Red Dirt who later changed their name to Snake Eye and Universe, who I have to say were both very good bands, but I suppose we were always used to getting all the attention. "They'll be alright they've got other bands they manage", was one comment I remember, but it wasn't as simple as that.

We had a couple of meetings with Wilf Pine and they had very plush offices in Central London. All dark mahogany wood furniture and chandeliers. This was certainly like walking into a different world. Come the second meeting we had to make a decision as to what we were going to do.

Wilf's plan was to take us off the road for a few months and take time to record a new album. He said we were going to be the next 'big' thing, "You'll be as big as Sabbath" he declared. He assured us Peter and Ivan would be compensated and increased our weekly wage and of that our road crew. So we did the deal with Wilf Pine/Worldwide Artists and were optimistic and a little bit excited as to what the future would surely bring now that we were with a major management company.

It did feel good for a while knowing that we didn't have to spend so much time away on tour, although for me it was sort of business as usual writing songs at home.

So now we had the new big management company and we, the band expressed our concerns over the record label, Transatlantic Records. To the best of our knowledge we were still signed to them for another couple of years. As I understood it, Transatlantic had taken up their further two-year options as detailed in our original contract. Just maybe they thought that because we had got ourselves in with a new, major management company, they would be silly to let Stray go. Wilf said he would look into our contractual obligations and get back to us on this.

After a while it became clear that we were tied into a very tight contract which would not be easy to get out of. I can only imagine that Wilf must have had a few heated conversations over the telephone with Nathan Joseph, the Head of Transatlantic Records, because one day we were summoned to the office and told we were going for a meeting to discuss leaving the record company.

Picture the scene, we quite literally marched into the offices, opened the door into Nathan's office, pulled up five chairs and with Wilf sat in the middle of the four of us and Nathan sat behind his huge desk. We waited for the talks to begin. I have to say that Nathan Joseph always reminded me of Napoleon Bonaparte, irrelevant, maybe, but I thought I'd mention it.

Wilf had told us before we went into the meeting that none of us must say a word. What I didn't expect was that it also included Wilf not saying a word either. So there we sat, bayonets fixed looking on at Napoleon and I for one am thinking 'what the hell is going on here?'

I think the gist of this scene was that after whatever Wilf had said to Napoleon, Nat Joseph, would tell us at the meeting, "Well guys, I am releasing you from your contract with Transatlantic Records". Nathan said a couple of sentences and what he said I can't remember because I think I was so amazed and confounded as to what was going on in that room, which actually was nothing! Wilf and the band didn't say one word!

After a few minutes of silence from our camp (although if felt like half an hour), Wilf stood up and said, "Okay guys, we are leaving". I didn't notice when we entered the offices if there was a balcony to the street but fortunately Napoleon's retreat wasn't downward to the pavement!

We were sort of amused by what had just happened, if not a little bit nervous, childlike and giggly if you know what I mean? Wilf thought that our actions might shock Nathan or persuade him (Wilf anyway), that we meant business. Something in my head tells me we did a repeat performance the following week, but I couldn't swear to it.

As a few weeks went by and we waited for news of our record contract update, we attended another meeting with Wilf at the offices in Dover Street. As far as we were concerned the bad news was that we were still with Transatlantic Records, well indirectly with Transatlantic Records, because Wilf informed us that he had negotiated a deal with them and that he had formed a new company called Gladglen for recordings, for which in turn there would be a lease deal with Transatlantic via Gladglen.

Gladglen (Wilf) would be in charge of the recordings and not directly Transatlantic. It all sounded complicated to us (we were still only bloody kids!), but it must be okay we thought because Wilf is our manager and he will make sure everything is okay.

# 13.

# Mudanzas

Steve Gadd was really getting into his writing. He had written the odd song or two before. 'Dearest Eloise' from the *Suicide* album was one of his first, a simple but beautiful song (oh yes and it featured that nominated Mellotron player, Del what's his name).

We co-wrote 'Come On Over' and one or two other bits and pieces that were stockpiled for another time. One day I went over to his house for a song writing session. He said he had an idea for a song and what did I think needed adding to it to finish it?

When I heard the song I thought it was great. He was playing it to me on acoustic guitar and as it was, it had that kind of Lennon/Dylan feel to it. I thought a funky bass line and piano would work well with it and had a bass line in my head virtually right away. I often think of bass lines not always following the route of the chord, which has over the years been something that by my own admission I incorporate in some of my songs.

In this case, the song starts in E minor then goes to D, but I suggested the bass line should play F sharp where the other instruments play D. It is a little trick that many of the classical composers used and I would continue to use it again as time went on. This song was called 'The Gambler' and I said to Steve the song is perfect and it doesn't need any input from me, just a bit of arrangement. So this became Steve's song and I have told this story in my live shows adding the comment that perhaps if I had even contributed one word to 'The Gambler' it would have become a Gadd/Bromham composition and I would have 50% of the song writing royalties!

By now we regularly rehearsed regularly at The Patmore Youth Centre in Battersea. As always, getting the songs in shape for the new album as yet to be titled. In the past we had rehearsed new songs and tried them out live, but as Wilf had decided to take us off of the road for a while to concentrate on the music we didn't have that opportunity. We rehearsed regularly and more often than not Steve was never ready so we used to wait for him not only to get up and get ready but to prepare his breakfast which was normally two boiled eggs and toast which he sat and ate in the car on the way to the rehearsals. You couldn't make it up.

We were summoned by Wilf for a meeting in Dover Street, right in the heart of Mayfair, London. He had arranged for us to go away for a week to Escape Studios in Egerton, Kent to begin recording the new album. Wilf had seen or heard a Spanish word 'Mudanzas' which meant to move or to change. As it was a time for change for Stray, he thought the word appropriate and had a good sound to it. I don't think any of us opposed this suggestion and we were looking forward to spending time putting the new album together. This all sounded so good because our previous three albums had all seemed to have been done in a hurry and then we were back out on the road. This was very different and quite 'hip' for the time as many of our peers had been doing what was known as 'getting it together in the country'.

Escape Studios was owned by Richard and Ted Roffey. It was a converted Oast House and barn area with accommodation and a recording studio. We had our own chef called Mick who cooked a good roast dinner and a studio engineer Tony Taverner, who went on to be a successful recording engineer.

One day our driver and tour manager Neil Darken arrived at the studios with a small package from the office to help us with our recording sessions. A little something that might add a different dimension to our music. As it turned out, it added a little dimension to our minds!

These were like little blue dots. L.S.D, trips whatever you want to call them. I had never taken anything before. To be honest, I had always been a little scared of the consequences. There were these stories of people having bad trips and jumping out of windows and I suppose because of my upbringing I always wanted to keep my feet firmly on the ground. I wanted to be in charge of my destiny and not let drugs affect me. Even today I am reluctant to take pills if I'm feeling unwell. I really have to have a bad headache to submit to the Nurofen.

Now then where was I? Oh yes, when I was told I was going on a 'trip' to the country, I never imagined that's what they meant and I would never have imagined what happened next.

Despite the thought of leaping from a window which was furthest from my mind because we were all mates together and looking after each other. I think a road manager or two were going to keep a watchful eye on us to make sure nothing untoward might happen.
So let the fun begin...

Don't ask me what time of day all the following events took place, but I think I must have been awake for twenty-four hours. When the trip started kicking in I started to get the giggles, to a point where I found everything funny. If anyone said anything, or anyone did anything, in my mind it was funny. Dinner was being prepared in the kitchen area which also had a large country dining table which we could all sit around. We didn't have mobile phones back then so people used to contact us on the house phone. My wife Jackie phoned to see how I was. Bad timing, the giggles had really taken hold of me at this point and what made it even worse was that I could not make head nor tail of what she was saying to me on the phone. Her voice sounded like one of the Chipmunks or a strangulated duck and one word linked into another. This was hilarious, I thought I was going to explode with laughter. Fortunately, Ritchie Cole was close by and I handed him the phone and told him to talk to her as he was not as advanced as I was in the giggling stakes. He managed to have some kind of conversation and probably assured her not to worry.

When it came to dinner, that must have looked like complete pandemonium from a 'fly on the wall' point of view. The scene in my mind reminded me of a chimp's tea party. We had, I am sure what would have been a lovely roast chicken dinner cooked and served up for us. I remember a serving plate with a mountain of roast potatoes on it. Someone (maybe me?) threw one across the table, which was followed up by another hurling across the room. Very soon there was a full-blown roast potato missile launch around the kitchen accompanied by wild laughter of course, because now I was not alone in the laughter department.

Midway through the roast potato missile incident, the door into the kitchen opened and the studio owner Ted Rofffey along with a couple of members of the band Jonesy walked in. He was giving them a tour of the studio for a possible future recording session booking. The potato hurling slowly ceased and we all looked up at our visitors and on consideration it must have looked like one of those scenes where the teacher walks back into the classroom as the kids stop misbehaving.

I can't remember exactly what happened after their arrival but I am sure there must have been one sane head in our group to try and normalise the situation. During the day we must have had many 'Adventures in 'Wonderland', but by the evening when our minds were really travelling, we decided it would be a good time to make some music in the studio to see what would come out of it? We jammed for ages. Ritchie on drums, Gary on bass, me on guitar and Steve also playing some guitar. I don't know why but at some point I headed straight for the Hammond C3.

This is what I remember most because with the aid of the L.S.D. that Hammond sounded out of this world. It was going through a Leslie rotary speaker cabinet, but in my head it was also going through a real psychedelic phaser. I had hooked into a riff which I kept playing over and over again. I still vaguely remember it. I was thinking about this the other day while preparing to write this piece and by comparison the band were sounding like we were playing not the song, but the sound like 'Tomorrow Never Knows' by the Beatles and the Hammond certainly had that 'Blue Jay Way' sound. 'Turn off your mind relax and float downstream', oh yes I certainly did.

We must have been playing for hours. Tony Taverner the engineer was there on call waiting to record. When we actually stopped playing we ran into the control room so that we could listen back. We were so excited to hear what we had done; it must have sound fab.

We had been playing for so long we found Tony sound asleep on the desk. Poor soul, we must have been in there for hours and it must have been so good it sent him to sleep! Consequently, he never pressed the 'record' button so we never got to hear what we had done. We were naturally disappointed so we adjourned to the house where over the next few hours more adventures ensued.

I remember walking around the house, running from one bedroom to another saying something like 'There's no time to lose' in a sort of Spike Milligan/Monty Python type voice. I remember walking into my bedroom which was now like a room in the 'Alice in Wonderland' story where the room sloped into the corner. I went into the bedroom and walked down the slope and stood in the corner of the room.

Of course it was pointed out to me the next day that because the building was an Oast House, all the rooms were round so I couldn't have possibly stood in a corner. Well it seemed real at the time.

A day or so went past so that we had slept enough to feel able to go into the studio fresh and resume recording.

One evening after dinner we sat around and decided we would have a séance. Both Steve and I had developed slight sore throats, so we decided to give it a rest for the evening and continue the following day.

I don't know if any of us believed in this sort of thing, contacting the 'afterlife', but we thought we would have a go and it would be a bit of a laugh. So we all sat around a table with all the letters of the alphabet and put a finger each on a glass on the centre of the table. I think like big kids, we had a few false moves with the glass going around the table and people being accused of pushing it. It happens with these things I suppose? On a couple of occasions, we picked up messages, one supposedly from Steve's grandfather and the next night we did it again and got Phil's grandfather and on both occasions questions were asked and answers were given that only Steve and Phil could have known.

The strangest séance of all was on the second evening the glass began to move and continue to get faster and faster and then slow down at which point our road manager Phil who was sitting next to me at the table leapt up in the air and said "Oi, someone just pinched my arse!" Then the glass began to spell the letters O S C A R, the name Oscar.

The more questions we asked, we realised we supposedly made contact with Oscar Wilde. Phil farted and the glass spelt out B U M and S M E L L S, and 'I LIKE YOUR STYLE'. Honest I kid you not! There was a lot of glass swirling and lots of messages being spelt out, but in brief we were being told that he, Oscar had a lot of aggravation in court and kept spelling out the letters MQ, MQ which we couldn't understand. There were various other questions asked but it soon came to an end when someone asked (what apparently is not advisable to ask) "How did you die?" The glass spun furiously and off of the table.

It was a calm evening and the glass doors blew open as if there was a wind blowing a gale outside and a couple of books fell off of the bookshelf. We were all shocked at this and decided we had better give it a rest for the night. We tried again the following evening, but could pick up nothing. The next morning at breakfast we were telling Mick our cook what had happened the night before and he said that he had some books about Oscar Wilde at his house. When he came back later, to our amazement he read from one of his books that apparently the person who contributed to putting Oscar Wilde in prison was The Marquis of Queensbury or MQ to us! It was MQ's son Alfred, who was Oscar's lover and MQ knew he could ruin Oscar as homosexuality was illegal and frowned on back in those times. Probably a good idea not to mess around with things you don't understand and no more séances were held.

Back to work in the studio we recorded the songs 'Come On Over', 'Pretty Thing' and 'The Gambler'. One song in particular stays in my mind which was the song called 'Soon As You've Grown'. A song very significant to me for a couple of reasons. Firstly, I wrote it thinking about mum, who if I ever asked her a question that she wasn't going to give me an answer to, she would say something like 'Children should be seen but not heard' and 'You'll find out one day when you grow up'. Secondly, for some reason, Steve didn't want to sing it, I really don't know why. Initially I don't think Wilf who not only was our manager but he was now the self-appointed producer of the album, wasn't that keen on the song or me singing it either. I really believed in the song and fortunately so did Gary and Ritchie, so the three of us recorded it and I sang it. Significant because this was the first song I had sung from start to finish on a Stray album. Wilf ended up loving the song.

We had not finished all of the album by the time our sessions at Escape had come to an end so I assumed we would be going back there at a later date. I couldn't be more wrong. For some reason Wilf was not happy with the results from Escape so we found ourselves booked into Olympic Studios, this time with engineer Alan O'Duffy .

I really enjoyed working with Alan. He fitted in with us so well almost like a fifth member of the band. He had a good ear for melody and in fact you can hear him singing the high vocal harmony on the song 'Oil Fumes And Sea Air'. We had the tapes from Escape, but I think we re-recorded some of the songs and recorded new songs to complete the album. I'm sure the backing track and vocals on 'Soon As You've Grown' might have been the only thing we used from Escape. But some overdubs were done at Olympic.

I know Wilf was really surprised with the songs we were coming up with because he thought we were going to be a heavy rock band, very much in the same vein as Black Sabbath. In fact, when we finished the album I remember him saying,

"I thought I'd found the new Black Sabbath, but I think I've found the new Beatles!"

Wilf knew how to say all the right things. He suggested we added strings and brass to some of the songs. Something I wanted to do particularly as I'd written a song called 'I Believe It' and I had a string arrangement already for it. It was one of those songs that as I was writing it I could hear where it was going. Cellos doing the deep line that the bass guitar would normally play. That little thing of mine where the chords would go Am-G-D but the cellos would follow A-G-F sharp. It's that classical music composition thing that I always liked, quite possibly from listening to those records of dad's when I was a kid.

Wilf said he'd found an arranger named Andrew Powell. I had not heard of him at the time. He was a new and up and coming arranger who had recently worked on the first album by Cockney Rebel. As soon as Wilf said Cockney Rebel, I thought "Yes", I had heard the first single called 'Sebastian' which has some fantastic string arrangements and production. I played it again today and it stills sounds amazing. I reckon that was the best thing Steve Harley ever did. Incidentally I met Steve Harley at a Festival in Minehead a couple of years ago. He was in the dressing room next door to ours and when he found out who I was, he told me that he and his mates used to go to The Greyhound Croydon on a Sunday night, to get there early so they could get down the front to watch Stray. Funnily enough Captain Sensible from The Damned recently told me that he too with his mates used to come along to the same venue and watch us.

Wilf pretty much gave a free hand for Andrew to come up with arrangements for some of the songs although I was adamant there were certain things I wanted for 'I Believe It'. So I discussed the arrangement with Andrew and we were on the same page.

We didn't go back into the studio for a couple of weeks, until Wilf invited us to hear what had been done to the songs. Overall we liked what we heard. I mean from our point of view hearing our songs with an orchestra was completely something else. However, there were some songs that I never thought benefitted from additional instrumentation. The song 'Pretty Thing' for example had a brass section added to it, which I felt detracted from the rocking power of the original which we had laid down. I always felt that the overall production of the album didn't truly represent the band either. 'Come On Over' in my opinion sounds drowned out somewhat by the orchestra. Wilf insisted it was the right move, to make it different from the previous Stray, an album that has a wall of sound.

I wasn't going to argue with Wilf and I can guarantee if you knew Wilf you wouldn't argue with him either. The album was finished and released as *Mudanzas*.

The opening track on the album was a song written by Steve originally titled 'Searching'. A short but beautiful song which said it all in a couple of minutes. So you can imagine our surprise when Wilf played us the album and 'Searching' came on with beautiful strings... but hang on "Where are the vocals?"

"That's because it's now called 'Changes' and it's now an instrumental to set the mood of the album" said Wilf. Funny thing is at that time I don't recall anyone ever questioning anything that Wilf said. We had become far too easy going for our own good.

We had a couple of shows planned to coincide with the release. What Wilf had planned for us could have been, to quote a previous Stray album title... suicide!

We played a show at Alexandra Place on Thursday 2nd August 1973. First on the bill were Fumble and then Jonesy (they didn't bring any roast potatoes with them!) followed by us, The Groundhogs and headliners Black Sabbath. People were used to seeing Stray as a loud four-piece rock band, so on paper along with The

Hogs and Sabbath, this bill was about as rocky as you could get at that time.

When I said doing a show like this could mean committing suicide that was because we played with a brass section, backing singers and a keyboard player. Andrew Powell was the keys player and one of the backing singers was Jimmy Helms, famous for the chart hit record 'Gonna Make You An Offer You Can't Refuse'.

To be honest I think it took the audience a couple of songs to get used to not only what they were seeing but what they were hearing, as this kind of line-up was pretty alien at that time for a heavy rock concert. Sound wise, I'm not sure any of the bands sounded great that day as it felt like you were in a huge aircraft hangar with the sound echoing around!

However, the show went well and nearly fifty years on, I still get fans coming up to me and saying they remember that show and how special it was. We went on to play another similar show at The Fairfield Halls in Croydon, only this time only with The Groundhogs.

We played some more shows although not a tour as such and by now we had dropped the lights the pyrotechnics and of course the brass section and backing singers. The idea was to let the music speak for itself. *Mudanzas*, overall received pretty good reviews, although where once we were criticised for using lights and pyrotechnics presumably because we were too young and it covered up our lack of musicianship. Now the critics were saying "Ah well, they are not as good now that they don't use all the pyros and stuff. You just can't win!

Once or twice we had been down to Minis Bay, Kent where Wilf had a house near the coast. As it turns out, the house belonged to his former boss Don Arden. There were some good parties there and a couple of months after *Mudanzas* was released, Wilf invited us all down to the house for a party to celebrate the release of the album. There was always a huge spread of food and this night was no exception.

To our surprise Nat Joseph was also there. I'd never seen Nat outside of his office in Marylebone, so I never expected to see him here, especially as we'd had had a couple of tricky meetings with him. However, all was good, the album was played from start to finish, drink was drunk and food was consumed. Then to our surprise Nat appeared with Wilf and Ken Mewis (Ken was managing a band called The Hollywood Brats and was based in our offices in Dover Street) he gave a little speech and gave us each a Gold Disc for 'Outstanding European Sales'. This seemed like such an achievement and with all that had happened in the past year, perhaps we had made the right decision after all?

A couple of days later, I drove down to visit mum and dad and took the Gold Disc with me. Mum never showed much enthusiasm or excitement for anything and the only time dad showed any form of enthusiasm was at Christmas, which he loved, or going on holiday, buying a new television set or a new stereo radiogram.

When I presented the disc, mum, who always underplayed her feelings, said something like "Ooh, dead posh aren't we. How much are your four penny haddocks?" She was full of those kind of sayings. Dad on the other hand on that day, I have to say, had never seen him look so proud and he was clearly quite emotional. He had never shown any feelings one way or the other about my involvement in music, but this must have topped it all for him.

"Can I keep it for a couple of days, son. I'd like to show it to a few people?" asked Dad. To be honest I didn't want to let it go, but I couldn't say no after seeing his reaction. I hope he doesn't leave it on a bus or go down the social club, get pissed and leave it there! No need to worry. I daresay he treated it like it was his prize possession. Probably loved it more than his medals he received during the war and that's saying something.

# 14.
# Going to America

**W**ilf had decided we were going to record the next album in America. This was to become the beginning of a new phase for Stray and certainly for Wilf Pine.

Wilf suggested that we record the song 'Move It' which was a big hit for Cliff Richard back in the 50s. We were used to only recording our own songs as we had got to the point where we believed that we had to show people what we had to offer. Once again Wilf and his powers of persuasion convinced us that this would be a good thing to do. He said to me that he wanted the new version to sound heavier and rockier, maybe a bit like if Sabbath were playing it. I found it hard to imagine Sabbath doing anything like it but I was very familiar with the song as it was another one that was played in my house when I was growing up.

I remember sitting at home with the guitar and taking that familiar lead intro riff and slowing it right down. Basically the same notes but making the rhythm chug along. We rehearsed it at The Patmore youth club and unusually Wilf came down to rehearsals and loved what we'd done to the song. Some months later after the song had been recorded and we were publicising the album, which was coincidentally titled *Move It*, I actually met Ian Samwell who was the composer of the song 'Move It'. I know how precious songs can be to the composer so I was really pleased to get his approval of our arrangement.

He also noted that I had changed the lyrics to the second verse, which was more accidental than on purpose. I got the lyrics direct from the record and these were the days where you couldn't go online and download the lyrics. These were the times where you played the record and lifted the needle or stylus stopping and starting the record to hear the words and then write them down. There was one line I couldn't quite make out what Cliff was singing so I used a bit of artistic licence and changed them from "Sambas and Calypsos that get nothing on" to "As bad as that calypso that gets nothing' on". Ian Samwell noted and liked the change and could see it sort of made sense in the musical climate of the day.

I don't know if it's a coincidence or not, but I recently saw Cliff Richard playing a version of 'Move It', in a live concert and it was nothing like his original but more like our Stray version. I'm sure he must have heard our version, so I wonder if, well you know what I mean?

We flew to the USA in January 1974 to Connecticut to be begin recording at Syncron Sound Studios. We stayed in a house which looked like something from the TV series *The Waltons*. An old-fashioned New England, wooden built house. 10 George Street, Wallingford, Connecticut. By the time we had arrived it was freezing cold and snow was thick on the ground. The house was occupied by a couple of guys who had their own band and I think they were quite happy to have some

English guys in the house. It was another adventure us blokes from West London were having. We woke up in the morning to really deep snow. I remember John the bass player who lived in the house looked out of the window and called out, "Where's my car?" The snow had drifted and had completely covered his car, which very inconveniently was a white Volvo. "It's out there somewhere" he exclaimed. We put our coats on and went looking for his car. The odd thing about this and the rest of the trip to Connecticut was although it was freezing cold, I have felt colder in the UK when the weather had been nothing like this. A different kind of cold that was for sure.

Our driver 'Woolie' Mick came to the USA with us and poor Mick was always in for it when we were around. He had a rather impressive 'Afro' hair style which Sly Stone would have been proud of. One of our favourite tricks was to sit behind him while he was driving and throw missiles at his head. Missiles like match sticks or bits of rolled up silver paper and then throw them and they landed in his hair like darts in a dartboard and he never realised what was happening. He used to get out of the car and go ballistic when he'd realised what we had done. In America he wasn't safe either. He did sleep very well and one morning we were all up and noticed he was still asleep in bed and lying on his back with his hands open. We did the old trick of filling his hands with shaving foam and then tickling his nose and then splosh, foam right back in his face. I'm sure he loved us really.

We got to the studio and met the engineer and all seemed very comfortable. We recorded the backing tracks live as we had done on the previous albums and overdubbed the vocals and additional instruments. I only took my Gibson Firebird with me, just the one guitar. On a couple of the songs I wanted to use an electric 12 string guitar, my own one was back in the UK. The studio engineer took me to a stock room and stacked in there were arguably some of the best guitars you would ever see. He pointed me in the direction of a 12-string Rickenbacker in red, just like George Harrison's one in *A Hard Day's Night*. It was wonderful and I wondered if they'd notice if it had gone missing at some point?

Not a good idea to remove one of their instruments, because what I was about to mention was that by what I could gather, the Mafia had an interest in the studio and as it transpires that is why Wilf decided it would be a good move to 'Move it' (you see what I did there?) to America. This was the beginning of Wilf's association with the Mafia, but more about that later.

I always feel at home in the recording studio. For me it's like painting musical landscapes and adding instrumentation just like adding colours to a painting. However, on this occasion, recording the songs was not the most comfortable of times. It was noticeable there were divisions arising between Steve and the rest of the band. Steve was on a song writing roll and it was apparent that he only wanted to sing his song or ones that I had co-written with him. It became obvious that the songs I had written generally speaking, Steve had little or no interest in. He was clearly moving in another musical direction. I went along with whatever the band wanted to do. I had no personal ego or expectation, I was what I always wanted to be, which was part of Stray whatever path it would take.

I did feel somewhat vindicated when we recorded one of my songs 'Somebody Called You' which Steve said he wasn't going to sing. The song was loosely based on mum and dad's next-door neighbours who had a daughter who was mentally handicapped. There was also a young lad I had seen in East Acton who was a Downs Syndrome child. I had also seen a programme on television dealing with problems faced with mentally handicapped people and their families and I was moved by all of this. I observed how people could be kind or patronising to their faces yet be quite cruel behind their backs.

"Who wants to know about all that?" said Steve at one of our rehearsals. To be honest I couldn't really answer that question. It was a subject that had affected me personally and as I found out in my life, music is the best way in which I can express myself. So I ended up singing the song. Steve however, did sing one line back to me in the song where there is another person or voice, which could be the devil's advocate or maybe someone's conscience — the little man on your shoulder type of thing, where I sing "Some people say that it gets too political, but what is politics, if it's not people" then Steve replies singing the line "Seems like some people are getting hypercritical today".

Remember the story I told you earlier about my first boss's brother and the line he said "But what is politics if it is not people". Well readers I waited about five years to use that line.

A guy named Irwin Schiff came to the studios to watch us record from time to time. He was involved in some way with the Mafia. You don't ask what he did, not with these kind of people. He was a big guy, always immaculately dressed (as they all are). We were near completion with vocals and overdubs on "Somebody Called You" and Wilf played the song back to us. When it finished there was a moments silence and then a voice said, "Excuse me, who wrote that song?" It was Irwin asking the question. "Er, I wrote it "said I nervously. Irwin looked at me and I noticed it seemed like he became very emotional. "It's a great song fella and I know exactly what you are saying with those words... thank you".

I was grateful for the compliment particularly as not everyone in the band wanted to record it, but I was even more grateful for the compliment when Wilf told me after Irwin had left the studio that he had a member of his family who had a mentally handicapped child and he totally connected with the lyrics. From that day, I have never been shy of writing what I feel because I know somewhere words are so important and can mean so much to some people.

On the subject of song writing, I have been both praised and criticised for what I have written. Generally speaking, I tend to write in the 'third person', writing an opinion which might not necessarily be mine, but maybe open for discussion. Having said that I have written songs on subjects which are my opinion, but I'll leave that for the listener to decide which is which, if one finds that necessary of course.

Some years later I was in Mexico and though I am not a particularly religious person, I do like visiting places like churches and cathedrals purely for the grandeur and works of art which are always on display. I think it was in the town of Puerto Vallarta where I went into this beautiful looking church and it inside were the most amazing works of art and sculptures. The walls were literally dripping with gold. I should have noticed when going in, although it wasn't until I came out and on to the steps leading in, that I noticed some very poor people begging outside. One little girl who could not been more than six of seven came up to me and said "Hey signor, do you want to buy some matches?"
It really stopped me in my tracks and I just couldn't get over the hypocrisy and the wealth inside the church and the comparative poverty right there on its doorsteps.

I vented some of my feelings some years later in a song titled 'In The Name Of God' which appeared on the *New Dawn* album. At this time the drummer in the band was Phil McKee and when I played him the song at his house, I realised that his father-in-law was the vicar of the church in Buckingham which could have been very awkward, but fortunately they were all okay with the song.

Back to the *Move It* album which was once again released on Transatlantic Records. The reviews were not great and the sales were not as good as the previous four albums. That was a bitter disappointment because we were supposed to be going up the ladder of success. I felt our live shows were becoming lack lustre for one reason or another. People wanted to know where was that exciting Stray that we used to come and see and that wasn't just down to the lack of pyrotechnics.

Steve insisted on playing guitar now on stage. The problem being was that he seemed to appear to look like he was concentrating so hard on the guitar playing it felt like he was ignoring the audience, so personally I felt I had to step forward and keep the attention, which I was not used to doing. I never had to before because Steve was there covering it. Where was the front man? Steve was one of the great front men. Had history been different, I have no doubt he would have been up there with the Jaggers, Plants and Rodgers of this world.

# 15.
# Introducing Mr Peter Dyer

It must have been around early 1974 when our driver/tour manager Neil Darken asked if it was okay if a friend and neighbour of his in East Acton could come along to one of our rehearsals. Steve had already met Neil's friend because at this time Steve was living in the same street. His friend was Mr Peter Dyer.

As time went on, I got to know Pete very well. His wife Jenny and my wife Jackie got on well also. Pete was a singer guitarist in a club/covers type band, playing the pubs and working men's clubs. One Saturday evening he asked if we would like to come and see him and the band play at the Cobden Club, near Ladbroke Grove in London. This was a typical working men's club, cheap booze and the smell of cigarette smoke in the air. Pete and his band played and we all had a good night. It was quite a regular gig for him and the band. Consequently Jackie, Jenny and myself went to see him play there a few times. The other guitarist in his band was a tall guy with a moustache named George, who to sounded like George Harrison when he spoke. A couple of times he handed his guitar to me and I got up and played with them. I can't remember what, probably 'Born To Be Wild' and 'Whiskey In The Jar' as I remember those songs were in their set.

The more we got to know each other we realised that Pete had actually played guitar in my brother's group The Traders a few years before I did. What a coincidence. Pete is a few years older than me, so I didn't remember him specifically, although I must have seen him rehearse at mum and dad's house. I have a recording somewhere of The Traders with Pete playing rhythm guitar on a few Shadows and Cliff Richard tunes.

It must have been around early 1974 when Neil asked if it was okay if Pete could come along to see us play at Loughton College in Essex. He brought with him a new guitar which he had just bought, for me to have a look at. It was a red Gibson SG and much to Pete's pleasure, I used it on a couple of songs.

Back in the Stray camp we were all concerned that Steve's attention to playing guitar on stage was distracting him from being the once great front man/vocalist. He maybe didn't realise it, but a lot of the time on stage he was either side on strumming the guitar or had his back to the audience. This was not the same old Steve we used to know. I think someone must have told him it wasn't cool to jump around on stage. We had a band meeting and we were quite open and frank about our concerns, but Steve was now convinced that if he stopped playing guitar, the instrument would be missed.

When you consider we had never had another guitar playing with us since we formed back at school this wasn't really a valid argument, but I think we all tried to understand his concerns as we had always worked things out together before.

However, someone suggested, well okay what if we get someone else in to play rhythm guitar, you could go back doing what you do best. Several times over the years we had tried out additional guitarists and keys players but it had never really worked. As I mentioned before, we were in our own little bubble, our little family, our 'members only' club and outsiders didn't seem to fit. I think it was me who mentioned that Pete played guitar. He already knew some Stray songs and he was a good bloke with definitely the same warped sense of humour as me!

I went to see Pete to tell him what the band had been discussing and asked him if he would be interested in coming down for a rehearsal to see how it sounded. He said that he would love to play with us. So I told him which songs to learn, which he did, we had a few rehearsals and he seemed to fit in very well. So what next?

If my memory serves me correctly we had an important show coming up (all shows are important actually) at The Fairfield Halls in Croydon with our friends The Groundhogs, so we thought that would be a good one to see if it works out live on stage.

The day of the show arrived and we set up in the afternoon for the sound check. As I said before we were never a band that did regular sound checks, but this was Pete's first show, so we wanted to make sure everything was okay.

Wilf Pine was out front watching and I don't remember if we knew he was there, but we had barely struck up the first chord when a voice from the darkness bellowed out, "Steve, Del, Ritchie, Gary, come here a minute, I want a word".

It was Wilf and us four naughty boys walked into the dark wilderness of the stalls where Wilf was seated to find out what we had done wrong. Then there was the realisation that we hadn't actually discussed or told Wilf, our manager, that we had recruited an extra guitarist for the show. The more I think about it now, the more I wonder how we managed to avoid telling him. Was it going to be a surprise? I really don't know? We sat down next to him. He turned to me and said, "Alright then, who the fuck is Eric Clapton?" We began to explain our concerns particularly referring to Steve and playing the guitar or rather not playing guitar, so it was felt another guitarist rather than Steve would be the way forward. Actually, Wilf was okay about it and as it transpired, it was something that he was going to discuss with us, or moreover with Steve.

"Right then get back on stage and let's have a listen", said Wilf.

He obviously liked what he heard and the show went ahead and we probably looked and sounded better than we had done for some time. Just to be clear, at this time Pete was only brought in for that one show and possibly others if it felt necessary.

This was now 1974 and Steve was really getting into his song writing. I would often pop around to his house to collaborate co-write, or maybe just make suggestions for song ideas and or arrangements etc. He did however, appear to have little idea what time of day or night it was, because if he had a new song he had to play it to me straight away no matter regardless. One time about 1am and I was in bed asleep when the telephone rang. "Hi, I've got this new song and I've got to play it to you" enthused Steve. "I've ordered a taxi and I'll be over in a while". How could I refuse?

The band went for a meeting with Wilf and he said it was time for us to record a new album. We had been rehearsing as usual and learning new songs, quite a few of which were Steve's. Rehearsals at this time were not a pleasurable experience. There always seemed to be an atmosphere in the room. Steve was adamant how he wanted his songs to sound and be played. He made it quite clear he was not happy with various individual's interpretations.

Our rehearsals had always been a private affair, just band members only, the four of us. Steve was now bringing his new girlfriend in to listen and we were aware that every now and then they would be whispering in each other's ears. She might say something in private to him and then he would blurt out some kind of statement. One time I became very frustrated and angry with all this and anyone who knows me will tell you that it takes a lot to get me angry. It all seems so irrelevant now but at the time it really was a big deal. The girlfriend whispered in his ear something like, "Other bands do this and that or someone does such and such" and then Roxy Music do this and Roxy do that. My head was completely full of hearing all this persistent bullshit of what others do and how we were seemingly inferior to everyone else, I just exploded and said "Fuck Roxy, we are not Roxy and Roxy Music can do whatever they like" I'm not sure what happened next because it was one of those see red moments where the brain doesn't think straight. I can't imagine I stayed. I probably decided to go home. These were like moments which reminded us of The Beatles' *Let It Be* film and for a while, Steve and 'the girlfriend' were referred to as 'John and Yoko'.

I was still writing songs as I always had done but I was beginning to feel like I was the odd one out and perhaps I should leave Stray and go solo. I did speak to Wilf about this and he suggested that I should make a solo album but not quit. He thought it was important that I stay.

The recording sessions were booked for the new Stray album at Majestic Studios in South London. A nice spacious studio which felt instantly very comfortable.

As before; Ritchie on drums, Gary on bass and myself on guitar set up and played what we had learned in rehearsal live but without the vocals. Over the first few days we had only recorded one of my songs which was called 'Smile'. Looking back, it appears we had also recorded the vocals with Steve singing the backing vocal because this was yet another of my songs which he didn't want to sing.

It is interesting to note that at this time prior to the recording we had been playing new songs on stage. Something we had always done in order to break them in live to see if they worked in front of an audience. There were songs I had written called 'Alone Again', 'Cross Country', and 'Down, Down, Down' which Steve was singing and we had included in our set, but it looked like my songs were not going to make it for this album. For the record (pardon the pun) 'Down, Down, Down' Pete eventually sang on the *Stand Up And Be Counted* album. 'Alone Again' and 'Cross country' I eventually got to record for the album *10* in 2001.

We spent several days working on about three of Steve's songs but it was slow progress on all of them. Steve didn't like the way we were playing them. He didn't like the bass, didn't like the guitar and certainly didn't like the drums. In fact, it was this last disagreement about the drumming which lead to a huge fall out! Steve was telling Ritchie how he should play the drums and Ritchie got so angry I thought he was going to leap off of the drum kit and stab him with his drumsticks!

That was it for me. I'd had enough. When I got home after the recording session I said to Jackie "That's it, I can't be in the band anymore. I'll speak to Wilf in the morning and I'm going to do something else".

Within a few minutes my telephone rang and it was Gary "I'm just ringing to tell you I'm quitting the band, I can't do this anymore!"

I really am not making this up but a few minutes after Gary phoned, Ritchie phoned and said "I'm leaving the band, I can't carry on like this. If I'm not good enough, you'll have to find another drummer!"

I told them both that I was leaving as well! This all seems so funny now I'm writing it down, but that is really what happened that evening. Three members of the same band all individually quitting the band.

As it turned out we were not recording the next day, so Ritchie Gary and myself went to the office and had a meeting with Wilf.

The meeting was not an easy one. Nobody wanted it but we needed to sort it out. Despite our disagreements and general falling out, no-one wished anybody any harm. It was just a situation when we had quite clearly grown apart. Wilf said he had noticed a difference in Steve's attitude and he didn't think the songs Steve had contributed so far were suitable for Stray.

I was relieved because Wilf suggested that Steve should leave but not to worry as he would look after him with his solo career and we should continue as a three piece and go back in the studio and finish the album.

I remember Steve phoned me later that day and to be honest it was not an easy conversation. I had to be honest and tell him how I felt. The conversation ended, not in a bad way, I have to add, but having said that I never spoke to Steve for a couple of years. I really hoped his solo career would work out for him.

$$****$$

I had never written a song to order before as everything I had written had come from inspiration or literally out of nowhere. As Wilf had decided that the album was to be called *Stand Up And Be Counted*, he wanted me to write a song with the same title. I surprised myself because I wrote the song quickly.

We were back in Majestic Studios on the 6th,7th & 8th May 1974 from 2pm-midnight and I think I played Wilf, Ritchie and Gary the new song. I know Wilf in particular loved it. I admit the song had a Beatle's influence and it was primarily a sit at the piano and play kind of song and even further removed from sounding like Wilf's new Black Sabbath. I think we set about recording the entire backing track there and then. By comparison to the previous sessions it was so easy and there was a good atmosphere. Wilf wanted a big production along with backing singers and orchestra. I wanted strings on the song 'Smile' so I said to Wilf if the orchestra was coming in they could do both songs, which duly happened.

I went to the studio to hear the orchestration and met up with two of the musicians. What happened next totally changed my attitude and gave me greater confidence regarding my abilities as a musician. I suppose I had always been the reluctant musician because I felt I was the songwriter first and also what seemed like the continual beating from certain quarters (media) that you were too young to be any good, quite possibly became engrained in my mind and contributed to my insecurity.

I was standing at the back of the control room listening to the play back of "Stand Up" complete with orchestra. It was impressive and I felt proud of what we had achieved here. I was standing next to the two musicians who had played on the recording. Both violinists, one of which was the orchestra leader I believe, turned to me once the track had finished and said, "Did you write that song?" "Er, yes" I replied. "It's a great song" he said.

"Did you play and write this without dots, you know sheet music?" "Yes" I replied, "I tried learning to read music, but found my brain worked faster than the reading so I gave up".

They were both most impressed. The lead violinist said to me "We think it's great you can just pick up your instrument and play or can improvise. We need the dots to play, we think it's brilliant". I was really taken aback and it gave me a new confidence and a very important conversation that I will value all of my life.

The recording sessions came to a halt at Majestic Studios. I sensed something was wrong but I couldn't put my finger on it. It's only years later that I discovered at this time Pat Meehan was winding up Worldwide Artists and this would have made a huge financial impact to Wilf and indeed Stray, but we were not made aware of this at the time.

**\*\*\*\***

We asked Pete Dyer if he would like to join the band on a permanent basis. I didn't want to be thrown in totally as the lead singer and I knew Pete could sing. I suppose having another person out front was moral support for me as well.

I had written some more songs but I had assumed these were going to be for my solo album project that I had spoken to Wilf about. I played the songs at rehearsals and everyone approved and decided we should record them. This was going to be a very different Stray both in sound and the look.

We were booked in to Mayfair Studios in Soho, London with engineer Richard Manwaring. The room where we played was downstairs from the control room and vocal booth, so communication was via intercom.

Recording was easier than it had been for a couple of years. We recorded nine new songs and with the two already done at Majestic we had eleven new songs for the album.

This was the first time I had been lead singer on more than one song. Pete sang lead vocals on five, and we sang vocal harmonies and a couple of twin guitar harmonies which was something we had never done before. I wrote a song titled 'The End'. It was a sad but soulful song and I had this idea of another voice singing a counter comment. Wilf suggested we ask Jimmy Helms to come in and sing the other part. Wilf was managing Jimmy at this time and we had already worked together before and got on really well.

So imagine me, I am now standing in the vocal booth about to do a vocal duet with Jimmy Helms who in my opinion is one of the great voices. It was obvious who had the better voice but he was as always, so lovely and in his own way helped give me confidence to sing my vocal part. Talk about being thrown in at the deep end.

'The End' is the story about a fella who knows he doesn't have long to live but he talks to his wife and tells her that she must move on after he passes away. When I played the album to my family, Aunt May felt that the song was about her husband, my Uncle Ted had recently passed away and he was only in his early fifties. I didn't knowingly write specifically about them, but it can't be denied it could have been in the back of my mind. The power of song can be quite amazing and emotional particularly when someone can connect in some way to it.

*Stand Up And Be Counted* was released in January 1975. The album cover was something of a surprise! It depicted four gravestones with our faces and names on it against a large cemetery possibly based on one of the large war cemeteries in Belgium and France. I didn't like the cover then and I don't like it now. I think it was in my opinion one of the worst album covers ever produced. There you go I've said it.

At least I felt the songs and music on the album were good although it was never received that well by the critics and some fans. Many felt that it was too soft in comparison to what we had done on the first couple of albums and I suppose I have to take some responsibility for that because the music was primarily written by me. But these were songs I was planning for a solo album so in retrospect what should have happened, particularly in the absence of Steve, was that we should have taken a bit more time to think about the musical direction.

Sometimes when you are in a band you just get on that hamster wheel and just keep going with little time to think. The other thing about the album and the new line-up is that as I have learned over the years, people do not like change. It's like comfortable shoes. Once you have them you don't want to change them or throw them away.

Tour dates were set up to promote the album and show off the new line up to the public and personally it was something of a hurdle to overcome because I had suddenly become front man for the band, something that I never wanted in the first place, that's why I got Steve to do it. I knew eyes would be on me and fingers might be pointing at me with disapproval. Dramatic as that may sound, when you take your career as seriously as I did (and still do) all these things jump into your mind.

Our first show was at Aberystwyth University in their large concert hall. As I looked out into the hall it was packed. I felt a bit nervous which may seem odd, but nerves are something I have never really suffered with. Heaven knows how Pete was feeling? I had taken him from working men's clubs and pubs into a full on rock concert hall with hundreds of people waiting to rock!

We were just about to begin when all of a sudden from nowhere a guy jumped on to the stage grabbed Pete's microphone and started shouting stuff in the Welsh language. I thought at first it was maybe the student social secretary introducing us on stage with a welcome something like "Ladies and gentleman, please welcome on stage Stray".

Oh no, quite the contrary, after a mouthful of the Welsh language he finished with "fuck off you English bastards!" Not quite the introduction we were expecting on our first show! The Welsh Nationalists had arrived and apparently anyone who was English were quite clearly not welcome. All of a sudden several other guys jumped up on the stage and were about to attempt to wreck our equipment. Our road crew leapt onto the stage along with a couple of students who were helping organise the concert. A couple of guys attempted to jump onto the front of Ritchie's drum riser in an attempt to pull his drums off. Another guy came past me and tried to grab one of the cymbal stands.

I had my heavy double neck Firebird on, but I managed to grab his arm and I got a punch in. It must have looked impressive because at the same time our driver 'Woolie' Mick, threw him off of the stage, so it looked like my punch had launched him into the audience. Henry Cooper would have been proud of me. Actually, thinking about, it if Wilf would have been too, he would have sorted them out on his own.

Quite clearly these rebels were in a minority because the majority wanted to hear the band play. You would think a ruckus like that would put us off playing, but it did quite the contrary. I think it made us feel 'right, this is our first show, let's do this'. It upped the ante as they say. The show went really well as did the rest of the dates on this tour. We took a hell of a gamble because it would have been so easy to play the older songs and crowd pleasers but most of the set was from the "Stand Up" album with only a couple of the old ones for good measure. It might have looked and sounded like a different Stray and although being aware that not everyone liked the album, we proved we could still do the business live.

# 16.
# First US tour

Wilf Pine had been going back and forth to the USA establishing contacts and part of his plan was for us to play and break it there. I think like Wilf, the new sound the band now had would be accepted more in the USA than at home.

The Glam Rock scene was happening with acts like Mud, Slade, Bowie, T. Rex, Queen, Roxy Music and for me personally it seemed far removed from what we were doing. Just a small point and blowing my own trumpet here. On the subject of Glam Rock I wore my mirror suit at the Reading Festival in 1972 before Noddy Holder had his mirror top hat. Was I the first Glam Rocker? How embarrassing, arrrgggh!

We were all listening to the music coming out of America. Steely Dan, The Doobie Brothers, Joe Walsh, The James Gang and Graham Central Station. The new version of The Isley Brothers were playing some great material. I had always been a fan of the music from America; Motown, soul, Stax, blues. Music coming out of Muscle Shoals, Little Feat, the list goes on. The UK just didn't compare with what was going on in the States. The music scene in America was where it was for me.

Often the boys would come on over to my place and I would put on the music I was listening too. Favourite albums at that time in the early seventies were *Music Of My Mind* by Stevie Wonder, *Still Bill* by Bill Withers, *His California Album* by Bobby 'Blue' Bland, *Can't Buy A Thrill* by Steely Dan and *Release Yourself* by Graham Central Station. I was always looking for something else. Not the sort of records a supposedly British rock musician was expected to be listening to.

It seemed like the UK were putting music into categories and almost encouraging people to be in little clubs and if you were in that club you disliked or hated anything else. To some extent it is still the same today nearly fifty years later. What happened to the multi bills that used to be in the UK? What was happening in the USA really appealed to me. It was appreciating music whatever the genre. You could like Bruce Springsteen and Earth, Wind and Fire — both who were starting to make a big name for themselves in the USA.

It was the 13th August 1975 and we boarded a flight from Heathrow to JFK Airport. Except for the PA we took all of our back line equipment and two road managers, Dave Flockton on sound, and Bob Sallows for the backline. I can't imagine what that would cost to do these days?

This was an exciting time and we were confident that once we would get to the States we would make it to the big time. What you don't realise is how big that country is. You could fly 5,000 miles from one gig to another or drive for 1,000 miles to get to the next one. I think you could fit Great Britain into Texas about three or four times.

We landed at JFK, New York and after showing our passports we were ushered into what seemed like a large room with glass windows so that we could see what was going on outside but not hear anything. We had paperwork with us with phone numbers and sponsors listed and presumably a phone call was made. Because after a while we could see coming towards us, Wilf Pine accompanied by two other very smart looking gentlemen. This really was the start of what would become scenes from films. Scenes that would be so far removed from what four young lads from West London could imagine.

My recollection is that Wilf and the two gentlemen started talking to the uniformed immigration officers. At one point it appeared that Wilf whispered something in one of the officer's ears. It seemed almost without little hesitation they gestured towards the door of our glass cage and allowed us to set foot on American soil. I obviously do not know what was said but as the day and the rest of the tour continued it was quite clear we had some very influential people vouching for us.

We were met outside the airport by two black stretch limousines. We were driving upstate New York to meet and have dinner with Joe Pagano but more about Joe later. The driver of the limo reminded me very much of Alfred the Butler who was in the sixties television version of *Batman* starring Adam West and Burt Ward. He was a friendly man who told us stories about the old days and the things he used to do — all the way on our journey, which was probably a good idea as we didn't have to think too much about the fact we were about to meet one of the heads of the Mafia!

I rarely talk about what happened in the USA, because even as I'm writing this it all seems unbelievable, so what would others think of these stories?

We arrived at the home of Joe Pagano in Rockland County and every time I have seen the film *The Godfather*, in my mind the house in the film looks very similar. Joe Pagano was part of the Genovese family who dominated organised crime in New York and New Jersey and were part of the American Mafia.

Joe welcomed us into his home. He was softly spoken with a Bronx accent. I am no linguist but that's what I think. In fact, he was everything you would imagine a Mafia boss to look and sound like.

For some reason he took Pete and myself aside and asked if we would like a little tour of his house, although it was more a small mansion than a house, exquisitely decorated. He took us to one room in particular that he seemed keen to show us. "This is my special room" he said. "Do you notice anything in unusual about it?" he asked. The room had no windows and the walls were reinforced with layers of concrete. It was bomb proof and he said if there were ever any family wars he would be safe in this room.

We had heard from Wilf about 'JP's bar and Joe took Pete and myself to one of the rooms that had a beautiful wooden bar with crystal glasses on display. "What would you like to drink?" he asked. "Scotch and coke please," we replied. Joe replied "Scotch, whiskey, how about some Bourbon, do you drink Bourbon"? "How about a Jack Daniels?" This was 1975 and we'd never really heard of or tasted Jack Daniels Bourbon. But we were about to and it has been my drink of choice ever since. In fact, I recorded a song titled 'The Ballad of JD' on my solo album *Nine Yards*.

It was soon time for dinner and we went to the dining room which had a perfectly set 'silver service' dining table laid. The conversation flowed as did the liquid and as I recall we had a very good steak dinner. Joe asked us if we had enjoyed our meal which obviously we had. He called out a name and a guy appeared from the kitchen. "I'd like you to meet the gentleman who cooked your dinner for you" said Joe. I can't remember what his name was but I think he was something to do with The Teamsters, a big union out in the USA. When we left Joe's house, he handed me a piece of paper and said that if you have any problems here is my personal private telephone number, call me anytime. I mean, think about it. What would a bloke from East Acton want to phone the boss of the Mafia for? Read on and you might find out!

It transpires that Joe had a son named Jimmy who was found shot dead in a car in mysterious circumstances. It was thought to be an inter family disagreement which led to his death. It seems that when Joe met Wilf, Wilf reminded him somehow of his son Jimmy who also had some connection with the music business too as I understand.

I cannot write down everything that happened on this tour which lasted about six weeks because it would take too long to document. Also the fact that it is now so long ago that some of the facts and details can get distorted in one's memory. When I've spoken to Gary and Pete recently it appears we all remember things slightly differently so the relevant stories are the ones I feel I should mention.

We flew from New York down to Atlanta for our first shows which were at Alex Cooley's Electric Ballroom and we were playing three nights with Canned Heat.

When we arrived in Atlanta, the aircraft door opened and the heat hit you just like opening an oven door. I think for the tour at different places we had Ryder trucks on hire. Consequently, the equipment was loaded into a truck and Bob and Dave followed us to the hotel. We were in a nice big estate car being driven by our new tour manager Roy Reich. He met us at the airport and introduced himself and said he had a little something for us as a "welcome to America". Roy worked for The Doobie Brothers and it transpired that Tom Johnson of the Doobies used to get Roy to pick up some of his "welcome packages" too. They weren't called The Doobie Brothers for nothing you know.

The humidity was quite a new experience for me. By the time I got to the hotel it felt that I was losing my voice and the humidity was drying it up. Fortunately, the first show was not until the next day.

Roy began telling us all about himself and was really happy to be working with a band from England, a place where he had always wanted to visit. When I mentioned the concern about my voice he said I should try a little of something he had brought with him in his welcome pack. It was cocaine, something I had never tried before. I'd always been very reluctant to go down this road but I suppose getting caught up in the moment it was a bit like 'When in Rome etc'.

I had a little toot and I felt great and whatever it did, my voice got better. The next day Roy went to a chemist and got me a bottle of Chloroseptic, an antiseptic throat spray. Although it is available in the UK now, it wasn't back then. What you get in the UK is a much smaller bottle and is very watered down by comparison to what you once could get in the USA. One spray of this and it worked miracles. We carried it with us all the time and I brought a couple of bottles back home to the UK with me. I think they eventually changed the recipe because like the original Coca Cola drink it had a small amount of Cocaine in it. If that is correct, that would be why it was so popular.

One thing that was noticeably different throughout the tour was the hospitality left in our dressing rooms at the venues. Some places there was enough food and drink to host a party (as we did from time to time and boy did we party!)

The venue, Alex Cooley's was like a big ballroom and there was a big stage and excellent PA and lighting. We were due to play three nights, two shows per night opening for Canned Heat. Even then, Canned Heat as a band, had become legendary. They had had hit singles and albums worldwide. The main vocalist and harmonica player was a guy named Bob 'the Bear' Hite. Called 'The Bear' because of his stature. Apart from liking the music 'The Bear' was featured on another of my favourite albums, *Blues from Laurel Canyon* by John Mayall. Laurel Canyon was a place I had always dreamed of visiting and did I ever get there you may ask? Well you'll have to keep reading to find out.

There had been a couple of line-up changes within Canned Heat. Only two of the originals remained for these shows, Bob and drummer Fito de la Parra. They were all extremely nice guys and always were interested to have a chat. We got on really well and soon there was a bit of banter between us. I've told this story many times at my live shows but I'll tell the story here for posterity.

One afternoon we were on stage doing a sound check, when I could see from the back of the venue Bob Hite and the rest of Canned Heat had arrived. Bob could obviously see we were there on the stage when he called out "Hey where is that skinny little English Cockney bastard", or something to that effect. Well I was skinny that was a fact and he was bloody huge and the difference in size was a thing we had going on comparing our sizes. It is such a shame that in those days we didn't have mobile phones with cameras on because I would have loved to have captured this particular scene. Bob and I were in the dressing room and we were both wearing Levi jeans. As you will be aware Levis always have the waist size on the label above the back pocket. The size on my Levis was waist 26" and Bob's was 56"!

After one of the shows, the guitarist in Canned Heat who I think was Chris Morgan, invited Ritchie and I back to his hotel room to play us some records which he had collected as he did while on tour. We were dropped off at their hotel and the others went back to our hotel. Chris had a portable record player and he kept pulling out old blues records. As he was putting them on he would tell us who the record was by and the year it was recorded and some added history if he knew any, which was often, as he clearly knew his stuff.

He also had a contraption called a Bong which was a glass tube with rubber tubes attached and grass or cannabis was burning and you inhaled through the tube. The effect was instant and we were well and truly stoned. Somehow Ritchie managed to phone down to reception and call a taxi. Under the circumstances that was quite a feat. We obviously got back to our hotel but I don't remember much about it. The next day, probably lunchtime, because I cannot imagine getting up too early, we were all sitting around the dining room table when the conversation of what everyone got up to the night before arose. Ritchie and I started to tell everyone of our little adventure and the blues records and the Bong and getting a taxi back home. At this point there was a moment silence when our roadie Bob said "You got a cab back?". We replied "Yes". Bob gestured to us to follow him. "Come here" he said. So Ritchie and I followed Bob to the front doors of our hotel. "You got a cab then did you?" said Bob. Well that seemed quite reasonable because we didn't know where we were. Bob pointed to the hotel on the opposite side of the road. "That's the hotel you would have got a cab from" laughed Bob. I bet the taxi driver had the biggest laugh. He probably knew that we were a bit worse for wear and quite probably drove up the road a bit and then back down to our hotel. I've no idea how much the cab fare was?

After three nights with Canned Heat, we packed our stuff and set off for the next stop in Cleveland Ohio. We were staying for a few nights at The Hyatt Lodge which I believe was also known as 'Swingos' Hotel, on Euclid Avenue and East 18th Street. To be honest I thought it looked like a bit of a rundown area of town, but despite that, I have since read that it was the place that all bands stayed at and a lot of rock and roll history and wild parties went on within those walls.

It was a big hotel, well it had to be because there was a board on the wall of the reception which said welcome to the following bands 'Mahogany Rush, The Faces, Uriah Heep, The Blue Oyster Cult, Stray'.

One day we took a walk out of the hotel looking for a launderette as the dirty washing was building up. I must admit to feeling a little wary as we walked the backstreets. The tall old brick tenement and factory buildings looked not unlike those seen in films where there might be a sniper or a street gang just around the corner. We found a launderette went in and loaded a couple of machines. While we were in there we began talking to a little guy who on reflection reminded me of the character coach in the US sitcom *Cheers*.

He was really friendly and struck up a conversation. "Hey, where are you guys from? Oh England, I was there about 1945, loved it" he declared. It turns out he was a G.I. stationed in the UK for a while. He then started to recite place names incorrectly as only you hear on TV comedies. PicAdilly (emphasis on the letter A) Circus, Licester Square BuckingHAM Palace the list went on and in his own way he was very interesting and it made a change from rock 'n' roll stuff.

One day I was in the lift going down to the bar. When the lift doors opened, who should be standing there waiting to get in but quite possibly two of the biggest stars on the planet back in 1975, Rod Stewart with his then lady friend the actress Britt Ekland. It's not a normal day occurrence and I could feel my inability to speak properly in such esteemed company. "Hello," said Rod, "Where's the beach?". If I'm not mistaken they both had a glass of something in their hands and Rod looked as if he was about to go on stage. If my memory serves me correctly, he was wearing a white sailor suit. He was meeting the rest of The Faces downstairs to make their way to play a big concert at The Cleveland Stadium.

According to records this would have been August 23rd. The other bands on the bill at the stadium were Blue Oyster Cult, Mahogany Rush, Aerosmith and Uriah Heep, but Stray, like Cinderella, didn't go to the ball. Our band by now were also assembled in the bar area, although we had no plans as such, somehow Roy managed to get a free access all areas pass so that we could go with The Faces and see the show. We had arranged to follow The Faces to the stadium, but the problem was we never saw them go, we missed them somehow, so consequently we stayed in the hotel and made our own fun!

I think it was the next day there was a huge rainstorm and around lunchtime I was at the bar and was joined by The Faces. I was sitting with Kenney Jones, Ian McClagan and Tetsu Yamauchi, who had replaced Ronnie Lane on bass. They were knocking back the whiskies and Kenney kept asking me if it was still raining hard because they were due to go to the airport and fly off somewhere and they were all terrified of flying in those weather conditions. If you had seen the rain, you wouldn't have blamed them.

As we sat there drinking there was a little noise in the background as if someone important had just entered the room. It was Rod and Britt accompanied by his manager Billy Gaff. I have to mention at this point that quite clearly the relationship between Rod and the rest of The Faces was not good, so you will appreciate that once again I will not name names. A 'Face' said to me without turning from the bar "Is that him?" "It's Rod" I replied. "Is she with him?" said The Face. "Er, yes", I once again replied. "Gimme a double scotch" said The Face "Yeh, I'll have one too" said Tetsu who already looked a bit worse for wear. They did leave for their flight and presumably everyone got to their destination safely. Ronnie Wood was also in the bar but talking with some others on the other side of the bar. It's also worth mentioning that Ronnie Wood left The Faces a couple of months later to join The Rolling Stones.

****

Now here's a funny story but I will not mention the names, the reasons why will become apparent. One evening, one of our road crew and the drummer of a certain band which were staying at our hotel met two ladies in the bar. After a few drinks the ladies went upstairs to the respective individuals' hotel rooms. I think Gary and Ritchie were in the room which Pete and I were sharing when we heard a huge row coming from the hallway outside our room. We opened the door to find our road manager chasing this lady he was with and shouting something like "Come 'ere you dirty fucking bastard!". Well even with high heels the 'lady' got away.

When we calmed our man down and asked him what was going on he reported that they were on the bed, he put his hand up her dress and inside her knickers to find a penis and a pair of testicles! She was a he! The funny thing was we never heard from the drummer and I never actually saw him in person for many years after this event and although I was fascinated to know how he got on, I really didn't have the heart to ask.

We were due to play three nights, at The Smiling Dog Saloon, a club in the heart of Cleveland. We were looking forward to this one, particularly after the shows in Atlanta.

The Smiling Dog was not a huge club, possibly the size of The Marquee Club in London. Cleveland seemed to be a bit of a rock 'n' roll city, if the hotel antics were anything to go by. It turned out to be disappointing, hardly anyone turned up, maybe about fifteen people at the most. It would take a while to conquer America at this rate. After the show we went back to the hotel and chatted about it and the fact we had a couple more nights in the same venue. It didn't seem at all worth the bother.

I'm not sure how this happened and the more I think about it, it is quite surreal. Either it was decided or maybe I decided to phone Joe Pagano. In retrospect, why didn't I just speak to Wilf? No, I had to phone the head of the New York Mafia for assistance. So the next morning there are I am in my hotel room in Cleveland and I telephoned Joe Pagano. The telephone conversation went something like this:

BRRRRRRR, BRRRRRRRRR, BRRRRRRRRR
Female voice answers: Hello, the Pagano residence
Del: Hello, can I speak to Joe please?
Female voice: May I ask who is calling please?
Del: Yes it's Del Bromham from the band Stray.
Female voice: Thank you. One moment please.
Joe Pagano: Hey Del how are you doing?
Del: Hi Joe, yes I'm fine thanks, but we've got a bit of a problem.
Joe: Problem, you've got a problem. Don't worry, I've got friends in Cleveland.
Del (in panic mode): No, not that kind of problem.
Joe: Well what's the problem then Del?
Del: We played a show last night and there were only about fifteen people there. We have a couple more night to play there and we don't think it's worth playing the other couple of shows.
Joe: (Slight pause) Del, have you heard of a little singer called Frankie Sinatra?
Del: Oh yeh, Frank Sinatra of course yes.

Joe: Well when Frankie Sinatra first started, he played to about fifteen people. So I figure if it was good enough for Frankie Sinatra, then I reckon it's good enough for Stray.
Del: Oh okay Joe, I understand.
Joe: Okay good. Is there anything else I can help you with?
Del: No Joe, that's all. Thank you, bye
Joe: Okay very good. Bye.

I got off of the phone and I think it might have been Ritchie who asked, "What did he say, what did he say? I tried to describe the conversation but it didn't alter the fact that we still had a couple more nights at The Smiling Dog Saloon.
Wilf wasn't too pleased when he heard I'd phoned Joe. I mean it's not the normal thing one does to phone the boss of the Mafia now is it? Well maybe it was a coincidence but when we were out in the car later that day we had the radio on. A DJ was promoting our show and playing one of the songs from the "Stand Up" album. You can probably imagine the kind of thing "Tonight live at The Smiling Dog Saloon, all the way from London, England the fantastic Sttay!" We had a few more people in that night and a lot more on our final night. So maybe it was worth the phone call after all. People with influence I suppose?
August 24th, next up was Lebanon, Illinois then Bellville Pennsylvania where we played a small club called Boot Hill. August 27th we heard that Uriah Heep and Blue Öyster Cult were at The Kiel Auditorium not far away in St Louis, so we drove up to watch the show.
While we were in St Louis, an interview on the radio station KSHE95 had been arranged. It was a live on-air show. The DJ played some tracks from the "Stand Up" album and had a good chat. Then we were given some KSHE95 station t shirts. Only problem was we had to check who was going to wear one on what day otherwise we'd all be walking down the road looking the same.

# 17.
# Hooray for Hollywood

**B**y the 1st September we flew into Los Angeles and drove to The Ramada Inn on Sunset Boulevard where we stayed for over a week and for me this was life changing.

We played five nights at the famous Starwood Club. I can't remember how many nights, but Caravan were also on the bill and to be honest I don't remember seeing them or meeting them.

Even when we weren't playing I really liked just hanging out in the club. The DJ there played some good records and one in particular grabbed my attention primarily for the bassline. I found out that the record was by a band called Crackin. I think they might have been a band from L.A. They had a really soulful sound, not the same as, but a similar style to Graham Central Station. This is what I meant when I said earlier that the UK were starting to put music in categories and here I was in a great club were all music was played regardless of the genre. Good music is good music whatever the category.

I managed to find the album in Tower Records which was conveniently a short walk away from the hotel we were staying in. Sadly neither Tower Records or The Starwood are no longer there. Looking for the album, I realised I was standing next to none other than Dudley Moore, the great comedian, actor and much underrated Jazz pianist. As a teenager I used to stay up to watch Peter Cook and Dudley Moore on their television show called *Not Only But Also* and Dudley's jazz trio always featured in it. Here is another example of me being a bit starstruck and the only thing I could say was "Hello" to which he replied, "Hello". Maybe if I had met him a couple of years later when I had heard the funny *Derek and Clive* album, I could maybe have replied with something like "Don't you hello me". Some of you will know what I mean by that.

Celebrities often used to pop into the bar and café area in our hotel. One day I was sitting in the café when I noticed Joey Molland and Mike Gibbins from the band Badfinger sitting there. Once again I didn't introduce myself so perhaps another missed opportunity. I saw Ringo Starr drive by one day and by some coincidence as I was walking from my room, possibly on the way to see my guys down at the pool, I passed by a room a couple of doors away from mine. I was wearing a pair of Ringo Starr's sunglasses. I had helped get my brother-in-law Pete get a job working for The Beatles at Apple Recording studios. Ringo had just released his album with him wearing the sunglasses with stars on the lenses. Pete often used to get goodies from Apple. He got the 'star glasses' I was wearing when a young lady came running to the door of her room and called out to me "Hi there, how are you?"

"Oh hello, I'm fine thank you. Are you okay?" I replied "Yes, I love your glasses and I must have them" she said. "Sorry but they are not for sale" said I. She was almost begging me to let her have my glasses, but I kept repeating I was not parting with them. She went on to explain that she had just spent the night with Ringo and wanted his glasses (which I was wearing) as a keepsake of spending the night with him! By this time, she was out of the room and up very close, face to face with me. "Please, I will do anything you want, if I can have those glasses, please oh please" she begged.

Now I have to admit she was a very attractive brunette and I am a helpless young 23-year-old, wearing Ringo Starr's glasses being propositioned in Hollywood by a 'Hooker'. Pretty surreal eh folks?

Many would have taken up the offer, I mean after all they were only sunglasses weren't they? No they weren't any old sunglasses. These were Ringo's sunglasses and you know what a big Beatle fan I am. I had to quite literally pull her off of me so I could carry on walking and as I briskly walked away I could still hear her calling after me trying to get me to change my mind.

This may well have been the day where I proceeded to the pool to meet the rest of my gang. We were often there in the daytime soaking up the sun. They had a big bin full of ice by the pool, supposedly for your cold drinks. As I walked by the pool, Bob pushed me in, fully clothed to everyone's entertainment. I had all my dollars with me and I began to pull them out of my jeans, one dollar note after another. I laid them out by the pool and they dried off in the sun. Talk about money laundering (groan, sorry about that one).

Roy Reich's trick was to jump off of one of the verandas a couple of floors up. Bloody dangerous, but he always managed it. My trick was to cut a piece of carrot very thin and get people to look in the pool while I gestured there was something in there. I would then plunge my hand in and pull out the carrot which in the speed of the moment appeared to be a Goldfish which I duly put in my mouth and started eating. An oldie but goodie.

After our first show at The Starwood, I left the stage and made it back to the dressing room. A little while afterwards Roy Reich came in and asked me if "We'd like to see the girls now?" "Girls, what girls?" I asked. "Come outside a moment" said Roy. Stepping outside the dressing room was a line of the most beautiful Hollywood ladies you could imagine. The queue went from the door and halfway down the corridor! ("I didn't see a queue outside Caravan's dressing room door "said the author smugly).

Well, we were quite well known in the UK, but I'd never seen anything like this, well not since we were chased to our dressing room by screaming fans at The Silver Blades Ice Rink, Streatham, London in 1968! These were by comparison classy looking girls none of which would have looked out of place on the big screen. Not one of them had pumped up lips and caterpillars for eyebrows like the girls seem to have these days!

We let them in to the dressing room, a few at a time and I know what you are probably thinking, but every one of them were saying how much they loved the music and I am sure once again they were quite fascinated by these four young British guys and in particular the way we talked. One or two of them commented on the accent. "Hey, say that again". The other surprising thing was that some of them brought gifts for us. To give you some idea, I came away with a couple of nice 'girlie' tops which I wore on stage for a while.

One of the nights in The Starwood, Ozzy Osbourne came to see us play. Maybe Wilf had told him we were in town. After our set he kept on saying in his unmistakeable accent, "Oi wanna prodouse yaauw" which translated from Brummie into English is, "I want to produce you".

We had a few drinks and then decided we'd make our way back to the hotel. Ozzy asked if we could give him and his young lady companion a lift back to his hotel which was no problem. So we all climbed in the car and set off towards The Beverley Hilton. On the way there our driver Roy inadvertently jumped a red traffic light! Within seconds there was a wailing of police sirens and a police bike pulled us over. Roy cleverly diverted the conversation from his traffic offence to the fact that he had guys/musicians all the way from England in the car and he was taking them to the hotel. He got away with it and the Cop sent us on our way. I was in the back sitting next to Ozzy and I couldn't help noticing that prior to be being pulled over by the policeman and during the questioning he was wriggling around next to me. To be honest I didn't think too much of it at the time. I thought he might just be adjusting his trousers or something. Anyway, we dropped Ozzy and the lady off at The Beverley Hilton and we made our way back to our hotel.

The next day we were out in the car again, off to somewhere and Gary was sitting where Ozzy had sat the night before. He could feel something sticking in his lower back. He put his hand down the back of the seat and there was a carved Elk horn with a stopper in one end. The Elk horn was filled with white powder, cocaine. No wonder Ozzy was wriggling about! Just as well the policeman didn't stop and search otherwise Roy or all of us would have got busted for carrying drugs!

On a Saturday night at The Starwood we met up with a well-known photographer named Armando Gallo and his wife. They invited us for Sunday dinner the next day "a good old English Sunday Roast". Armando and his English wife said they thought we would look forward to a typical Sunday roast dinner. Next day we went to their house and I think I am right in saying it was right on Venice Beach and also in the house were his wife's parents who had come over from the UK to visit. It was a lovely day indeed.

I couldn't help but notice a lady who was often in the hotel. Sometimes helping out in reception or just being around. She was a tall, slim, blonde and everything you would expect a Hollywood lady to look like. She reminded me of the actress Candice Bergen, so anyone old enough to remember her will know what I mean. We got talking on a few occasions and one day she offered to take me out for a ride in her convertible (Mustang or a Chevy, I really can't remember) and show me the Hollywood Hills. Her name was Linda and driving around that day was like heaven. Seeing all these places I had only ever imagined. Wishing I could meet up with the likes of Crosby Stills Nash and Young or John Mayall. Maybe famous actors and actresses and all the other musicians up around the Hollywood Hills and Laurel Canyon area.

Seeing where my childhood silver screen heroes like Errol Flynn, Fred Astaire, David Niven, and Gene Kelly used to live. We even went up on the hill and stood behind the big famous 'HOLLYWOOD' sign. It seemed like I only had to go and knock on a door and tell them who I was and they'd invite me in. I'd pick up a guitar and we'd make a hit record and then I'd move into Laurel Canyon... yeah right... only in my dreams. Linda insisted we should go barefoot as we walked part of the way. Well not for the first time, I found my feet were not used to the hot sand and I suffered a bit later, but I wasn't going to let on now was I?

We went to her place up in the hills which was a lovely little bungalow and we talked and talked into the early hours of the morning until it was almost light again. It seems she had a sad childhood, abandoned as a baby so she never knew what her real name was. She was never even adopted so she never really had a surname.

She told me she had once got together with an English drummer she had met called Bugs Pemberton. So she took his name and she became Linda Pemberton. I looked up his name and he was in fact Warren 'Bugs' Pemberton who was the drummer with The Undertakers, a well-known British group in the sixties. He went on to play with Jackie Lomax (Apple Records) The Burrito Brothers who coincidentally featured Gene Parsons from The Byrds, who I told you about I had met in Cannes and Ken Hensley to name but a few. He continued to live in the USA and died in 2013.

Another time Linda took me to The Starwood Club where Buddy Miles the drummer was having a birthday party. We went into the club and sat at a table. She seemed to know everybody there. Celebrities were in town and she seemed to know them all. "Hi Jimmy" she said as Jimmy Page walked past us! You see what I mean now? We were both very sad when it was time to leave Hollywood and we hoped we could meet up again sometime soon, although sadly it was never to be. I only knew Linda for a couple of days, but she was a beautiful human being and made a huge impression on me and I often wondered how life treated her.

On September 9th we arrived in Houston Texas and then picked up a small plane to Beaumont Texas. The plane only had us, our equipment and about six other passengers. We were going to be in Texas driving for a few days and I remember one time we were stopped by a Highway Patrol car. Bob and Dave had a Ryder Truck with our gear in and we followed behind in the car. Having been brought up in the UK where the police are not armed it's quite a daunting experience seeing the American Police force with their guns. They don't have to pull them out, you just know they are there ready to fire if necessary! Two cops were in the car, a male and a female. They were checking we were not hauling drugs as there had been reports of this happening at that time. We co-operated and they were very polite and surprisingly enough they didn't make us unload the truck or the car.

I think it was in Beaumont that we played a small club and opened for the legendary blues guitarist Freddie King and his band. I'm slightly embarrassed to say that back in 1975 I was not really aware what an influential blues player he was and if I'm honest I don't remember much about the set he played because it was by far overshadowed by the scenes backstage after he'd played the set.

A room had been set backstage presumably so no-one could be disturbed. A table and chairs were laid out and Freddie, the promoter and several other guys sat themselves around the table. Freddie pulled out a huge pile of dollars as did the other players. The room was smoke filled and dimly lit. The scene looked like something from a film and if a gun had been pulled from under the table, it would not have been a surprise. I watched for a while but I didn't feel too comfortable and felt it best to leave.

September 11th we arrived in Nacogdoches. I could be wrong but it struck me as a really small western town, once again the like that I'd only seen in films. Regardless of where it was the venue was really nice, but we just hoped people would show up to see us play later. The venue was basically a big bar and there was another bar which had a Pool table in. Pete and I both played snooker back home in the UK and Pete was a snooker champion of sorts at his local club. Pool, however was not a game we were very familiar with because once again like some of the alcohol we'd sampled, Pool as a game had not really arrived in the UK. We were watching two guys playing. No disrespect to the guys but they would not have looked out of place in the film *Deliverance* or some hillbilly-based film. The two guys had been watching us watching them and every now and then would direct a comment our way. They were fascinated by our accents and probably had never spoken to English people before. When they finished their game they called over

"Hey do you guys wanna shoot some pool?" We approached the table thinking they were going to leave, but after getting acquainted, they suggested we all play a game together. UK versus The USA. We explained that we had never played Pool before but we'll give it a go.

Pete and I soon got the hang of it and I was playing okay but Pete really got into his stride and we were knocking balls in, racking up the points. One of the guys, a bit overweight, beard and baseball cap was really making us laugh. Every time either Pete or I made a good shot or put a ball in a pocket he would shout out "Well kiss my ass, are you sure you fellas have never played this before?" Every time, yes every time, he kept repeating that phrase "Well kiss my ass" and it really made us laugh. We often recall that scene all these years later. It would have made a good scene in a Mel Brooks film. In retrospect, he sounded like Slim Pickens. Well what do you know, we beat them! We shook hands, said our goodbyes and went back into the live band room.

I was talking to Pete about this gig recently and we are sure this was the night that our drinks got spiked. As usual the dressing room had plenty to eat and drink in there. There was a particularly large jug of Tequila Sunrise and this was another new drink which we had discovered in the USA. I had taken a particular liking to this and by no strange coincidence so had Pete. So before the show we had a couple of glasses of it and I can only speak for myself when I say that when I walked on stage I felt fine, but the moment I picked my guitar up, strange things started to happen.

I can relate back to my story of being at Escape Studios and taking LSD and the part in a trip where the sound starts changing and phasing and the room starts moving and this all began kicking in. I wasn't totally out of it fortunately, but I remember looking over at Pete on the other side of the stage and him looking back at me and we both knew instinctively that we were on the same trip if you know what I mean? It felt at the start as if I was levitating slightly but I was in control, as was Pete. Although it was different from acid in a good way, we were not totally out of it and we played the show which went well. Those Rednecks never threw anything at us so that was a relief. Pete and I decided that a couple of beers might be safer than further Tequila Sunrises. I wondered what was in the drink and who did it? Was it our pool table opponents trying to get the last laugh? We will never know.

On September the 12th we arrived in Dallas and Pete and I were once again sharing a room (it makes you wonder if the others wanted to keep us apart from them, ha ha!) We had not been in our room for more than ten minutes when we heard a bang-bang noise out in the street. To be honest we didn't pay much attention to it initially, as it could have been a car backfiring, but all of a sudden one of our guys (possibly Ritchie) came rushing into our room and said to look out of the window because there was a car pulled over and a gunfight going on in the street with the police. Welcome to Dallas, Texas boys!

While we were in the hotel we were invited up to the Penthouse suite of a guy who said he was the manager of the band Trapeze. If so at that time it would have been Tony Perry. He seemed a nice guy, we had a couple of drinks but as I recall we didn't stay too long.

I have to say the details of the shows over the next few days are a bit sketchy because the records I'm reading from in old diaries seem a little incomplete and mixed up.

We played a really good club maybe in Dallas or maybe Fort Worth, which I have on the itinerary but Pete seems to think this show in Fort Worth was cancelled, I am not so sure. One show in particular I can remember was really enjoyable partly for the fact that the band opening for us were very good. They were a local band called Frenz or maybe Phrenz (I think that's how they spelt it?). In particular, we were really impressed by the guitarist whose name was Danny Brandt. He looked great and was just oozing with charisma. He looked like a star on that stage. He was from Fort Worth and having seen him perform we talked about and really considered if there was some way he could join the band and bring him back home to the UK with us.

Danny liked the sound of that idea. Like most Americans, they had as much desire to go to England as us English had to go to America. We had just seen Lynyrd Skynrd and they had three guitarists. We soon made friends with Danny and his band and I might be wrong but I had it in my head that we played a second night in this club but I can't find any record of it.

Here is some useless information which some of you might be interested in. While I was there I managed to get a Maestro flanger effects pedal at the club, which I recently showed to my friend keyboard player Simon Rinaldo, which he now has in his studio plugged into a Wurlitzer electric piano. It had three rocker switches, the first switch creates a slow phase, the second switch a faster phase and the third switch a fast almost tremolo effect. A couple of years later while on tour with Rush, Alex Lifeson used one, but his broke down so he used my one for the tour. Also just over a year after we had played a show with him, Freddie King died in Dallas on the 28th December 1976.

Bruce Springsteen was having a good year in 1975. It seemed like wherever you went at this time there were Billboards erected advertising his name. Bruce was in town, he and his entourage may have even been staying in the hotel, but I 'm not sure. Anyway, we met up with one of his road crew and we were invited to see Springsteen in concert which was literally just across the road from our hotel and according to records it was The Electric Ballroom.

We were all invited to the concert, but don't ask me why but we didn't go? I don't know what the others were doing but Pete and I found ourselves in the bar again! The Hyatt Lodge had a good bar and a lovely waitress called Loretta. Only in Texas would you find a girl called Loretta. I mean have you ever hear of a Loretta living in Cleethorpes? As it turned out it must have been Loretta's night off because there was a young G.I. behind the bar on this night.

So we perched ourselves up on two high bar stools and tried to decide what we wanted to drink. Behind the bar there were a list of cocktails none of which Pete and I had tried and some we had never even heard of. We got chatting to the bar tender and we were getting on great. I think we were the only two people in the bar all evening so we were his captive audience. "Why don't you try one of these?" he said pointing to the first one on the list. He proceeded to give us a details of what goes into this cocktail which incidentally I can't remember what this first one, the second one, the third one or the fourth, fifth, sixth maybe was?

I had lost count but I'm convinced we went down the list on the board. Apart from the Tequila Sunrise, there was the Singapore Sling, Alligator, Cosmopolitan, Planters Punch, Screwdriver (remember him) and various Sour drinks and drinks with fruit in, so at least we were drinking healthily! When we asked for the bill he said it was okay as we were guests in his country and we were having free samples, so we had sat there drinking all night and there was no charge. Don't you love America?

I think it was safe to say we were both pissed, so we made our way upstairs to our room. I'm not sure how or which room we ended up in, but not for the first time there was a party going on. All the band were there and Danny Brant our new guitarist friend. Then Bruce Springsteen's road manager arrived with a beautiful young blonde lady who for no apparent reason began taking her clothes off and dancing around the room naked, even though there was no music playing. I don't honestly remember much more and even if I did I wouldn't print it, but when I got home I wrote the song 'One Night in Texas' and that folks, is all you need to know.

As I said earlier, some of the show details and time spent in and around Dallas are somewhat sketchy. It seems we also played The Electric Ballroom in Dallas, this time with Spirit and Pacific Gas and Electric, two bands I had become familiar with dating back to buying the CBS Record samplers around 1968/69 called *The Rock Machine Turns You On*.

These were great albums of various artistes which I believe in some ways were quite influential to young bands like ours finding new music. In fact, when we first began to change our image back in the late sixties one of the songs we played was called 'Fresh Garbage' recorded by Spirit and was on one of these albums. It was quite possibly in our set on that first memorable performance at The Roundhouse Chalk Farm.

Who would have thought that when I was sixteen years old I would be hanging out with Spirit and Pacific Gas and Electric? Over the years I was lucky enough to meet many more artists like these. Before the show, one of the guys from Pacific Gas came over to us and recognising our language seemed thrilled to tell us that we should meet their bass player who was also from England. It turned out to be Kim Gardner who had had a couple of hit records with his band Ashton Gardner and Dyke. He had decided following the bands break up he would move to the USA where he became a successful session musician right up to his death from cancer on the 31st October 2001. He seemed like a really nice guy and seemed well pleased to be hearing familiar English voices again.

Spirit as some of you may already know, were just a three-piece line up with Randy California on guitar and vocals and the very charismatic Ed Cassidy on drums but I seemed to recall they were a four-piece that night and when I looked up the history of Spirit they did indeed employ a second guitarist for a while so I could be right. Both bands sounded really good, so there were no disappointments there to be had.

Next stop was Norman, Oklahoma on the 16th September and Ada, Oklahoma on the 19th September. Finally, up to Long Island to play a venue called My Fathers Place. I can't remember much about any of these places I'm sad to say.

We returned home to the UK on 24th September and as we stood at JFK Airport I will always remember Wilf turning to me and pointing at another airplane which was heading back to L.A. and asked me which plane did I want to get on. To London or Los Angeles?

Wilf knew how much I had fallen in love with the USA and Los Angeles in particular. I was sure I could make it there if I stayed. Linda back in Hollywood was friends with Don Kirchner who produced the famous legendary *Don Kirchner's Rock Concert* TV shows and could introduce me to him and work with him in some way as a starting point for a new career. I have to say I was surprised at Wilf's suggestion as if I had decided to fly to L.A. then he would have had to find another guitarist to replace me. Not that I am irreplaceable, but it would have been inconvenient to say the least, being the main songwriter as well. I was torn between the two destinations, but I think that my upbringing taught me to be loyal to those close to me. So it was to be London and continue with Stray and also back to my wife Jackie.

Hindsight is a wonderful thing and if I knew what I knew now and how things eventually turned out personally, I would have taken the flight to L.A. I often wonder how my life would have been had I gone to L.A. Like I said at the beginning, you don't get a rehearsal in life. You make your choices and have to live with them.

Interestingly enough, it was around this time that Wilf was establishing himself in the USA, so maybe, just maybe, he might have been offering me an alternative because he might have been thinking he was considering doing the same thing himself? We will never know?

# 18.
# Back To Work In The UK

**B**efore our trip to the USA we had mainly been playing headline shows and sets no longer than sixty to ninety minutes, primarily containing material mainly from the "Stand Up" album which Pete played on. We had played longer sets in the States, sometimes even two sets so we had to re-introduce some of the older songs. To Pete's credit in particular, it was quite an achievement for him to learn. I think it showed how very together we were at this time and we sounded really tight.

We were looking forward to recording the next album which we began in October 1975. This time we used the PYE studios in Marble Arch, London. I liked this studio and I felt very comfortable in it. The atmosphere was good and we approached this recording with renewed confidence. We had two engineers, Terry and Kim who fortunately had the same warped sense of humour as us. Sometimes we got into fits of laughter with childlike things like making farting noises (with your mouth), particularly effective when you are just about to record a vocal and then over your headphones you hear a fart.

I had written a song called 'Houdini' which Wilf thought would be a good album title. Although I had plenty of songs left over prior to America, the new album would feature all brand new songs. I think that all of the songs in their own way were quite commercial and radio friendly. I had played keyboards (Hammond organ/ piano etc) on all of the previous albums, but I thought we could probably do with someone else coming in and adding some keys parts on certain songs.

We didn't really know any keys players at that time but Terry and Kim had contact numbers of a couple of players. Basically we had a couple of session guys come down and try to add the keys parts to a few of the songs, but what they had to offer didn't seem right. Something I have found is that quite often keyboard players are often technically gifted but rather than listen to the song they want to show you how clever they are. After what was to be the last session player to come in and try to add to the songs, we all sat there and thought we haven't found anyone to play what we wanted.

"Del, I think you should play the keyboard parts, you know what they should sound like" said Ritchie and everyone agreed. That was a great compliment and gave me the confidence to go in and do what was required. So I added the various keys parts as required.

Around this time, I had met Bill Gammond, a close friend of Pete's. I remember Pete telling me that when he told Bill he had joined Stray and that my name was Del Bromham. He asked Pete "Has Del got a brother called Allan?" It turns out to be another coincidence. It turned out that Bill played bass guitar for The Traders for a short while as well. When I found out, I did vaguely remember a young left-handed player with ginger hair playing in my mum's front room.

Like Pete, Bill was a few years older, although I never knew him then. Bill came up to the studios a couple of times while we recording. One time I was working on the vocal which I think was 'Houdini'. I was showing Pete what the vocal harmony would be on the chorus and that I would go in after and put a high vocal harmony on top. Bill heard what I was suggesting to Pete and he started singing the high harmony in the studio like I had suggested. "Well, I tell you what, why don't you come in with Pete and me sing the third harmony?" I asked. We went in the studio and sang the three-part harmony I think in the first take. It sounded good. We had another song for the album that I wanted harmony vocals on called 'Gonna Have A Party'. Same thing, the three of us went in the studio and added the vocals to that one as well.

Our good friend Jimmy Helms came along one day and added some vocals and Trumpet to one of my favourites 'Wait Another Day'. Quite different from what we'd done before with a slightly jazzy, funky feel to it. I also added Fender Rhodes piano to this one which for me not considering myself to be a proper keyboard player was something of a challenge as there are some tricky jazzy chords in there. It gave the sound I was looking for. I had been listening to people like George Duke, Chick Corea and Joe Zawinul, so I was trying to do the kind of thing they might do. I think it worked?

While recording the *Houdini* album, Wilf had invited a couple of agents down to meet the band, one being Richard Cowley of Cowbell Agency and Rod McSween of ITB Agency. He was trying to get Stray new agency representation as it seemed over the past couple of years we had quite a few agents and Wilf seemed to be taking us from one to the other.

I remember we were with Good Earth Agency for a while in 1976 and we needed to promote the *Houdini* album. The booker at the agency was someone we kind of new from many years ago as he was the Social Secretary at Brunel University in Uxbridge, Middlesex. Wilf was rarely available and appeared to be spending a lot of time out of the country, predominately the USA. Worldwide Artistes had been sold off in 1975 by its owner Patrick Meehan and consequently so was the financial backing received by Wilf at our Dover Street office. On the rare occasion we did see Wilf it was at his house in Worcester Park, Surrey.

The irony was that the gigs we were playing were going very well and the audiences were returning again. Where some of the old fans whose allegiance to the original line up had now departed a new audience was coming along to see us. No words needed to be said really as it was obvious that without backing from Worldwide Office we were very much on our own and the weekly wages ceased.

However, the wages had to be paid and for the first time since I was about sixteen we had to set about managing ourselves. Ritchie, being the grammar schoolboy became the band's bookkeeper and I suppose I was the one who spoke to the agencies, venues or whoever would "give us a gig". The problem is that when the guitarist phones up looking for gigs the promoters know you need the money because you should have representation doing that, so it was not a good move but something which had to be done to keep the work coming in. The words of my dad saying "Put pride in your pocket son, pride doesn't pay the bills" kept resounding in my ears.

We had been hiring trucks and I thought it would be better to have our own truck. I also thought it would be better now we were self-sufficient to have our own account. Some venues paid by cheque and it got complicated when there was one made out to Stray. Fortunately, my bank knew me and allowed me to sign my name on the back and they would give me the cash. One day I arranged a meeting with the bank manager and he was willing to help. I opened up a Stray bank account and furthermore a small loan which was immediately deposited into the account so that we could go out and buy our own truck. No more van rental.

At this time, we were down to just two on our road crew. Dave Flockton remained as sound engineer and new addition, Paul Cantwell driver and backline tech. Our personal tour manager and driver 'Woolie', Mick Crickmar had been offered a job with Hot Chocolate so we didn't replace him. In future we would hire a car when necessary and drive ourselves.

Pete and I went to a dealer over East London and we bought a 7-ton Leyland boxer truck with a tail-lift on the back. Pete had been an HGV driver in a former life and knew more about these things than any of us. It was a big yellow bus which belonged to the Kodak Company. Pete brought it back to my house where we painted it black. It looked really smart. We managed to get a good deal on rental cars from J. Davy a new car rental company in Putney, so we were self-sufficient and up and running again. So bring on the shows.

Ah here's a bit of light relief and something funny which I've just remembered. Pete's wife Jenny cut his hair and I thought it looked good, so I asked her if she would cut mine too. Gary like it so she cut his and also cut Dave our sound engineer's hair too. Not quite a mullet, but the top was layered and the back remained long. I thought we looked pretty good, so as well as being our chemist (that's another story) she became our hairdresser too.

We had played a couple of shows at The Roundhouse and both shows were sold out. One Roundhouse show I remember well was 28th December 1975. Stray, UFO, Judas Priest and Strife. What a good bill?

Despite being listed on the bill, for some reason Judas Priest turned up but didn't play. A year or so prior, a guy turned up at a gig we played in the West Midlands who I'd spoken to at our shows before. I cannot remember his name but he introduced me to his friend, a guitarist, Glen Tipton. I remembered Glen because I was particularly impressed with him when I saw him play with his three-piece band called 'The Flying Hat Band' one time at The Marquee Club. He told me he was going to manage the band and the band were called Judas Priest and they were going to be Big! Er, whatever happened to them?

Some forty years later, I have seen televised concerts from the Roundhouse with some top names and it would be hard for people not around at that time and even hard for me to acknowledge that Stray were so popular at that time, we could sell it out, this was the main reason why promoter John Curd of Straight Music invited us to open for both Rush and Kiss on their first tours of the UK. He knew with Stray he would definitely get an audience. More on that in a moment.

Following the release of the *Houdini* album we asked Bill Gammond or Billy as we called him if he'd like to play some shows to cover those extra vocal harmonies. He was a bass player, but with us he was going to play rhythm guitar. I suppose we still had Danny Brandt in mind.

John Curd of Straight Music was the main promoter at this time for The Roundhouse Concerts and he had noted that we pulled a crowd and always went down really well. I just thought it worth mentioning at this point that around this time we broke the house record for attendance at London's Marquee Club one time.

He phoned me to tell me about a band he had coming over from the USA and would I fancy nipping up to his office in London to have a meeting about it. What I am about to tell you is another story I have that many will not believe, but it is absolutely true and gives those who do not know how big Stray were on the live gig scene in the 1970s.

I went to see John and he told me more about the band. They had a big show and were getting rave reviews back in the US, but he wasn't sure how many people they would pull into the venues in the UK. So he wanted an opening act who could guarantee an audience should this particular act not pull on their own merits so to speak. The band he was talking about were Kiss. I know what some of you are thinking, "yeah, right". To be honest I didn't know much about Kiss either, but I trusted John and his judgement (well he believed in Stray when not many others did) there were some good venues and the fee he offered was surprisingly good. With the lack of money coming from our office, the wages could be paid.

The dates were as follows:

13th May Free Trade Hall, Manchester
14th May Birmingham Odeon
15th & 16th May Hammersmith Odeon

It's funny how time changes things in your mind, because I had forgotten there were only four4 shows. I was thinking there were a few more.

The first show we arrived early and watched their sound check. To be perfectly honest they didn't sound great, but it was a sound check in a huge venue with no people in it. We got to meet all of the crew and they all seemed like nice guys. These UK dates were part of their European tour and it must have cost them a fortune as they had brought everything over from the USA with them. One of their crew showed us one particular flight case which was full of large jars of white powder which was their pyro technical and flash powder (they were well known for their stage show), except he gave us a little wink and pointed out that two of the jars were actually not what you thought they were, sniff, sniff, if you understand what I mean?

We were about to go on stage for the first show and we still had not actually met or come face to face with the band themselves. As we were walking from our dressing room, four guys appeared in full stage costume and make up, looking like characters from Marvel Comics and called out to us, "Good luck guys".

Like promoter John Curd, we didn't know if we would get good audiences on these shows, but we need not have worried because every show was sold out and a lot more shows could have been added.

The well-known DJ on the scene at that time was Andy Dunkley and he announced us on stage from the wings. I remember waiting to go on, but there was a huge fire curtain in front of the stage. I heard Andy say something like the usual "Please give a warm welcome to Stray" at which point the heavy fire curtain began to raise. As the curtain rose the roar of the crowd got louder and louder. I will never forget that. I looked over to my right and Billy gestured to me something like 'I think I'm gonna be sick"

Every show was great and we had proved we could still do the business if only we could get people like John Curd to believe in us.

We had been very disappointed with the backing and publicity etc we were getting from PYE Records and so was John Curd. For example, Ritchie and I would run around the venues prior to the show putting up our own posters. We never saw or heard anything from PYE (Dawn) Records on these shows or any others for that matter. There was one exception: PYE Records A & R man, Colin Ricardo. He was a nice guy who quite clearly had his hands tied by the senior management. I felt sorry for him on the night he showed up to see us at the Hammersmith Odeon. John Curd was so pissed off with PYE Records with the lack of support they were giving us, that he would not let Colin in the building. We really had to persuade him that Colin was okay and to allow him in.

The final show at Hammersmith was entertaining and very good for us, being in our home town and seeing our name up in lights outside the Odeon was quite something. To think I used to go there to the cinema and there I was actually going to perform there was quite something.

As our set ended the Kiss guys came out and hit us with custard pies! Apparently it was an end of tour prank they did on a lot of the bands they got on with. They did the same thing to Rush when they toured with Kiss the year before.

When Kiss came on stage they had a guy come on stage to give them the 'big introduction'.

He was a big black guy with quite a deep booming voice. I was standing at the back of the Odeon next to the sound desk and their sound engineer gestured to me "Hey you watch this". As the big guy opened his mouth he began his introduction something like, "Ladies and gentlemen, the greatest rock 'n' roll band in the world... Kiss".

Except tonight the sound engineer had plugged his microphone into some kind of vocoder or octivider and as he was introducing his voice was getting higher and higher sounding like he'd inhaled a good dose of Helium. It was hilarious, we were all killing ourselves with laughter. He was not amused and he tried several times to announce Kiss, but every time the sound engineer tampered with his vocal microphone. After several attempts he stormed off of the stage and you just about heard him shout "Ah, fuck it" sounding slightly like the character, Alvin from the Chipmunks.

So many times over the years I have heard people say how unfriendly Gene Simmons and Paul Stanley are, and not nice people. I can only speak for myself but I found them to be really nice guys. The line-up was Gene Simmons, Paul Stanley, Ace Frehley and Peter Kriss on drums. We could tell there was a bit of an atmosphere between Peter and the rest of the band and I believe he was fired a little while after. It had also been noted that Gene and Paul has stood side stage watching us play and they had been watching Ritchie on drums in particular. It all kind of makes sense now, they must have been on the look-out for a replacement, or maybe I am totally wrong.

Kiss were extremely friendly to us. On the last night in Hammersmith they invited us and our entourage backstage for drinks and one thing I remember was Ritchie and his wife Lyn standing with their little daughter Emma who was maybe only about five at the time. We were talking to Gene Simmons and Emma only came up to the height of Gene's waist. She started tugging at Ritchie's jacket, not actually saying anything just tugging the jacket with one hand and pointing with the other. Gene had a huge leather belt and it had a glass buckle and behind the glass was a spider possibly a Tarantula! I know Gene Simmons in particular has noted on many occasions how special the first UK tour was for Kiss and how important it was and how much they enjoyed it.

I was really surprised when I got a message from Guy Griffin guitarist with The Quireboys. Guy and fellow band members Paul Guerin and Keith Weir were on tour with Joe Elliott from Def Leppard (also a Stray fan), with his other project The Down 'n Outs. They were at Sheffield City Hall and Guy messaged me to tell me that Gene Simmons had come into their dressing room and he was reminiscing about that first UK tour and about how good it was with Stray. Of course the guys followed it up with telling him they were friends of mine. It's good to know that someone like Gene still remembers those times over forty years later.

It was becoming difficult to find an agency to represent us. For a short while Bob England ran an agency called Good Earth. After a while he decided to close the agency and move to the USA. The main booker at Good Earth was a guy named Paul King, who we had known way back in the early seventies when he was the social secretary for Brunel University. Paul called me to say he was starting up his own agency called Outlaw and he would like to represent us. This was good news because he believed in the band and he had been working for us indirectly for Good Earth. So more dates started coming in up and down the country.

One band we got to play with on many occasions were three guys from the Liverpool area called Strife. Paul was also representing them and we became good friends and always looked forward to meeting up on the road. They were like no other band on the circuit at that time. Some of the impromptu moments during their set when they did a song with a long solo where there might be a bit of jamming going on did remind me of Stray when we first started playing and musically we would wander off into something different. We were always looking forward to playing shows with Strife. We used to nickname them 'The fuzzy hair and flying arrows'. I told bass player Gordon Rowley that some years later which made him laugh. Together we always gave the audience a good show and we shared a little something in common in that both Stray and Strife were bands that some name bands wouldn't want on the bill with them because of going down too well. That's a fact. Strife at this time were Paul Ellison on drums, John Reid on guitar and vocals and Gordon Rowley on bass guitar and vocals. Gordon and I have remained friends and I will tell you more about our relationship later.

# 19.
# The Final Countdown

**A**lthough our work had picked up with Paul King at Outlaw Agency the finances were still very tight. We had been paying Billy to come along and play with us but it was no longer financially viable to do so. We went back to being the four-piece line up of Pete, Gary, Ritchie and me. We began rehearsing songs for a new album. Even with our backs against the wall so to speak, we seemed to be just as determined to forge on. We had a new song for the album titled 'Lonely Road' and there is a line in the song that mentions 'Hearts of Fire' which we thought would be a good album title.

We still had fire in our bellies and our hearts with the desire to play our music. It felt right at the time. I cannot say that Wilf Pine was doing very much in a managerial roll at this time but he did come in and negotiate the new album being recorded once again with PYE Records for their Dawn label But this time we recorded at Air Studios London with producer Neil Slaven. He had worked with many artistes notably Trapeze on their *You Are The Music ...We're Just The Band* album. Neil was good to work with and along with engineer Ross Cullum we produced a good sounding album.

In the background Wilf had resurfaced and it appeared he was trying to get back in with Don Arden once more. Don seemed to be keeping a pretty low profile also rarely leaving his office at Jet Records in Wimbledon. Don was managing Lyndsey de Paul, ELO and Widowmaker. Widowmaker were a new band featuring Steve Ellis from Love Affair and Luther Grosvenor from Spooky Tooth and I have a story about him later.

It appeared there might be a co-management deal coming up for us with Wilf Pine and Richard Arden, who was Don's son. It may have been Don's suggestion that while he was too busy Richard should start handling an act or two. I had a couple of meetings with Wilf and Richard, but I was getting the feeling that nothing much was happening and my feelings were confirmed when neither Richard or Wilf seemed contactable. I spent many hours waiting in the offices of Jet Records in Wimbledon in the hope of having a meeting with Don. I got to know Arthur Sharp an A & R man for Jet Records (he was the singer from The Nashville Teens) and also got to know Sharon Arden (who later became the world famous Sharon Osbourne). I always found Sharon a really nice lady. Totally different from the person you see on television these days. She seemed a quiet polite lady and always very helpful when I met her in the offices.

One day I was at the offices of Jet Records and Arthur said to me "Ere, you'll never guess who's coming in here today for a meeting?" "Who's that then?" I asked. "Only Charlie Kray" he replied.

It transpires that Charlie had been released from prison and was trying to get a deal for his autobiography and it was recommended he should speak to Don Arden.

The waiting room in the offices had two leather settees facing each other. I took my usual place on one of the settees and waited for my meeting with Don. Not unusually I had been waiting for some time with no sign of Don calling me in. To Sharon's credit she did pop out from time to time and apologise. While I was sitting there, in to the reception area walked a very smart gentleman in a blue suit and sat down right opposite me. It was Mr Charles Kray, elder brother of the infamous Kray Twins, Reggie and Ronnie.

Blimey I thought, Charlie Kray! I was kind of nervous but not, if you know what I mean?
Something I can't explain but I suppose it is when legend or facts precede someone about that person you have only heard about, it puts many things into your mind. Charlie said hello and quite clearly was very friendly. We had a conversation something like.

"What do you do then boy?"

"I'm in a band and I'm hoping we can get Don to manage us"

"Oh nice one, I used to be in the music business you know?"

Yes, I did know. He had links with personalities such as Judy Garland and actor George Raft, before he went away to spend time in one of Her Majesty's hotels. Charlie and I must have been sitting there together for at least 45 minutes.

"How long have you been waiting here then?" Charlie asked

"Well about an hour and a half, but it's not the first time. I've been here a few times and not actually seen anyone" I replied.

Charlie seemed a bit restless and then said to me. "Look, I think I've waited long enough. I don't know about you but I don't like being given the run-around. I know a few people in the music business. I could have a word if you like?"

"Oh, sounds great" I replied, or something like that.

"How did you get here?" asked Charlie

"I drove here. I came by car" I said

"Oh great" said Charlie "Are you going anywhere near Bethnal Green?"

Er well let me see, I was living in West London and he wanted a lift to Bethnal Green, East London.
Was it on my way, no it wasn't... err yes I was! Like I was going to say no to Charlie Kray.

I had a really nice mini at the time. Sporty looking, white with 'John Player' markings on the bodywork and alloy wheels, irrelevant I know, but I just thought I'd mention it and it wasn't too shabby a vehicle to drive a celebrity to Bethnal Green in now was it?

As it happens, we got on well and had a good chat all the way. We exchanged phone numbers and he said he'd be in touch. I dropped him off at his mum's house in Bethnal Green. All the way home I am thinking to myself and looking at my passenger seat. No-one is going to believe who I have had sitting in my car!

Charlie also gave me a contact in the music business. The number was for Laurie O' Leary. It transpired that Laurie knew almost everybody in the business and quite clearly everybody knew him. He used to run the famous Speakeasy Club in London where many of music's celebrities hung out. He was involved in music management and coincidentally was a good friend of the Krays.

I rang the number and someone picked up the phone, but it wasn't Laurie, it was Robin Greatrex. "Hi Del" said Robin "Laurie isn't here at the moment, but let me take your number and I'll get him to call you back". Sure enough later in the day

Laurie did call me back. He knew Wilf Pine. In fact, like I said, he knew everybody it seemed. We arranged for me to go to his office where I met both him and Robin. Although we didn't talk about anything specific, it was a good meeting in as much as we chatted about everything and about the state of the band. It appeared that generally speaking he was more advisor and an artist/management liaison capacity and not strictly a sole manager.

I am sure it was his idea that Charlie Kray would ultimately wind up being the new Stray manager. It was supposed to be great publicity for both parties. Once again we, the band went along with this idea. Very soon we were in the daily papers. The *Daily Mail* had a big article with a photograph of Charlie standing with the band. We actually looked like Charlie's gang, The BBC also came to a small venue and filmed us on stage with Charlie watching his new protégés' from the audience. It went out on national television.

Following this big statement, we began playing UK dates up and down the country. The first was at The Penthouse in Scarborough, a good club which we had played before. We were sitting in the dressing room when the promoter came in and asked if we were expecting any trouble? Trouble? No none that we were aware of. He said that some plain clothes police had arrived and were in the club's reception to check if Charlie was there and to have a word with him in the event there might be a problem. The whole situation was ridiculous, not that they knew, but Charlie was not that kind of guy and if he were it would be unlikely there would be any trouble in a public place.

Although nothing like that happened again, I could really sense a different atmosphere when we arrived at gigs. As if they had to be very careful what they said to us. You didn't want to upset Stray! One of the last gigs we did on this run of shows was at The Marquee Club in London. There was only one dressing room, so it was odd that we had not seen the support band to speak to all evening? They didn't even come in the dressing room after they played their set.

We were sitting in the dressing room after we had played our show, just generally cooling off, when a couple of heads poked around the door. A voice said something like "Hello, great set, thanks for having us on with you". I said "Thank you, no problem. Why don't you come in?" "Come in? We can come in? Is that okay?" said a nervous sounding voice. Two of the band came in and sat down and we had a little chat, but the thing that completely astounded me and it shows how false rumours circulate. They told us that they didn't enter the dressing room earlier because they had heard that we were a hard bunch and they might get beaten up! I hadn't heard words like that since I was in Secondary School. This wasn't right at all, but how do you quash rumours like that?

Here's a funny story. One day my phone rang and it was a young guy who I had first met when he used to come along to The Greyhound, Croydon and help the road crew load in and out the equipment. His name was Mel Wesson. He phoned to tell me that he had received a message from a guy who had stolen one of my guitars from the show we had played in Croydon a couple of nights before. Apparently the guy had found out that our manager was Charlie Kray and he had been shitting himself ever since and was scared that someone was going to go and pay him a visit. The guy new that Mel knew me and the band and asked if he returned the guitar to Mel to pass back on to me and nothing more would be said (he would remain anonymous of course). I went to meet Mel and got the guitar back which was a new Dynelectron guitar which was a new reissue of the old style Danelectro. Having Charlie as your manager did have its benefits!

By the way Mel Wesson went on to become a successful keyboard player and composer writing scores for films such as *Black Hawk Down*, *Pirates of the Caribbean*, *Batman* and *Mission Impossible* to name but a few.

Charlie and Stray had a very short relationship. Although it gained publicity, certainly for us it backfired. The parting was amicable and I still spoke to Charlie from time to time for years after.

We had yet another all but short encounter with another would be manager and I've spoken to Pete and Gary and I have no idea how we met up with Mr Barry Bethell, of Thomson/Bethell Associates. It may have been someone that Charlie knew, I really don't remember. Barry was a one time 'bit part' actor. One of those actors who pop up in the background in films from time to time. Never a starring role. I realise now looking back on it, even trying to be our manager, he was playing out an acting roll but without the knowledge of what the job entailed.

The company may have been accounts or financial advisors primarily so perhaps the thought of someone handling finances on our behalf was the attraction? Barry met us and could certainly 'talk the talk' and he gave us the impression that financing the band in some way would not be a problem. Ironically one of the first gigs we had with Barry managing was on the Isle of Wight and guess who was the promoter? Wilf Pine.

Wilf didn't have to dress up to look 'the part', but when Barry turned up at the gig, with the leather coat and doing 'the walk', well even Wilf looked him up and down and turned to me and said with a grin "Is that your new manager?". Barry decided he should get up on stage and introduce the band. I can't tell you what words he used, but it made us cringe, it felt like he was the master of ceremonies at a working men's club. It may have been a scene or lines from one of his 'B' movies.

A little while later we had a week or two without any gigs, but we were under the impression that Barry would be coming up with the wages for the group and road crew. I tried to contact him and his partner Fred Thomson but could not speak to anybody. Then my phone rang and a frantic lady who turned out to be Mrs Bethell, Barry's wife was having a go at me for hassling Barry for money. "We haven't got money in our bank account to give you lot" or something like that she wailed. I didn't know what to say to her to be honest. I'd never had the wife of a manager call me before. Quite clearly Barry had never told his wife how he intended to manage this band.

Consequently, we never heard from Barry again. While doing research for this book I discovered that Barry was the television face of the *Slimfast* advertising campaign in the early 1990s. Fortunately, Paul at Outlaw was getting some shows in but not nearly enough, so I started speaking to promoters myself.

News travels fast in the business and since signing with Wilf we had been with so many agencies in a short time. Our connections (however loose) with Wilf, Don Arden, The Mafia and the Krays scared everyone off. "I don't want to get my legs broken" was a phrase I heard in connection with Stray on more than one occasion.

Then of course bands like Stray were deemed to be old hat. Yesterday's news. The rise of Punk and acts coming out of the independent labels were taking over the live gig scene. The irony of this is that we were the same age as some of the punk bands and younger than some others, but we were put in to that older bands categories.

Many of the bands like us at that time had good management and had the foresight to see what was happening and played more shows abroad, especially the new Eastern Bloc market which would gradually open up.

Fortunately, we still had one ally in John Curd. He phoned me and I had another meeting in his office which had a very similar tone to the conversation I had the year before regarding the dates with KISS.

It's another story that some would not believe if I told them, but here goes. John said that he wanted to bring this band over from Canada, but he wasn't sure if they would pull enough people in the venues. He was so pleased with what Stray did on the Kiss dates that he wanted us to do it again. This time with a band called Rush. As before I trusted John and he offered us a pretty good deal. I told him that it would be good for us too as it tied in nicely with the release of our new album *Hearts Of Fire*. He clearly wasn't impressed that the album was once again coming out on PYE Records but it didn't change his mind that we were the right band for the Rush shows, as follows:

| | |
|---|---|
| 1st June | City Hall, Sheffield |
| 2nd June | Free Trade Hall, Manchester |
| 3rd June | Odeon, Birmingham |
| 4th June | Hammersmith Odeon, London |

Rush then left to play a couple of shows in Europe, before resuming in the UK:

| | |
|---|---|
| 11th June | City Hall, Newcastle |
| 12th June | Apollo, Glasgow |
| 13th June | Empire Theatre, Liverpool |

I knew nothing about Rush and had never heard any of their music at this point, so I didn't know what to expect. I didn't even know what they looked like. Social media was non-existent in 1977, so it wasn't like you could look them up on YouTube or anything.

We were in our dressing room at the first show, following our sound check, when there was a knock on the door and a head popped around and said "Hi guys, I'm Neil. I'm the drummer with Rush". He went on to say that he had lived in London for a while and saw us play at The Marquee and it was great we were doing the tour with them.

Well that was a surprise, not only that he'd seen us play, but I don't think I could ever recall anyone from a headline act purposely taking the time and trouble to introduce themselves and say hello. As it turned out that was typical of Neil, a warm and friendly guy and a hugely talented drummer. We soon met Alex and Geddy, both of whom were very nice guys also. When I first heard Geddy sing I thought he was singing through some kind of effect but as it turned out that was the sound of his voice. Fairly high pitched and it took me a while to get used to it I must admit.

John Curd need not have worried about audience attendances, because every show was very well attended and both bands went down very well. Like the Kiss tour, I think this tour was a good launch pad for the start of the popularity of Rush in the UK.

Incidentally, this was called the 'All The World's A stage' tour and for them it certainly was. If you look up their tour itinerary, this tour began in August 1976 and they were arguably the busiest band I had ever seen. It didn't stop for them when this tour ended. They toured continually over the years, night after night, releasing one album after another!

This was another tour where both bands and crew got on very well. They had a great sense of humour which was just as well. I think it must have been at The

Liverpool Empire which was the last night of the tour, I spotted hanging up just off of the stage, two old brown overall type coats and a couple of yard brooms. I grabbed Ritchie and said, "Here you are put that coat on and take a broom". Well into Rush's set, Geddy was just about to introduce the next song when Ritchie and I came onto the stage pretending to be sweeping up. I don't think Geddy saw me at first, so he was still talking over the microphone while I was behind him with my broom, muttering something like "C'mon now, time to pack up. Ain't you got any homes to go to?"

Alex had a wild sense of humour. One night after the show we went back to their hotel for drinks. Geddy and Neil were there but there was no sign of Alex. Then Alex walked into the bar area holding a cigarette holder with his hair slicked back, a pencil moustache, dressed in a silk smoking jacket and shorts, and proceeded to talk in a fake German accent. He kept that up for the duration of the evening as if it were quite natural.

The tour ended and I didn't see them again until the following year when I went to The Hammersmith Odeon to see them on their 'Farewell To Kings' tour and say hello again.

Around this time, we had a rather unusual request to play a Christmas concert at Wandsworth Prison for the in mates. It was John Curd who suggested it. Well you might not believe it but I had never been to prison before and the feeling when entering the prison walls was like no other that I had felt before. The building looked like something I had only ever seen or imagined in TV and films. It all looked antiquated and could do with a lot of refurbishment. There were prisoners wearing arm bands helping unload the equipment with our road crew. These were the guys on some kind of good behaviour, rewarded away from their daily mundane routines within the prison walls.

We had a small room to the side of a big stage in a large hall. The thing I remember most was one inmate who was serving a life sentence saying "I suppose all the shops have got Christmas decorations up in them now?"

"Yes they have" I replied. "I bet it looks lovely" he replied. This scene has remained in my mind all these years. It was one of the saddest conversations I think I've ever had. The look on his face and his words are something I will never forget (sad regardless of whatever his crime).

We played our usual rock set which went down very well. Not exactly Johnny Cash at Fulsom Prison but a strangely rewarding experience.

Speaking of rewards, the following week I received a letter from the Governor/Chamberlain of Wandsworth Prison. He thanked us for performing a concert for the staff and inmates and offered us a £20 note as a token of appreciation which he thought might help cover our expenses. However, there was no sign of a twenty-pound note in the envelope! I think of Ronnie Barker in the TV programme Porridge and imagined his character Fletcher on good behaviour just like the fellas we met with the arm bands, being asked to go and post the letter, but stopping off to steam the envelope open and take the money out! Maybe the governor actually forgot to put the twenty-pound note in, but I still think the possibilities of my story are funnier.

I wish I could say that 1976 and 1977 had been as successful for Stray as it had been for Rush, but even though with some good shows and two good albums things were tough.

I got to know Laurie O'Leary and Robin Greatrex who at the time were also managing The Heavy Metal Kids and The Tyla Gang although they didn't do anything specifically for Stray, they did put a bit of business our way with regard to hiring our

PA system. We always 'right from the start' (another Stray song title by the way) had our own equipment and our PA was one of the best around at that time.

A couple of years before we had played a show at The Roundhouse. Also on the bill were UFO. When we arrived we were concerned to find that our own PA was not set up. When we questioned our crew, Dave our sound engineer had been talking to UFO and they wanted to sell their PA. Dave was impressed by the specification and it was agreed we could use it on the night with a view of buying it. It was a fantastic sound system and looked very impressive. I called it 'The Berlin Wall'. I'm not a technophobe but apparently it was a 5,000 watt Kelsey Morris system with Amcron (Crown) power amps and a 32 Channel Soundcraft desk. Having used it, we had to have it. Somehow we got the cash together and it became ours. So anyway, it became a good asset because as the gigs were getting harder to find, the PA hire at least kept the crew in wages.

As the year was drawing to a close we had gigs up and down the country. We were aware that some promoters were taking advantage of us and some shows we were being paid far less than we had been paid before as well as taking other shows for less money just in order to survive. It was a frustrating time and after all we had been through over the years it was becoming a struggle and I could see no light at the end of the tunnel.

Our final show of this year was on Saturday 10th December, a gig we always enjoyed at The Nottingham Boat Club. It was a good night, plenty of people in and the band played well. We said our goodbyes at the end of the evening, but little did we now that was going to be the last show we were to play. There might have been tears if we had known!

\*\*\*\*

I mentioned the Heavy Metal Kids and I have to say that their lead singer Gary Holton was a great front man. I first saw him when we played a show together at The Roundhouse. Well talk about making a disadvantage into an advantage. He had either broken his leg or his ankle and he appeared on stage in a wheelchair still wearing the green hospital gown. He and 'The Kids' put on a great show and I thought they were best British band I had seen for a long time.

Sometime later, we were playing a show at Barbarellas in Birmingham. I was sitting backstage in the dressing room, when the door opened and a little head poked around the door and said "Allo son, do ya fancy a lemonade?" It was Gary. I've no idea what he was doing in Birmingham but there he was. I was on the stage and during the set I could sense that there was someone standing behind me. Then as I turned, a voice shouted out "Go on son, rock 'n' roll". Then he disappeared off of the stage and in retrospect I thought he might have stayed and grabbed the microphone or something. The stage was certainly his home. He reminded me of the Artful Dodger. I don't know if he was ever in a stage production of *Oliver* but he would have been perfect in it.

A couple of years later Robin Greatrex called me and said he'd had an idea about Gary and I forming a band together. Lots of maybes. Maybe we could call it Stray or maybe we could use the rest of Stray with Gary fronting it or maybe call it something completely different. The main objective was to get Gary and me together. As Robin put it, I could write the songs because Gary wasn't a songwriter and Gary could be the lead singer and front man. Robin felt it could launch both our careers. I thought it was a great idea and waited to get moving on it.

A few weeks went by and then Robin called to say that Gary had been offered an acting part in a play somewhere, so the project would have to go on hold. This happened on a couple of occasions and Gary was getting a name as an actor, but what finally put a stop to our project was that he was offered a part in a new TV drama series called *Auf Wiedersehen Pet* about a gang of builders working in Germany. The series turned out to be a huge success and consequently no more was discussed about the band project. Sadly, Gary died of an overdose of morphine and alcohol on 25th October 1985. He was only 32.

In recent years I have got to know the drummer Keith Boyce and have met up with him a few times at gigs. It's surprising how things have changed because these days I know more people/musicians from that era now than I did back then. Maybe it's an age thing, but people seem more sociable (self-included) than back in the seventies.

andad Private Ernest Jewell 1914.

Mum circa 1930.

Mum, Allan, Raymond and
Norman, 3rd December, 1940.

1-Private John Edward Bromham, 1941.

Dad, Italy 1943.

Pre School photo 1956.

Great Yarmouth, July 1956.

Butlins, Clacton, 1965.

School photo 1966. Front row, centre Mr Ryder, Del, Steve Gadd, Alan Dennis third row left to right six along Gary Giles. Back row top left Steve Crutchley, third along Gerald Blankensee

Mod Gear, 1967.

With Mum and Dad, 1967.

First newspaper photo as The Stray, 1967.

Stray, 1968.

Stray with A&R man John Whitehead signing our recording contract January 1970.

Wedding day with Jackie, 1972.

Ivan Mant and Peter Amott PFAIM Int. (Stray first managers)

Stray, Pye Studios, 1975.

With Andy Viccars.

With Steve Harris.

Stray, 1968.

Stray with A&R man John Whitehead signing our recording contract January 1970.

Love bug 'bites' stray

Del Bromham, lead guitarist of the local group Stray, with the girl-next-door Miss Jackie Collins, who is now his wife

A love bug certainly seems to have hit the local pop group Stray, with Gary Giles getting married a couple of weeks ago and now another member of the group, Del

Bromham, doing the same.
And incredible though it may sound Del has actually married the girl next door.
She was Miss Jackie Collins, and the pair had lived next door to one another in Hilary Road, East Acton, for most of their lives. They were married at St. Katherine's Church in Westway on Saturday afternoon.

Jackie is a secretary, while Del is Stray's lead guitarist and writes most of their numbers. They plan to move into a house in Hendon on their return from a secret honeymoon.
Gary Giles, bass guitarist who married Miss Sandra Knowles in Acton register office on May 6 is also taking a delayed honeymoon at the moment.

And it seems that for the moment the love-bug stops there — no weddings are planned yet for the other two members of the group, Steve Gadd and Ritchie Cole.
They do, however, have one consolation, with Del and Gary both on their honeymoons, Steve and Ritchie have been able to take a holiday at the same time.

Wedding day with Jackie, 1972.

Ivan Mant and Peter Amott PFAIM Int. (Stray first managers)

Stray, Pye Studios, 1975.

Stray with Nathan Joseph of Transatlantic Records.

Stray with Wilf Pine (centre) and gold discs.

# Introducing Charles Kray, late of Maidstone Jail, now manager in Tin Pan Alley

Charles Kray and group. From the left : Gary Giles, Ritchie Cole, Del Bromham and Peter Dyer

Picture : TIM GRAHAM

**CHARLIE KRAY**, eldest of London's notorious gangland brothers, has moved into rock group management.

Surrounded by his proteges yesterday, he said : 'I have a lot of friends in showbusiness. I am sure I can look after the boys all right.'

Mr Kray, 50, whose brothers twins Ronnie and Reggie, are serving life in Parkhurst Prison for murder, has taken over the management of Stray,

### By KEVIN COSGROVE

a four-man rock band from London who already have one gold album to their credit.

'I met the boys at a party,' he said. 'They were having trouble with their management. They asked me to help them and I agreed.'

Mr Kray was released from prison 18 months ago after six years of a ten-year sentence for being an accessory to the murder of Jack 'The Hat' McVitie. He served part of his time in Albany, Isle of Wight, and the rest in Maidstone.

Since then he has been taking things easy and put-

ting the finishing touches to his life story, Me and My Brothers. It is, he says, a book that will put the record straight about the Krays and their gangland empire.

'It's hard after you've been away,' he said. Not once did Mr Kray mention the word prison. Everything changes, decimal currency was brought in while I was away and look at the way fashion changes.

Yesterday he was dressed at the height of fashion in a pale blue safari suit, broad blue and white striped shirt and enough gold on his fingers and wrist to make it seem a strain to lift his arm.

'The group gives me a chance to do something again,' he said. 'I like rock music

and I used to be a show business agent before.' Again he shies away from saying what before means.

The group, Del Bromham, Gary Giles, Ritchie Cole, all 21 and Pete Dyer, 20, are enthusiastic about their new manager. 'He's the first honest bloke we have met in this business,' said Mr Bromham with a smile.

What about Mr Kray's infamous history ? 'You can't break people's arms and make them buy your records,' said Mr Giles, the bass player.

Mr Kray's view : 'I don't think anyone will take notice of my past.'

Ritchie Cole, the drummer said: 'We hate go, someone very reliable.

'Yeah,' said Mr Dyer — 'We've already lined up a few banks, whoops, I'm sorry, a few gigs.' — Mr Kray feels that Dyer has a great future as a comedian.

Mr Kray smiles benignly, smokes the occasional cigarette and takes all pointed remarks with quiet good humour.

But the smile did slip a little when Barry Bethell, a showbusiness agent who is to act as co-manager of the band, was emphasising Mr Kray's good reputation in showbusiness.

'You know,' said Mr Bethell intensely, 'he's been out of it for a while, but old friends die hard in this business.'

Charles Kray and Stray, 1976.

Stray, Del Bromham, Pete Dyer, Ritchie Cole and
Gary Giles, circa 1976.

This was when I started up Bromham's Stray.
Left to right: Dusty (Graham) Miller, me and Phil McKee.

Gordon Rowley and I formed a project band Razorback. When the album was released on Angel Air Records we found out that there was already a band named Razorback, so the album was named BRB Razorback.
Left to Right: Steve Bartley, Gordon Rowley and me.

With Jackie and our daughters Zoe and Jodie.
Inset: Zoe and Jodie, 1980.

Daughters Jodie and Zoe.

Linny Meakins & Annie Paterson
AKA The Merch Maidens.

Zoe marries Darron Ayres.

Jodie with grandsons Liam and Jaxon.

Zoe marries Jason Herron, 2015.

Stray 2001-2004.
Left to right: John Bootle, Paul Watson and me.

With Mountain's Leslie West, 2004.

With Zoe in Australia, 2015.

With Annie in Spain.

With Spike (Quireboys) and Terry Reid.

With Danny Baker.

With Luther Grosvenor.

Stray 2005-2018.
Left to Right: Me, Stuart Uren and Karl Randall.

With Cherry at Birmingham Symphony Hall, 12th November 2013.

With Cherry Lee Mewis.

With Andy Viccars.

© Noel Buckley

With Steve Harris.

Stray reunion show at The Borderline, London, 2016.

© Ken Ansted

Del Bromham,
Steve Gadd,
Ritchie Cole and
Gary Giles.

© Ken Ansted

With Paul Newcomb at
The Borderline, London.

© Ken Ansted

Stray 2019 to present.
Left to Right: Me, Colin Kempster, Karl Randall, Simon Rinaldo and Pete Dyer.

Publicity shot by Lee Scriven.

# 20.

# Shut Up Shop

**M**y recollections of this time are a bit of a blur. Life was becoming a mess, full of one problem after another. Christmas 1977 passed. I don't recall the band had any shows booked in at all for 1978 and it just seemed like all of a sudden one bill after another was coming through my letterbox, or someone knocking on my door trying to issue a writ for unpaid bills which started to pile up.

The worrying thing was that a lot of these bills were for vehicle hire, car purchases and various other sundry items which appeared to have originated from our Dover Street offices. Remember we had our own truck, our own equipment and for the past couple of years I had rented cars from J Davy in Putney all paid for with bills to prove it. Ritchie also had kept a book of monies going in and out when we found we had to fend for ourselves. It also transpired since we had joined Worldwide Artists in 1973 our tax and National Insurance contributions had not been paid.

I think Gary and I were coming off worse in many ways because we were both home owners. I was paranoid about hearing the letterbox go because it seemed every letter was a bill. The paranoia still remains with me today although not as much. I find it hard to open some envelopes. I have to leave them and come back to them later in the day. In fact, I wrote a song on my solo album *Nine Yards* titled 'Bills' which in a way reflects my memories of that time.

I contacted the Musicians Union who were very helpful and put me in touch with an accountant Bob Shapiro who I duly had a meeting with. I went to his house and no disrespect to Mr Shapiro but it seemed really untidy with books and paper everywhere, almost like a modern day scene from an Alan Bennett play. He was obviously well versed in the problems musicians got themselves into and if anything it was good to know that it wasn't just me and Stray that got themselves into a mess like this.

I also had to be very careful not to mention too many names from the past and implicate them in any way as this would have not been very sensible if you understand what I mean?

Somehow I had become the bands spokesman and representative, primarily because all the band's tax letters and summonses had come to my address and I had arranged things with Mr Shapiro.

I had to appear in court in London, I think somewhere near The Strand, I'm not sure now. Like I said it was a bit of a blur. I managed to get the court hearing postponed explaining as best I could that the matters were in hand and my accountant would be in touch in due course. Once Mr Shapiro was satisfied he had enough information and I don't know how but he managed to put together a log of accounts dating back several years and accountable explanations of our finances which were acceptable to the court and a deal was done. Thankyou Mr Shapiro.

Bills still had to be paid and the only way we could do it was to sell our assets, our equipment. The reality kicked in. If we sell our equipment, then we can't play and we will no longer have a band. Sad as it might seem, I think at this time we all needed a break and new careers because being part of Stray had become stressful and not pleasurable.

I was pleased for Dave Flockton and Paul Cantwell our two loyal remaining road crew as they managed to find new jobs fairly quickly. I think Dave worked for the well know equipment stage hire company, John Henry, and Paul went to work initially for The Boomtown Rats then Suzi Quatro and many of the big rock artists of the day.

Gradually I found buyers for the PA system and backline equipment. The truck was the last thing to go which in a way was quite fortunate as I am about to tell you.

One day, out of the blue, Laurie O'Leary who I hadn't spoken to for a good few months, called. Laurie had heard that Stray had split and wondered if we had sold everything yet, but mainly he was interested if we still had the truck which was still parked outside my house.

Laurie was helping Steve Marriott out with his personal affairs. Steve was moving house and needed someone to help. It was good to know someone like Steve Marriott was having problems and it wasn't just me. I called Pete as he still had his HGV licence and we set off to Steve's almost legendary Beehive Cottage, Moreton, Essex. When Pete and I arrived, Steve's friend and road manager John was there doing the final clear out of the house and studio. We put all the equipment from the studio into our truck and drove back to London where we met Laurie.

Laurie then took us to a lock up just around the corner from his house in Bethnal Green which incidentally was close to Charlie Kray's mum's house. In the evening I phoned Steve who was staying at The Kensington Garden Hotel just to let him know that his gear was safely with Laurie at the lock up. I will try and explain how the telephone conversation with Steve went. If you can, try and remember Steve's voice to get how funny the conversation was:

"Allo?" says Steve.

"Hiya, it's Del, just thought I'd give you a bell a let you know your gear is all nice and safe at Laurie's lock up" I said.

"Oh nice one, cheers, yeah" replied Steve.

"Steve, are you sure you don't want that Humble Pie drum skin you were chucking out, cos I still have it?"

"Nah, I don't want the fuckin' thing, you can 'ave it".

"Oh cheers mate, I'll hang it on the wall. Anyway, how are you?"

"Well I'm alright now, but I nearly got killed earlier!"

"Eh, killed, what happened?"

"Well I was walkin' daan Kensington High Street when some cunt drove up on the pavement and nearly run me over, the cunt".

"Oh shit".

"Yeh fuckin' cunt, didn't catch him, he shot off whoever he was? Fuckin' cunt".

"Ok Steve, well look I'll leave you to it, if you need anything just give me a call, here's my number or phone Laurie"

"Okay mate, hang on what are you doing tonight?"

"Nothing much, why?"

"Well I'm recording down at Maison Rouge Studios, why don't you come down. We can meet up, have a listen see what you reckon?"

"Oh nice one, what time?"

"Anytime you like mate, I'll be there all night".

"Cheers Steve, see ya later".

In the evening I drove down to Maison Rouge Studios and Steve was sat at the piano, tinkering around with some tune or other. We had a chat about nothing much in particular as you do. He was recording with The Small Faces again. Ian MacLagan, Kenney Jones and new man on bass, Rick Wills.

I must say, I found Steve more subdued than the Steve I'd had a lively conversation with earlier that day. They had recorded a backing track to a new song so Steve was going to show them how the vocal line went. What happened next was unforgettable. He walked over to the control desk and told the studio engineer to play the backing track back to them loud over the speakers.

"Turn it up a bit mate" said Steve to the engineer.

By now it was coming out of the speakers nice and loud.

Steve starting singing the vocal line and the power of that little guys voice was unbelievable! He soared above that loud backing track without a microphone. I had never heard anything like it.

Well to be honest I had done and it was with Steve singing with Humble Pie at The Hammersmith Odeon a couple of years before where I think it was during their song called 'I Don't Need No Doctor' he walked to the front of the stage and sang out to the audience without a microphone in a packed out concert hall.

I don't know how long the session was going to last but I didn't want to outstay my welcome as I know what it's like to be recording and there are people standing around as we say in the business 'ligging' and I'm no ligger. I said goodbye and I didn't actually meet Steve again until a few years later when I played a show with him at The Open University in Milton Keynes. He had a three-piece band then called Packet Of Three and he seemed in good spirits. He had a new lady in his life, Toni who I noticed carried his amplifier in ("Cheapest roadie I've ever had, ha ha" he laughed) and seemed in good spirits.

Blimey I thought Steve could swear, but Toni, she could string a few choice words together. We sat chatting about all sorts of things. I was telling him how when my Stray first started we wanted to look like The Small Faces and we used to go to Lord John either looking or clothes shopping. We talked about the fashion of that time and he found it really amusing. 'All Too Beautiful'.

He liked my Firebird and I told him I liked the little Epiphone Coronet he used for a while in Humble Pie and I suggested he should get that one out again. When I came off stage he said he liked my hat and the western string tie I was wearing. He said it was a good image. Funnily enough he told me that he had not long returned from the USA where he met up with Peter Frampton again and were talking about possibly playing some shows together, maybe even as Humble Pie. He said he was also probably going back out to the States again. He did go and tragically died in a house fire when he returned home after the journey on 20th April 1991. He was just 44.

A sad loss to one of the, if not the greatest white soul singer to come out of the UK.

**** 

The truck was the final piece of the equipment to be sold and I managed to pay off the last of the debts, or at least I thought so, because a few years later, the Inland

Revenue came after me again as they had uncovered more unpaid taxes. I tell you what, once they know you exist they never let you go.

I had a meeting with a tax inspector. To cut a long story short he finished the interview by telling me that they wanted a particular some of money within the next seven days! (A few grand I couldn't spare). As I had to show him my bank statements, I asked him how he thought I would be able to find that sum of money within seven days?

I was aware that he had a small tape recorder in the top draw of his desk. I saw him reach down and I could clearly hear the click of the machine being turned off. He looked up and told me that they knew how much my house was worth and to be quite blunt didn't really care how I got the money as long as they got their money.

Anyway moving on… the next chapter please author. But first…

It is Sunday 10th January 2021. I heard this morning that William Jellett passed away on the 8th of January peacefully in a London Hospital. Some of you will not know who he was but there are some of you who will know him better as Jesus. He was a regular at London gigs and also attended many festivals. I remember seeing him first of all at Hyde Park where they held free festivals between about 1968 to 1970. Yes folks free festivals where I saw acts like Pink Floyd, Blind Faith, The Rolling Stones to name but a few and yes all for free!

Jesus, as he became known was clearly visible as many of these outdoor festivals. People sat and watched and Jesus would stand and dance and generally groove along to the music. He often stripped down to the waist and danced and on a couple of occasions was totally naked, but nobody deemed it unusual because it was Jesus and it was accepted.

By 1970 Jesus used to turn up at our gigs in London. He would always bring with him fruit, usually a bag of grapes which he would come into the dressing room and share them out. Jesus was becoming very well known for his appearances at gigs and there was a certain amount of Kudos connected if he should be seen at one of your shows. I daresay that he rarely had to pay to get into a venue because it was good for the venue that he was in attendance.

He had become so popular that a couple of the main music papers had written articles on him which was something that every up and coming band would strive to achieve. He carried a shoulder bag which would contain a tambourine or maracas the latter piece of percussion caused us a problem while we were recording our *Live At The Marquee* album back in 1983. The studio control room was above The Marquee Club so consequently you could hear the music but not see the stage. Gordon Rowley who was producing and engineering the recording had real problems mixing the last song 'All In Your Mind' because Jesus had jumped up on the stage and proceeded to shake his maracas but unfortunately he was right on my vocal microphone.

When mixing a live recording if you try and take a microphone out of the mix it can change the whole sound. Consequently, he had the problem of trying to remove the sound of the maracas without affecting the whole sound of the band recording. Gordon persevered and made a good job of salvaging the recording. The words 'Living Legend' are not always appropriate when describing someone but William Jellett aka 'Jesus' was indeed a living legend. If there is an after life then I'm sure he is up there freaking out with all his old musical friends. RIP 'Jesus', you were definitely a one off.

# 21.
# The Road Crew

All through my career I have been lucky enough to work with some very good road crew, so I feel I should give them a mention.

Ivan Mant partner to Peter Amott as our first management team, spent a lot of time on the road with us, driving our first proper band bus and setting the stage lighting and pyrotechnics. In those early times one of our school friends Gerry Blankensee often came along and worked the light controller which Ivan had made. 'Blank' as we used to call him, didn't stay with us for long as we became very busy and he couldn't do all the gigs along with his full time job at that time.

'Blank' has kind of become semi-famous due to a line in one of our songs. So let me explain. Iron Maiden recorded the opening song from our first album. As the B-side to their single 'Holy Smoke', 'All In Your Mind' also appeared on their album *Best Of The B sides*. When I actually heard their version, I noticed that the second verse was different to our original album version. We had recorded two or three versions all with slightly different lyrics. I was fascinated to know why Maiden had recorded that version.

When I spoke to Steve Harris he said that it was on the single version that he had. I had completely forgotten that Transatlantic Records had released 'All In Your Mind' as a single and this was a much shorter version more suitable to get airplay on radio because of its length. The second verse includes the line 'Even Blankenheimer's in your mind'. I asked Steve if he had any idea what or who Blankenheimer was that his vocalist Bruce Dickenson was singing about? Of course, he didn't!

There was a well-known American DJ and celebrity named Rodney Bingenheimer and I can't remember if it was Frank Zappa or Mick Jagger who was heard to sing or call out 'R O D N E Y  B I N G E N H E I M E R' so Steve Gadd and I used sing out 'Blanks' name in a similar vein i.e. 'B L A N K E N H E I M E R', which I think irritated him a bit which made it even funnier.

When we turned professional Peter and Ivan decided it was time we hired a couple of roadies to take care of the equipment and also to give Ivan more time to work in the office with Peter. Our first two crew members were Phil Griggs and Bob Sallows. They were the same age as us and from the same area. Phil primarily handled the sound and PA while Bob did the backline. At this time, we all drove around together in a large purple Ford Transit parcel van, fitted out inside with aircraft seats. We had lots of laughs on the road and we somehow had accumulated a selection of what we called 'The silly hats'.

In these days before Sat Nav one thing we did from time to time was to stop and ask directions from an innocent pedestrian. We would pull up alongside a stranger, wind the window down put on a silly hat and ask for directions to the venue where we were due to play. We had a Pith helmet, a sailor's captain hat, policeman's helmet a cowboy hat to name but a few. It was so funny the reactions we received. Funny how some things stick in your mind. I remember one time Steve and I were sitting in the two front seats and we arrived in a town, Phil pulled over to the kerbside, Steve wound his window down wearing the sailor's captain hat and called out to this innocent pedestrian, "Hey man where's the gig?" It was hilarious, but to our surprise he knew exactly what we were talking about and gave us the exact directions to the aforementioned gig!

As time went on our equipment was expanding. Another who joined our road crew was Marty Haynes. He was an Australian who'd been living in the UK for quite a while. He had worked for several bands on the scene at the time so had plenty of experience. He was a lovely guy with a big droopy moustache and always in a cowboy hat. He was a few years older than us but fitted in no problem. Sadly, he passed away in 2019.

We could have got a car but we decided to get a small single axle Transit bus which could accommodate plenty of luggage, guitars and also wives, girlfriends and friends, which I know wasn't a popular decision with Peter Amott. We got in a fourth road manager an old school mate and fellow East Acton resident Neil Darken. Neil and I had the same sense of humour and I always thought he could make a living doing something like being a Butlins Redcoat he had that people thing going on. In fact I think he may have worked at Pontin's Holiday camp as a Blue coat for a while. Sometime later, Mick Crickmar (known to everyone as Woolie Mick) replaced Neil. I wrote a song titled 'Woolie' on the *Stand Up And Be Counted* album that loosely tells the story of a guy who goes and works for a band, so you could say it was based on him.

It must have been around 1974 that our then sound engineer Phil Griggs was offered a job working for RAK Records but on the road with Suzi Quatro. So we were on the look-out for a replacement, which was harder to find than we imagined. We played a show with Argent who were having some success at this time with a hit single 'Hold Your Head Up'. It was noticed during the evening that one of their crew was being given a particularly hard time. Phil had been chatting to him and he mentioned that he was leaving within the next couple of weeks and that would he be interested in talking over? We met up with Dave and offered him the job. We had a guy named Phil Lacy working with Dave for a while until he decided to move up north. Dave went to work for John Henry and still works for them today as far as I am aware. When Phil Lacy left, Paul Cantwell joined. He and Dave Flockton remained with us until the shows came to an abrupt halt in December 1977.

There was a guy who used to help out on the road crew occasionally around 1976 ish whose name was Dave Cross. One thing I remember about him was that he used to eat Ginseng in chunks. I think it was Dave Flockton who found him, quite a quiet guy but a good worker as I recall. I don't know where he came from and I don't know what ever happened to him. He disappeared just like he appeared!

The early seventies a 17-year-old joined the road crew with Phil and Bob. His name was Noel Buckley. He did a lot of shows with us over the years, not as a full-time member but whenever he was available. Noel and I have remained good friends over the years and he has turned to being a photographer, photographing many top artists (and me, ha ha).

Another person who turned roadie for a while was Paul Newcomb. We first met Paul in 1976 when even at 16 he organised a big concert in Carshalton Park which attracted a couple of thousand people. He was telling me that he originally wanted Thin Lizzy for the concert, went to the offices of Lizzy's management, knocked on the door and told them he wanted to hire Thin Lizzy. You must admit, it takes some front to do that especially at that age.

They weren't available but Stray were, so in brief that is how we got the festival and how I met Paul. Dave asked Paul what he was doing the next day and ended up taking him to our next gig was at JB's Dudley. After that he did quite a lot on the crew. Paul went on to live in a couple of different countries and when he returned from New York in 2001 we met up again when I played a show with Ian Hunter. He went on to be my tour manager for a while, notably on the European tour dates in 2003 with Iron Maiden and also tours with Mountain and Leslie West. Paul now runs the company Monstrous Child Management Co and represents me and Stray as well as several other acts. Like Noel, our friendship goes back forty years or more.

Stray played some shows in the early eighties (I was not involved at this time) but they had two road managers Andy Law, Barry Goddard and Brian on PA, better known as Catweazle. I re-joined the band to record the *Live At The Marquee* album and a few other shows with Andy and Brian. Dick Hammond has been working with me on and off for the past twenty-five years (he is also famously known as Biggus Dickus).

When Paul Watson was on drums he brought with him his friend and drum techie Jay Stewart. Jay is an excellent drum tech and when Paul left the band and Karl Randall joined, Jay occasionally came along and would set up Karl's drums. Karl was amazed because on the first occasion, Jay had never seen Karl's drum kit before but it was all set perfectly for Karl when he got on stage. It's worth mentioning that Corky Laing, the drummer with Mountain offered Jay a job to be his personal drum tech, but he turned down the offer to remain in the UK.

I have known Nigel Hart for many years. He has worked as sound engineer for many artistes over the years. My friends who run Rock Hard Music in Wolverton, Milton Keynes have a rehearsal studio/recording studio within the building.

When I decided to run through some demos, I chose Rock Hard Music to record the demos. Nigel was working as engineer and together we worked on my second album *Nine Yards*. Like I said, the idea was to demo the songs and then record them elsewhere. I was pleased with the sound we were getting with the demos. It was just what I was after. So I decided to record the whole album there. Nigel has since been sound engineer on some Blues Devils and Stray shows.

Peter Perks has been an all-round helping hands type roadie. He has looked after my guitar equipment and occasionally been selling the merchandise. He has been helping me out for a good fifteen years or so now. The last couple of tours bringing it up to date is Dick with Andy Law back again, and Paul Chapman.

# 22.

# Leslie West

I had a message on Tuesday 22nd December 2020 that my friend and legendary guitarist Leslie West had a heart attack and was seriously ill. In fact, his brother Larry said that it would take a miracle if he would last the day! Indeed on Wednesday 23rd Leslie passed away.

This was such a shock because my good friend and mutual tour manager, to both Leslie and me, Paul Newcomb, had spoken to him only the previous week. He said that Leslie sounded happy and had just moved with his wife Jenni down from New York to Florida to a lovely new home and was looking forward to recording a new album.

Leslie had not been in good health for some years. He was a diabetic, which he said was down to eating too many Crispy Cream Doughnuts. He was on tour in the USA in 2011 and he was taken ill on a flight from New Jersey to Biloxi, Missouri. Apparently the pilot radioed ahead and an ambulance was waiting to take him straight to hospital where a lifesaving operation was performed and part of his right leg was amputated above the knee. He did recover, but spent the rest of his life in a wheelchair, although it didn't stop him from performing as he took to the stage in the wheelchair.

It was 2001 and Don McKay of Rhino Agency contacted me and offered me the tour with Leslie West and Mountain which was the first time he would have been on tour in the UK for many years. I said yes because it would be a good opportunity to play the venues to different larger audiences.

Leslie wanted all the equipment supplied for him. He wanted the classic big stage line up that always looks impressive even if not necessary these days. He wanted three Marshall amplifiers and 4 4x12 speaker cabinets, 2 x bass rigs and a large drum kit. By this time, I was only using small equipment a Marshall Silver Jubilee amplifier and one speaker cabinet. I telephoned Steve Yelding, someone I knew at the Marshall factory in Bletchley, Milton Keynes. Fortunately, I had a good relationship with the people at Marshall Amplification and they gave me everything I had asked for.

I had heard that Leslie could be very difficult to work with so I was quite prepared, or I thought I was prepared but quite clearly from the first show I could see that he could be unpredictable with mood swings and temper tantrums. The guy I felt really sorry for was his guitar tech, Mark, who surprisingly had worked for Leslie for quite some time. He would really lay into him if something, in his mind, wasn't right. That also applied to his band and whatever sound engineer was at a venue. So I'm thinking, at some point it would have to be my turn. However, he had better not upset me I thought, because I have got all his equipment for him and are trucking it around the country. He wouldn't want to upset me because I would go home and take the gear with me! Try and play without any gear Mr West! To be honest I wanted to play the shows as much as he did. Over the years I learned a lot about Leslie and got to understand something of how he reacted to people.

One of the first shows we played was at The Brook in Southampton. The owner of the club Bryn passed away a few years ago. Coincidentally I played The Brook with my band in 2019 and it's now run by Bryn's son, who I told the following story of that night all those years ago on the first tour.

I am not sure exactly why, but I don't think Bryn wanted Del Bromham or Stray on the bill that night. I don't know if he just wanted Mountain or whether for some reason he had taken a dislike to me or the Stray band name as a brand, I really don't know?

The equipment was all set up and ready for the sound checks. I was sitting on the edge of the stage at the front. Bryn, who I'd never even met at this point, walked past the stage and shouted up at me "If you're too loud, I'm turning you off!" To which I replied "This isn't my gear, this is Mountain's". "I don't care. If you're too loud, I'm switching you off!" Great, I thought, I'm getting a bollocking and I haven't even played a note!

So the evening of the performance arrived and we began to play our set. I think I must have only been into about the second song when my amp went off! I looked around to find Bryn and the tour manager Paul Meredith behind my speaker cabinet (only one cabinet remember), with the cable in his hand. "I said I'd turn you off if you were too loud!" This was crazy. When things like this happen to you when you are actually on stage, mid performance it can really throw you. I don't' ever recall before or since having an intervention like that. My only hope was to get a message to the sound engineer to maybe turn me down out front. Sometimes bands do get the blame because we don't hear what's going on front of house.

With my one cabinet plugged back in we finished our set which went well I'm pleased to say. Bryn would have probably loved it if we'd got booed off!

Something else did happen during the gig which did change I am sure, Leslie's attitude towards me. I don't remember all of the details, but after the shenanigans of the day at The Brook, I was not in the best of moods and someone said something about something that Leslie had apparently said.

I really can't remember what it was, but my response was something to the effect of "I don't care who he is, Leslie can fuck right off!" or something to that effect.

The following day at the next venue, it was either Paul or Mark came up to me and said, "Leslie would like to know if you would like to come back to New York and work for him?" I said "What, are you serious, why would he want me to work for him?"

It turns out he was standing side stage and heard every word I said in my little outburst! No-one ever told Leslie straight what they thought. I believe that he had years been surrounded by 'yes men' for so long he might have found this skinny little cockney bastard (where I have heard that one before), quite a challenge.

Having heard this, I must have been partly dreading a confrontation with Mr West himself. Obviously I never took up his offer. In retrospect I'm not even sure if he was serious, but he and I were fine and over the years we played several tours together and I only ever had one other confrontation and that was in a club in Hamburg in 2004, but that's a story for another time.

I have to say that things between Bryn, myself and Stray were fine after this first show and Stray has played The Brook several times over the years. The story gave Bryn's son a chuckle too. He said it sounded typical of his dad being a miserable bugger one moment and lovely bloke the next.

That tour was good for me and the Stray name because it got us back in front of some larger and different audiences that we had not previously played in front of.

I must mention Marshall Amplification again at this point. When we played a show at The Shepherd's Bush Empire, my own amplifier a Marshall Silver Jubilee cut out just as I walked on stage! So with a bit of fumbling around I had to plug in to one of the other Marshalls which I'd never used before. However, the show must go on as they say and we played and went down really well. John Entwistle was at this show. He had known Leslie some years ago while touring the USA and coincidentally Steve, the drummer Leslie was using was playing on some recording with John around this time.

Anyway in the morning I telephoned Phil who was the service engineer at the Marshall factory in Bletchley. To my surprise "Oh hi Del, we've been expecting your call" said Phil. Simon Alexander was in the audience and saw what happened to my amp. Simon worked for Marshall at that time and over the years he and I have been involved in the promotion of Carlsbro Amplification. Anyway, back to the Marshall Factory, Phil said he wouldn't be able to fix my amp there and then but they had ready for me a brand new 'Slash Signature amplifier', which I had on loan for the whole tour and a bit more.

There's another story here regarding the 'Slash' amp. My Silver Jubilee was in the factory sometime before being serviced. Slash came over and took a tour of the factory. He spotted my Silver Jubilee and asked to plug in and play it. He loved the sound of it so much that they modelled the amp for Slash on my Silver Jubilee. Some years later, Joe Bonamassa bought several Silver Jubilee amps. He heard that I had one and one of his representatives contacted my friend Ronnie Orme at Rock Hard Music in Milton Keynes and enquired if Joe would like me to sell it to him. Believe it or not I said no. I've said no to a few well-known people in my time. Yet another story for another time! More about Leslie later.

# 23.
# Personal Stuff 1972 & 1976/77 And Beyond

**B**ack to the seventies, another significant thing which happened to the band at the time: Gary and myself announced that we were going to get married to our respective girlfriends, which I know didn't please Peter Amott in particular. He always wanted to keep girlfriends invisible in case it affected our female fan base. That may seem a daft thing to say, but that is pretty much how it was back in those days.

Jackie and I had been going out together since we were about sixteen and you can imagine that a lot of the time we were apart due to the band touring. I'll be perfectly honest and say that I wasn't bothered one way or the other about getting married, but it was something that Jackie particularly wanted with the opportunity of setting up our own home. We announced we were going to get married on Saturday 3rd June 1972 and shortly after our announcement Gary and his then fiancé, Sandie announced they were going to get married on Saturday 3rd May. Jackie and I were more fortunate in a way because the band had been gigging solidly and there happened to be a few weeks off in June, which was quite unusual.

Our wedding took place at St Katherines Church, East Acton at 3pm. It was a cloudy day but the good thing about a cloudy day was that nobody had to squint for the photographs. Even though we didn't make a big thing about getting married, there were some fans of the band who found out about it and were waiting outside the church gates. I bet Peter Amott loved that! I can't remember the vicar's name, but I remember he seemed quite young. What I do remember which made me chuckle was that he was wearing long clergy robes and you couldn't see his feet, so I had this vision of him sliding along on casters.

I had hired a white Rolls Royce to take us to where we were holding the reception which was the very glamourous George and Dragon public house in Acton High Street. We hired the function room at the back of the pub, which brought back happy memories as I had played there many times with The Traders at various functions. The Traders played for us and I got up and played a couple of songs with them, as did Stray and we played a few of the old covers songs we had been playing some years before — none of the heavy long haired beat music at my wedding!

Another thing I remember is that during the evening, it may have been Steve Gadd or his then girlfriend Isobel, who suggested we nip down the road and have a cup of tea in the café along in the High Street. A few of us walked down the street in our finery and I think Jackie may have still been in her wedding dress. Imagine leaving your own wedding reception to go and get a cup of tea! The Traders were still playing and everyone had a good night. Well they must have done because I put quite a bit of money behind the bar. That went quickly and then apparently as I discovered later, Uncle Ted put some money behind the bar and so did dad.

The local press was at the church and took some photographs which were published in an article by the West London and Acton Gazette. A few weeks later there was an article in the same newspapers about Adam Faith, standing proudly in front of his white Rolls Royce. I thought that Rolls looks familiar and when I looked at the number plate I realised it was the same one which I had hired for the wedding! It wasn't Adam's Rolls after all and I don't think he owned a chauffeur hire service to my knowledge.

When the evening drew to a close, Ivan drove Jackie and I to Paddington Railway Station where we boarded a night train down to Devon where we spent a few days and a few more days in Cornwall. Gary and Sandie joined us during the week down in Cornwall as they had not had the chance to take a Honeymoon as the band had been busy working.

When we came back from Honeymoon aside from getting back to the touring schedule, Gary and Sandie eventually bought a place in Hanwell, Middlesex and Jackie and I came back to our first property which we had bought in Southall, Middlesex. It was only a small place but it was ours and we had a good few years there. Friends used to come over and quite often the band would stop over after a gig. We would listen to music into the early hours of the morning. I wrote most of my songs there and it was my base throughout those heady years of the seventies

## Zoe is born
Jackie and I wanted children and we had tried but to no avail. Then in 1976 Jackie discovered she was pregnant. In those days you didn't know whether you were having a boy or a girl and I don't think we would have wanted to know even if we'd had the option, On February Friday 11th 1977, a little girl Zoe was born. All dad's will say this, but she was beautiful. She had a lovely head of hair and we all kept saying it looked as if she had been to the hairdressers. She was born by caesarean section which in those days, unlike these days, you were left with a scar like you had just suffered an attack by a shark!

Well the show must go on as they say and fortunately there was nothing I could do at the hospital as both mother and daughter were resting and doing well. The band had a gig at Maidstone Technical College that evening. We got there for a sound check. I remember standing on the stage having just checked my guitar when in walked three guys, the support band. I recognised the first guy who spoke up immediately. It was Lemmy Kilmister, who I'd known for some years and worked as stage manager for the promoter John Curd mainly at The Roundhouse. Lemmy used to come into the dressing room and show us to the stage shining his big torch in the darkness of backstage.

"Hello Del" says Lemmy, "This is my band, we are playing tonight". "Oh okay" I said. After a few moments he pipes up with "Have you got a guitar lead I can borrow", "Yes of course no problem" I said.

"Oh great, have you got an amp I can plug it into?" asked Lemmy.

They arrived at the gig with a drum kit a Marshall 4 x 12 cabinet with a Marshall amp. That was it. They played their set. To be honest it was a bit of a racket and I never would have expected Motörhead to be so successful in the years to come. Unlike Stray they had the management record company and the marketing just right.

Our dressing room was the students' common room and we were in the room when they came off stage. They were having a real shouting match. Lemmy, Eddie and Phil (Animal) who played drums with his arm in plaster that evening. I believe it had been documented that he had fallen out of a window. There was a one-armed bandit in the dressing room with a glass top. Coincidentally, Phil who was also a one-armed bandit that night, punched the glass with his arm in the plaster and as you can imagine it shattered into lots of pieces.

A few days later I received a call from our agent, Paul King, informing us that the college were sending us a bill for a couple of thousand pounds for smashing up their common room. I explained what actually happened and that it was not us that smashed up the room. Consequently, we never had to pay the bill and I don't know if Motörhead or their management paid it either.

A week or so after Zoe was born, I felt I had to see Steve Gadd again to at least share with him my good news on Zoe's birth. I hadn't spoken to Steve for about three years in those troubled times after he left the band. I really don't know why, I can only assume it is because my feelings for my old friend Steve run deep and despite everything life has thrown at us we are still good friends today. It was a good 'ice-breaker' meeting up and seeing Steve again. He was living in Earlsfield, London with Jan. We had a good evening and I was so pleased I had made that decision on that night. Another piece of trivia is that I had the Stevie Wonder *Songs In The Key Of Life* album on cassette in my car. As I drove home from Steve's, the song 'Isn't She Lovely' came on. I think of Zoe and Steve when I hear that song and of that moment in my car back in 1977.

During the year Jackie and I had been planning to move house, but we were planning on moving towards Denham, Amersham, Great Missenden or Aylesbury. Allan and his wife Pat had moved to Prestwood in Buckinghamshire and we'd had some good times there. We wanted a bigger house and somewhere that had good schools for Zoe and any other children who might come along.

Bill and Jill Gammond had moved to Bletchley, Buckinghamshire with their two daughters Louise and Charlotte and we had spent a couple of weekends visiting, so we were getting to know the place and their friends. Bill had a band called Teaza. They were going into a recording studio and Bill asked if I would go in with them when they recorded. They had booked two or three days in the studio. I went with Bill and the band and Jackie spent the days with Jill.

I telephoned Jackie on the Sunday and she told me she had seen a couple of houses advertised with a local estate agent. On the Tuesday we went back up to Bletchley and viewed a couple of houses and put an offer on one which was accepted. We got back and immediately put our place in Southall up for sale. The furniture we had would not have gone with the other furnishings in the house we were buying and fortunately the people who were buying our house wanted to buy all our furniture, therefore the move would be fairly easy. Just luggage baby stuff, oh yes and a few guitars.

The completion date was on the Friday and the couple who were buying our house came around the day before on the Thursday and paid us cash for the furniture. They left at 5pm. The phone rang at 6pm from the wife of the couple whose house we were buying. She rang to tell me that they were sorry but they had decided not to sell the house after all! That's the night before we were due to exchange contracts. I could not believe it. That confused mist entered my brain and I'm not sure if I was polite or rude, but upset and confused I definitely was. What do we do now? We had sold our place the next day as arranged but we had nowhere to go. We arranged to view a couple more properties in Bletchley during the week and also arranged to stay at mum and dad's back in East Acton until we could find a new home.

Bletchley was still quite a small town and had not yet been swallowed up by Milton Keynes as it did years later, so there were not that many house for sale to choose from. We did find a house and our offer was accepted. We had visited the offices of Brown and Merry in Bletchley and we were given the property details by a lovely young lady. It's funny how sometimes you meet someone and they always stay in your mind? I told the guys in Teaza that we were going to move to Bletchley and that we had bought the house via Brown and Merry. The guitarist said "Brown and Merry? My sister Annie works there. The guitarists name was Don Hollis. More to come later about Don and Annie.

# 24.
# Back To Reality

It was now March 1978, Jackie Zoe and I had moved into our new home in Bletchley Buckinghamshire. We had very little money left and I no longer had a band with the ability to earn a living. So what was I going to do? I made endless phone calls to record labels and agents but no-one was interested. That word bills had reared its head again and bills had to be paid.

There was an employment agency in Bletchley, they may have been called Quality, I'm not sure, well anyway I went along there one day and managed to have a chat with a lady on one of the desks. I had very little work experience except for being the 16-year-old trainee telex operator and no written CV. I don't think I even knew what a Curriculum Vitae was to be honest! I told her my story so far as it were and the name Hammond Organ came up in conversation. As luck would have it, the company Hammond Organs had just moved their European distribution centre from Belgium to the UK, Bletchley to be precise and furthermore the company turned out to be just a walk away from my new house.

She thought this would be an ideal place for someone like me. She arranged for me to have a meeting at Hammond Organ UK as they were then called and I went to the office and met Graham Sutton. He has been a Hammond Organ engineer virtually all of his career and had and still does work for some well known keyboard players. He knows just about all there is to know about Hammond organs. Our meeting went well and I started working for Hammond almost right away.

I was introduced to Dave Chapman and he was going to show me around and give me an idea what I was expected to do. We got off to a good start just generally talking about music and as it turned out his brother Steve was living in the USA and was now the drummer for Poco. I told Dave that I had seen Poco on my trip to Cannes a few years before, although his brother was not in Poco back then. I met another guy there called Steve who worked in the warehouse and he remembered me and Stray because around the time Stray played at The Nags Head in Wollaston and The Blisworth Hotel. Steve used to come to see the band play and apparently one night after one of our gigs, he was hitchhiking trying to get back home to Bletchley and we stopped and gave him a lift in our van. Something he always remembered.

Any spare time I had, I would have a go on one of the organs that Graham was testing. Kid in a sweet shop springs to mind. I have to say at this point in the story, working for Hammond Organs was not the only 9 to 5 or what one would call a normal job which I have had. I have heard about or known many musicians who for whatever reason have had to take on a day job to pay the bills. On many occasions over the years, I have had people speak to me assuming I have been living the rock star life living in somewhere like Los Angeles or New York, or maybe a mansion in the country somewhere. That has not been the case.

Anyway, after working for Hammond Organ, I worked for a while for T Mathews a designer/point of sale printers. I've worked in warehouses, done stock control, quality control, point of sale marketing and advertising for companies such as Nina Ricci, Rockwell and Fossil UK. I have to say I have met some interesting people outside of the music industry, some who have remained lifelong friends.

While working for Fossil, I met Marcus Richardson who is a talented graphic designer. We got on really well and we had the same sense of humour. I'm sure there were times when the people around us didn't have a clue what we were talking about. Marcus went on to design the cover for the *Nine Yards* and *White Feather* albums.

Someone else I met around the same time was Terry Boss. My goodness we had some laughs together. We ended up having fancy dress costumes in the office and sometimes, for no apparent reason, we would get into character, dressing up, putting on wigs and generally going a bit mad. Probably there were some management types who didn't approve but we had fun and I know we made a few people laugh. When he could he came out to gigs and help set up the equipment. He should have been involved in the entertainment industry. Terry is a natural entertainer and he would have been ideal to work as a Butlins Red Coat or something like that.

Back to the story... I had been in contact with Laurie O'Leary. He said he wanted to repay me in some way for helping him out with Steve Marriott's house move as I wouldn't accept payment. I mentioned in conversation that I had a couple of songs which I wanted to demo. Laurie said he had a couple of friends who owned a studio and he could get me some studio time. Laurie called again and said he'd got me a weekend Friday until Sunday evening at Escape Studios, Egerton Kent.

Of course I knew the studio, but I was slightly apprehensive because they might remember who I was, I wasn't sure on what terms Wilf Pine had left them on and finally they might remember the roast potato fight? Nothing was mentioned and Laurie was quite an influential individual anyway so everything was okay. The only problem I had, was that there was not a house engineer available so I would have to engineer and play myself.

I phoned Richard Manwaring who worked on *Stand Up And Be Counted*. He said he would love to come down for the weekend and record a couple of my songs if we could record one of his as a favour. He had a song he wanted to place with a publisher or artist. That was no problem, so I now had the studio engineer I needed.

The year before, 1977, I had met a drummer named Romek Parol. I had been to a rehearsal studio he had been looking after. Gary Giles came with me and we went along and jammed with Rom (Romek) a few times and it felt fresh particularly in those troubled times. I could just play and not have to think about it being a Stray song, strange as that may seem. I asked both Gary and Rom if they fancied a weekend in the country and they both said yes.

I hired a van and we all went together and spent the weekend at the studios staying in the Oast House. I remember it to be a lot of fun and found a renewed sense of freedom. I was doing this for myself and no-one else. We rehearsed and recorded Richard's song 'Right or Wrong' and two of my songs, 'Talking About You' and 'Who Do You Love'. It all went so easy. Three songs rehearsed, recorded, overdubs and vocals and all mixed in about forty-eight hours. Sunday was the final day and by the evening we were just wrapping up when the telephone rang in the studio to ask if we had finished? It was the studio owner Ted Roffey.

"Oh hi Del" said Ted "I was just wondering if you'd finished in the studio yet?"

I replied "Yes we have finished recording. We have just got to pack our gear up and we will be out of here".

"Oh that's great, how long will you be. About half an hour?" asked Ted.

"Yes that should be okay" I replied.

"Oh that's great I'll let Jeff know, cos he wants to come down with some friends" said Ted.

"Okay fine... Er Jeff who?" I asked.

"Jeff Beck, he only lives up the road and he's had some friends at his house and wants to come down to the studio" said Ted.

I finished off what Richard and myself were doing and then I walked from the studio to the Oast House to let Gary and Rom know to get packed up because Jeff Beck was coming! As I walked over to the accommodation, I looked up the hill and I could see a set of car headlights coming down the hill, followed by another set and another set and another set. I stood fixed to the floor as I counted about fourteen sets of car headlights coming towards the studio.

I ran into the house and told Gary and Rom what was about to happen, so we ran back to the studio and finished packing the last pieces of equipment away and loading it into the van. When all the cars pulled up it seemed like there were a constant stream of people filing into the studio. I remember a couple of guys had acoustic guitars with them and they sat down and started strumming away. This whole scene seemed a bit odd and eventually Jeff Beck came over to speak to us. Now I apologise if I got the next bit wrong it but did seem pretty obvious to Gary, Rom and myself that Jeff was happy to see us although some of the people who followed him down to the studio were what we call in the business ligger's.

Jeff came over to us and started chatting and asking what we were doing down at the studio. "Where's all your gear?" asked Jeff. "Oh, we packed it away because we thought you were using the studio" I replied. "Ah that's a shame, we could have had a jam" said Jeff. "Oh sorry, we've got to get back to London" we said. So we said our goodbyes then went to the house packed our bags and left.

If you knew Rom and what his voice sounded like, this next scene would sound even funnier. I was driving the van on our journey home. It was quite quiet in the van when all of a sudden a voice from the back cried out "oh for fuck's sake!" "What have we just done?" "We've just said, no to Jeff Beck". "No to Jeff Beck for fuck's sake" said Rom. And the more we thought about it, the more ridiculous it sounds. I still think of it to this day. We actually told Jeff Beck, words to the effect of, no we can't stop and play with you Jeff, we've got to get home to bed. I wonder how many times Jeff Beck has been turned down?

# 25.

# 1970s Into The 1980s

In 1978 I had been speaking to Gordon Rowley and he was telling me that since his former band Strife, he had formed a new band Nightwing. They seemed to be doing okay, particularly in Europe and they had got a record deal with Gull Records and suggested that I should call the boss at Gull, David Howells.

I phoned David, we had a good chat and he invited me to his offices for a meeting. I have to say that it was and probably is, very unusual to speak to a record company executive and arrange a meeting there and then on the phone. My experience is normally "We will let you know" or a message from a secretary saying "So and so isn't available at the moment, can you call back". Alternatively, if you're lucky, you get a letter saying words to the effect of "Thanks but no thanks".

Gull Records had an office above Morgan Studios, Willesden, London. Meeting David was a breath of fresh air, purely because he was nothing like many of the record company people I had met in the past. He was polite, quietly spoken and considering the people he had worked with, very modest. Something I have noticed over the years, those in a similar position have the tendency to tell you all about themselves when it's me they should be hearing about!

David and I spoke generally about the business and what I had been doing and what I hoped to do. The main objective was to secure a new record deal. I was after all contract free and basically for the first time in my life a solo artist. I gave David the tape which I had recorded and said that I believed that the song 'Who Do You Love' was quite commercial and would make a good single. That may have surprised him because, I daresay that he may have thought I would be presenting something in a rockier vein, bearing in mind that Gordon and Nightwing were on Gull and so were Judas Priest at this time.

David put on my tape and listened without barely saying a word, although I sensed that he liked what he heard. So much so that when the tape finished he echoed my thoughts and agreed 'Who Do You Love' would make a great single. He played 'Who Do You Love' again and while we were talking had it playing in the background. He said he would like to re-record it and would like to use a new young engineer named Chris Tsangarides, who was working downstairs at Morgan Studios and bring in a couple of session guys he had used to work with me.

He mentioned Simon Phillips on drums and Mo Foster on bass guitar. Now that's a rhythm section. The meeting finished and I left his office feeling very optimistic. He was going to put something together on paper and organise studio time etc. It was about a week later that I had a second meeting with David and he had secured studio time and Chris to engineer. Simon Phillips was not available as he was just about to go on tour. I assumed that because Simon was not available, David had not pursued Mo Foster for bass. I said not to worry, because if it was okay with him, if I could play bass and if I couldn't find an available drummer I would do the drums as well.

I had arranged to drop by and visit Rom who was living in Ealing at that time. I began to tell him my good news and barely before I got into his living room he pointed to a guy standing by a window and said "He could play bass for you". I recognised this guy but I couldn't think specifically where I knew him from, but as we talked I remembered I had seen him at a Stray gig or two in the past and he was a friend of one of my road manager's Bob Sallows.

I also knew him as he worked for Marshall Amplification who had a shop in Ealing that I used to go into. His name was Stuart Uren. "I thought you were a guitarist" I said. He said he was and still is but he had recently changed over to bass and been playing with Rom, so they were becoming a tight rhythm section themselves. I knew Rom well enough to know that he wouldn't play with someone, particularly a bass player if it didn't feel right and I instinctively felt good about it. To be honest I can't remember if we even got together before the recording, but the three of us went into Morgan Studios and recorded three songs with Chris Tsangarides. It felt good and little did I realise that I would have a lifelong friendship with all three of these people.

We recorded three songs 'Who Do You Love', 'The Best Friend' and 'Love My love'. The sessions was a real pleasure. Stu was playing a fretless bass which is something I had only really heard with Jaco Pastorius, and recently Pino Paladino, who was playing for Paul Young at that time.

Chris had some great new ideas for recording techniques too which I found interesting, but above all the four of us together laughed so much together over those few days it's a wonder that I never had a dislocated jaw. It had been a long time since I had enjoyed recording that much.

David loved the recording and decided that the 'B' side was going to be 'The Best Friend'. I must mention that at no time was there any mention of me making an album as is often the case. Gull were going to put out the single and see what would happen.

David had a guy named Alan McGowan who handled some of his 'PR' work. Alan was well known in the business particularly on the media side of things. Consequently, he secured quite a few radio plays and also got me a few personal interviews on local radio stations up and down the country.

'Who Do You Love' was released on Gull Records on Friday 9th March 1979. I really had a good feeling about this record and I was over the moon when Andy Peebles, one of the top BBC Radio DJs played the record for the first time on Radio 1 on Monday 12th March. Andy played it a couple more times on his daytime show.

As well as Gull Records, the offices above Morgan Studios were the offices of Mr Sam Music who were music publishers. Unlike these days, they were the type of publisher who would give new young songwriters a chance by booking them studio time to hear their songs. Chris Tsangarides called me one day and asked if I, along with Rom and Stuart would be interested in doing a session for him for Mr Sam Music to record a new young female songwriter called Cathy Feeney who also sang and played piano. These days Cathy is better known for the band Never The Bride.

Actually it turned out to be a few sessions and financially quite well paid. These sessions went well and we were then asked to do a few sessions for LWT (London Weekend Television) who had formed their own record label and were planning to release records by some of their artistes from their TV shows.

Once such person was the actor Chris Blake. At this time, he was starring in a TV sitcom *Mixed Blessings* with co-star Muriel Odunton. They played a mixed race couple which was possibly the first time that kind of scenario aired on television. We recorded three songs 'Take It From The Top' which I think was planned to be the single; 'It's Not All Over Yet', and the old favourite written by Bobby Womack and made famous by The Rolling Stones called 'It's All Over Now'. As well as my session fee, I was also paid an arranger's fee. Coincidentally we had recently jammed at a rehearsal a version of 'It's All Over Now' in a reggae style, more in the vein of 'I Shot The Sheriff'.

Both Chris's and the session producer Ray Singer liked this suggestion and that is the version we recorded. We got quite a few sessions out of this although I have no idea if LWT did anything with the single. Just a bit of name dropping here, Chris had an actor friend who used to come along to the studio with him. He was an up and coming actor called Peter Davison, now well-known actor as a former *Doctor Who* amongst other things. Peter, like Chris was a really nice guy. He turned up the first day with an acoustic guitar and wasn't afraid to use it! I remember him sitting in the control room with the guitar, singing away.

Rom had been playing various London venues with his own project, Payroll. Quite often as I understand, put together with a pretty fluid line up which could change from time to time depending on who was available. Along with Stuart he had found a keyboard player called Vic Donnelly and they were having a rehearsal. Rom invited me along to see what would happen. We had got on so well in the studio it would be interesting to see what would come out of a rehearsal.

This was actually quite a challenge because since school I had been basically playing with the same musicians, so I was not sure what to expect. I was meeting up with three guys from the Ealing set who had played with more musicians than I'd had hot dinners, many I daresay were far better musicians than I was but nevertheless I jumped at the chance to play with them.

I had got to know Rom and Stu quite well but I didn't know Vic at all and my experience with keyboard players had not always been satisfactory. If I were to make a comparison, Vic was like Chick Corea, very jazz orientated and played a Fender Rhodes electric piano with a Juno synth on top. We did a bit of jamming at the first rehearsal and it definitely had that jazz funk feel to it. Rom naturally had that funky soul feel to his style. Stu was quite into Jaco Pastorius and along with Vic it all seemed to gel pretty well. For the past couple of years, I had been listening to players like Chick Corea, Stanley Clarke, Al Di Meola and many of those new wave of Jazz funksters. I saw Stanley Clarke and George Duke live in concert around this time and it sounded really refreshing to my ears. Something I would never have tried with Stray. Probably the closest Stray ever got to this style would have been 'Wait Another Day' on the *Houdini* album.

I think Rom suggested we try an instrumental that Vic had written titled 'Fly By Night' where the main melody line is played in unison by the keyboard and guitar. This was a challenge for me, something totally different to what I had been used to, but I think I managed to learn it and was very rewarding. In fact, I started to write new songs and incorporate little sections with the jazzy funky influences.

Rom said that he could contact a few of the venues he knew of and I said I could approach a few people myself. Although I was sceptical if anyone would want to touch an ex member of Stray considering the reputation we appeared to have gained. We set about rehearsing a set. I had some new songs and a couple of covers and they seemed to come together very quickly. We couldn't really decide on a band name. I think we did a couple of shows as Del Bromham's Payroll (incorporating both names) and The Del Bromham Band. We even chose the name Oasis and that was probably before the Gallagher Brothers were even born!

One of the first shows we played (it might have even been the first) was at The White Lion in Putney. The gig itself was upstairs in the function hall and it was packed out. For someone who doesn't normally feel nervous I have to admit I was feeling it a bit on this night. It must have hit me that this was the first time my name had ever been on the poster as the attraction. I'd always been part of a band and I could feel that a lot of eyes were on me. We played well, these were all new songs in a set that had never been played before and there was surely nothing wrong with the way we performed them.

I could sense a bit of unrest within the audience which did put me slightly on edge. At various times throughout the evening there were shouts or requests for Stray songs, none of which we had learned. I never ever gave it any consideration that I would have to play the old ones. This was a new project but I soon realised that you have to play some of your previous material. People have paid money to put you on that stage. When I go and see an artist or a band I like to hear some of the older stuff as well as the new. It's only natural. I was learning how to do this all over again starting at the bottom. It was a lesson I have never forgotten though!

As the year went on we played more shows but financially they were never really rewarding and Vic kept asking "Where are the roadies?". He probably thought that playing with someone from an ex-name band he would have others to carry his gear around for him. Fact is many times we could hardly afford to pay ourselves let alone the roadies.

Around this time my friends Teaza in Bletchley were starting to get more gigs in. Just before I did that recording for them they had a front man singer called Eddie McErlane. He was and still is a great front man and is still a friend of mine today. You will often see him singing at various blues festivals and he is also a great blues harmonica player. Back to Teaza, Steve or Wixsy as he is known as locally, had virtually taken over as lead singer whereas prior he was the back-up vocalist and guitarist.

In the early seventies there was a club in Bletchley, The Derwent Drive Youth Centre which was run by two guys Barry Fields and a very young Phil Banfield. Getting to know people in the business Phil ended up working for a music agency in London. Coincidentally he now lived just around the corner from me in Bletchley and was an old friend of Teaza guitarist Don Hollis.

I met up with Phil as he had suggested to Don and the Teaza guys that it might be a good idea if I played a few gigs with them as guest guitarist. It might help them gain a few more extra shows if the promoters knew that I was guesting. I agreed and rehearsed with Teaza and it sounded really good. I played quite a few shows with them and one in particular I remembered was at The Marquee in Wardour Street. I think they/we, were supporting The Ian Gillan Band. What I remember most about it was a couple of voices from the audience calling out my name followed by a couple of requests for Stray songs. So there it was again, just like the Putney gig, people want to hear songs I'd written which they knew.

# 26.
# Thin Lizzy

Let me take you to the morning of Tuesday 21st August 1979. I woke up and told Jackie that I had dreamt that I'd played with Thin Lizzy. I've no idea why I dreamt that. I was in the office at Hammond Organs when the phone rang and it was Jackie telling me that a guy named John Salter who was the road manager for Thin Lizzy had phoned our home number.

At first I thought she was just winding me up. It took her a while to convince me. I called the number and sure enough John Salter, Lizzy's tour manager answered. He told me that their manager Chris O'Donnell had given him my number and that they were looking for a new guitarist to replace Gary Moore and could I be at Shepperton Studios tomorrow... yes tomorrow... at 2pm!

Well the rest of the day my mind was in a big fog. I couldn't think of anything else, but furthermore I didn't have any Thin Lizzy albums at home to listen to. I went around to a friend's house and borrowed the *Live And Dangerous* album. Which I hastily played through in the evening and in the morning before I drove to Shepperton Studios.

It was a very hot day and I arrived at the studios at 1:30pm, but the band didn't arrive until about 2:45pm, so I had ninety minutes standing around waiting when all I wanted to do was to get on with it.

Scott Gorham arrived first and I must admit I found it difficult to get a conversation out of him. We were standing by a big pool table and while I was trying to make conversation he was just standing there occasionally grabbing a pool ball and rolling it along the table. To be honest, it looked like he couldn't be bothered to be there. They'd had so many problems with guitarists Brian Robertson and Gary Moore seemingly coming and going, he must have been fed up going over the same material. I would have probably felt the same way in all honesty. Next arrived Phil Lynott and drummer Brian Downey. Phil seemed really 'out of it' and actually spent the rest of the afternoon spitting on the floor! I think it might have had something to do with the heroin addiction or certainly the excesses of drug use.

At this time, I was never a big fan of Marshall Amplification I'm almost ashamed to say. However, when I plugged into the rig that they had there for me it sounded fantastic. I was using 2 x 100 watt amps and 4, 4 x 12 speaker cabinets which were linked to a small 100-watt combo on Scott Gorham's side of the stage. He had the same set up so I could hear him through the combo on my side and he could hear me on his side.

So here goes, I put on my guitar, John Salter showed me where to plug in. I got a sound and I had no idea if I was loud enough or too loud, but I was ready. No-one was talking much, then Phil said something like "Let's just have a jam". He started playing a bass line with the same chord progression as the old Ben E King song 'Stand By Me' C, A minor, F and G. No vocals just guitars bass and drums. It seemed to go on forever. When it came to a stop everyone looked around, Phil continued spitting so I suggested we play some of their songs. Phil replied with something to the effect of "Oi don't really feel like playing that shit, let's just jam".

I looked around at Brian up on the drum riser and I must have looked a bit helpless and Brian, who seemed to be the nicest and most sociable of them all said, "Maybe we could try one of your songs?" Well I didn't see that one coming! I'm not sure how I got out of that one but I emphasised that I felt it was really important to play a couple of your songs so that you would know whether or not I was the right choice as replacement guitarist. I had never done an audition in my life so the first one I get is with Thin Lizzy and now they don't want to play their songs. As if being there in the first place wasn't daunting enough!

One thing I was very aware of was that quite a few of their songs had the twin lead breaks in and how was I supposed to know which one was which? Which harmony was the one I play? I had listened to the live album that day and I was familiar with their songs anyway. I had found over the years that I had a good ear for picking things up pretty quickly. I think the first song we played was 'Jailbreak' and about six songs in total. When it came to a harmony guitar piece, having Scott's combo over my side, I could hear clearly his first note so I could tell if I was going to play the route note or the harmony and I think I got away with it.

I asked Phil if we could play 'Still In Love With You', which is a great song. It has a long guitar solo in it which I knew Scott didn't play and it would give them the opportunity to hear what I could do on my own to one of their songs. They agreed and we started to play the song. I don't know if it was my imagination or whether Phil had warmed up a bit but this now sounded more like the Thin Lizzy I knew. Phil was singing it with conviction just like on the album. When it came to the solo, I have to say my Gibson Firebird plugged into those Marshalls sounded fantastic. That day my 'bird' really sang. The song finished and I will always remember, there was a moments pause and then Phil Lynott looked over at me with a slight grin and said to me "Well, you can sure play the fuckin' thing". After all that, that made my day.

Then almost like it was perfect timing, John Salter came over and said to us all, that the next guitarist to audition was here. So I unplugged my guitar and said my goodbyes and thanked them for the opportunity at which point Phil stopped me to tell me that he thought I was really good and that he would like me to come back next week and play some more of their songs, and in his way apologised for not feeling himself that day.

That meant a lot actually and it proved to me that he was getting back into it as the day rolled on. The only disadvantage now was that I had helped warm them up for the next guitarist who was about to play. As I was leaving they were really ogling the beautiful very old, Les Paul guitar which was in the case belonging to the next guitarist to try out. I'm not sure but I think it was the guitar belonging to Snowy White.

I went home and waited for a phone call to see what the reaction to my audition was and what day next week was I due to rehearse as Phil had said. The next day, Wednesday, they sent me a few Lizzy albums and throughout the week I set about learning as much as I could and also deciphering who was playing what note when it came to the harmonies. The rest of that week passed as did the weekend and I think it was sometime Monday their manager Chris O'Donnell phoned me personally to thank me for attending and that the good news was that they had narrowed it down to three guitarists and I was one of them on the shortlist so to speak.

The bad news was that I would have to wait a good few weeks as he had just accepted a Japanese tour worth a lot of money that they couldn't turn down and that Scott Gorham's friend Dave Flett (with Manfred Manns Earthband) was sharing a house with Scott, so they could work through all the guitar parts together.

A few weeks later Lizzy were appearing at The Milton Keynes Bowl and if my memory serves me correctly Midge Ure of all people was playing guitar. They were good and went down well at the Bowl. Chris told me that they still had not decided on a guitarist yet but he would be in touch. As most of you know Snowy White got the job which for me was a shame, moreover because I have read in recent times he found it a miserable experience being in the band. I'm sure I would have loved every moment, but I'll never know now will I?

I was looking at the final entry of my diary on the day of the Thin Lizzy audition Wednesday 22nd August 1979.

I wrote, 'I left Shepperton at 5:15pm, felt good but have the feeling a friend of theirs will get the gig'. I have often wondered what would have happened if I had got the gig with Lizzy. Another turning in the fork of the road of life.

# 27.

# Jodie Is Born And A New Music Opportunity

I had bigger things to concentrate on now because on Monday 10th September our second daughter Jodie was born, by caesarean section at 8:03pm weighing in at 7lbs 5 1/2ozs at Stoke Mandeville Hospital. Back in those days, Caesarean births were a much bigger operation than they are these days and consequently as the father I was not allowed in during the birth. I knew it didn't take that long because Zoe was born the same way. So I was waiting in the corridor along by the operating theatre and there was nobody around and no-one to tell me what was happening.

The longer I waited, the more concerned I became. Eventually I saw a nurse walk along the corridor who I thought was one of the nurses who went into the operating theatre. I asked her if there was any news yet? And this must have been about an hour later around 9pm. "Oh yes, you have a lovely baby boy" she said.

A baby boy! I couldn't wait to see him. I waited and waited and still saw or heard nobody? On reflection it's hard to believe how quiet that hospital was by comparison these days. A little while after I had spoken to the nurse, the doctor who I recognised, who must have delivered the baby walked towards me down the corridor. "Hello" I said "I hear I have a baby boy?"

"A baby boy?" he replied "No, I don't think so, it's a little girl".

Well it was now 9:45pm and nearly an hour and a half later I got to see my new baby daughter. It was such a surprise because she looked so different to Zoe. This baby had very fair hair and looked much taller. We decided to name her Jodie. Jackie had a stepsister named Thelma who had been on holiday and said she had seen a little girl get up on stage and sing a song. Apparently she was a really pretty little girl but moreover she loved the name Jodie as at that time it was unusual and she thought it was a lovely name.

Jackie and Jodie stayed in hospital for about a week. Jodie had not been home too long before it was obvious there was something wrong! After her feeds, she could not keep liquids like milk down. The way it came out was projectile vomit, not even vomit. It was the milk flying out of her mouth like the jet from a hose pipe! We took her to the doctors and we were told to take her to the hospital immediately. They were going to keep her in and may have to operate. It appears there was a problem with a valve in the stomach. Fortunately, they didn't have to operate after all and after about ten days in hospital the problem was cured and we could take her home.

Towards the end of 1979 I was contacted by Rod Linton who was working with the agent John Sherry. I knew John Sherry from the early seventies when we were managed by Peter and Ivan as they shared their office in Dryden Chambers Central London with The John Sherry Agency. John had asked Rod to find me as he wanted a meeting. This was quite a coincidence because Rod had been the guitarist in Rupert's People all those years ago when we walked in on them rehearsing, looking for our first deal. Now Rod was potentially offering me a deal.

After Christmas, now into 1980 I had a meeting with John and Rod. Basically John was interested in me reforming Stray. Three days of rehearsal were arranged at a rehearsal studio in Chiswick, London and then, one-day recording at Fast Buck Studios. I had spoken to Ritchie and Gary and we had decided to record as a three piece primarily because we had not spoken to Steve for some time. Pete had not played guitar for a while and was working away quite a bit. I had written some new songs, some I had already played with Rom and Stu.

I gave John a copy of the recording and he thought a song I had written called 'Burning The Candle' was a strong song so he wanted to record that one to start with. This is a song I had been playing with the four-piece band including Vic on keyboards. Ritchie Gary and I went to De Lane Lea Studios in Kingsway where some years before we had recorded the *Saturday Morning Pictures* album. We recorded for two days. Then Rod and I went in and mixed the song for John to hear.

A week or more went by and we met John and Rod for lunch at a French Restaurant in Putney. I had inadvertently ordered Snails (Escargot) and the biggest plate of snails you could imagine was served to me. Well, I admit I wasn't keen but I had a try. My apologies to any French readers but I thought they were disgusting and as far as I was concerned they can stay in the garden next time! I tried a couple. Fortunately John and Rod had reasonable appetites so they ate some of mine.

During the meeting John explained that he wanted to represent me for management and agency and that they had formed a record label called Valiant Records. The downside of the meeting for me personally was that he wanted me and not Ritchie and Gary. He didn't think the Stray he came down to the rehearsal to see and hear was as strong as the line-up he had seen me perform live with (I didn't know he had been scouting and seen me play).

When the meeting was finished it left me with mixed emotions and I could think of nothing else driving all the way home. I was dreading the phone calls I had to make to Ritchie and Gary, but it had to be me who had to tell them what John had told me. John offered to make the calls but I said no, as they were my very old friends it had to come from me. It was not a good experience. These kind of phone calls are very short on conversation once the point of the conversation has been spoken about! I felt sick all evening and it took me a while to get over it.

I contacted Rom and Stu and suggested we try some new songs which I had written as a three piece along with a few old Stray songs to see how they worked. After just one rehearsal we could all tell there was something special going on here. Even my old songs had a freshness about them. Rom had that solid jazzy funky feel which I liked. Guitarists like Hendrix and Trower would have been happy having Rom as drummer in their three-piece line ups. Stu was now predominately playing a fretless bass and being a guitarist to begin with created a whole fusion of ideas in those fingers of his. With all three of us singing vocal harmony, it was a big sound for three people.

I decided that I wanted a band name and not my name. I came up with the name Javelin which I thought had a powerful direct sound to it and soon we had some good shows lined up for us to play.

The very first show by Javelin was at The Red Lion, Gravesend on Saturday 22nd March 1980.

John Sherry and Rod Linton arrived with a large wicker type picnic hamper with food and champagne to celebrate out first gig and new relationship. The gig was well attended and for a first show we played well. John and Rod were very complimentary and we were now looking forward to a new beginning.

During the year, John's agency got us some good shows and coincidentally one of the booking agents that was working for Rod was Phil Banfield an old acquaintance as you may recall while reading earlier chapters. We played The Marquee Club in our own right as well as a few gigs with a new band the agency were trying to promote called Sledgehammer. We played other shows with Krokus, Diamond Head and Samson.

I particularly remember the first time we played with Samson. The band took its name from their guitarist, Paul Samson. Paul turned out to be a really lovely guy and an excellent guitarist and we got on really well right from the start (there's that song title again!). He, like a couple of the others in his band were Stray fans and had seen me play a few years previously. Paul told me he felt embarrassed that I was supporting him on a couple of shows, but that was okay by me.

Samson to their credit seemed to be on the way up so to speak and they were one of the first to have the NWOBHM tag credited to them. NWOBHM = New Wave of British Heavy Metal. They had a solid rhythm section in Chris Aylmer on bass and Barry Purkis on drums. Barry was better known as Thunderstick and appeared on stage behind a huge cage. Paul had not long recruited a new lead singer named Bruce Dickinson. I was particularly impressed with the vocal range which Bruce had and he also had a good rapport with the audience. I never found it easy being the front man and holding a guitar you are certainly limited with hand and arm gesticulations. Gesticulations, that's a word mum would have loved.

I spoke to Paul many times after those shows and he came to see me play at a few gigs, often with their road manager Rob Grain. I still see and hear from Rob from time to time. Sadly, Paul died from Cancer in 2002 he was only 49 years of age and Chris Aylmer also past away from cancer in 2007. Barry has launched his own band Thunderstick and have seen him a few times recently. As for Bruce Dickinson, whatever happened to him? Oh yes, Iron Maiden, but more about them later.

I can't go into details as there are always two sides to every story, but while I was playing as Javelin, I received a phone call. If my memory serves me correctly it was from none other than Phil Banfield and the office needed to see me urgently! I was intrigued to say the least. Why would the agency want to see me and why hadn't John wanted to see me himself? They gave me a little hint at what I was about to find out, but I wasn't to mention the meeting to John should I speak to him. Very odd all this. Why was I going to a hush hush meeting?

I arrived at the office and was introduced to the company accountant who I think was called Leonard Richenburg. I was told that John Sherry was no longer to be part of the company! It sounded like all the agents working for John were staying, but the boss was being fired! The agency was now to be called PAN or Performing Artists Network. Big question was where did this leave me and Javelin? It seemed things were going so well and despite what internal business affairs they might have had, as a band, Javelin were getting a good reputation and went down really well at all the gigs we had played. I was told that they would have a meeting and discuss the future of me and Javelin. I actually thought that with Phil Banfield still there, I might stand a chance from still having agency representation. No such luck as once again it was that name association that would cost me once again.

Because I was John's act the agency would have to let me go. It was total nonsense as I never even had a signed agreement with John. It was a 'gentlemen's agreement', but quite clearly as I have found in my lifetime there were very few 'gentlemen' in the music business. As the year went on, we played the shows we had left, but then as before I found it difficult to get more shows booked. So although we still rehearsed regularly, there were no shows for Javelin on the horizon.

Chris Tsangarides phoned one day to tell me he and a guy called Grant Black, who was the son of Don Black the well-known songwriter, were going to form a new music company called Hit and Run Music. The name in itself was a coincidence because I had just written a song titled 'Hit And Run' which Javelin had just been rehearsing. Chris asked me what was happening with the band and I brought him up to date with recent events. He suggested that we record a few songs in a studio he had access to and see what we could come up with. So we went to a small studio off of Regent Street, London and spent three days Monday 6th, Tuesday 7th and Wednesday 8th April 1981 and recorded five songs. Four of my songs the titles being 'Need Your Love', which was the song I gave the new Stray line up to record. 'Survival', 'Daily Papers' 'Hit and Run' and a song Stu had written titled 'Hold On My Love'.

All songs were fully recorded including vocals and instrument overdubs. Rom, Stu and myself had been rehearsing regularly so we were well prepared. Chris and I spoke on numerous occasions where it appeared there was interest in the recording, but as time went on it was obvious that nothing much was happening both with Hit and Run Music or with Javelin. The gigs were few and far between and those we played were not particularly well paid. It is not like we decided to split up or anything like that. Javelin just ground to a halt. Stu went off to do some guitar tech work with various artists, so that took him out of being available for a while and Rom was playing with various people.

In the meantime life was as near normal as can be, bringing up two small children and earning enough to keep a roof over our heads.

# 28.
# The
# Milton Keynes Music Scene

Having a bit more time on my hands, what was going on musically where we lived (which was now part of the ever-growing new city of Milton Keynes) was starting to interest me. There were some good little bands springing up which seemed to be fusing all the elements of post punk, dance music with a little bit of rock thrown in for good measure. A lot of the music seemed to be coming from a place called The Peartree Bridge Youth Club. In 1980 The Police played at The Milton Keynes Bowl, who were arguably the biggest band on the planet at that time. They were managed by Miles Copeland, who at this point I have to mention, was one time a partner with my now ex manager John Sherry. Miles had very generously donated a sum of money to the youth centre to help with the arts and music.

There were two bands which really got my attention. The first was called Fictitious. They had real energy and they asked me if I would go in the studio with them and record a couple of songs. I had recently found a recording studio in a little village called Thorpe Mandeville situated near Banbury. It was called Stables Studio and was run by two guys Steve White and Phil Down. It was a converted barn, very conveniently in the large car park of a pub called The Three Conies. I booked them into the studio and we got some great results.

While I was working for Hammond Organs a young guy came in as a temporary worker. His name was Glen O'Halloran. Along with his brothers Joe, Brent and Larry they had a band called the Dancing Counterparts. He invited me along to see them playing locally. They were nothing like Fictitious musically, but they had a certain something about them that I couldn't quite put my finger on, but they did fascinate me. Both of these bands were taking me into new territory.

The Counterparts had a session booked at Earhole Studios. I got to see quite a bit of The Counterparts and became good friends with them. One of the brothers, Larry suffered a stroke which obviously was a shock as he was very young, so Brent changed from rhythm guitar to bass guitar. The Dancing Counterparts were now the three O'Halloran brothers, Glen on lead vocals (sometimes bass), Joe on Saxophone, Brent on bass guitar, Howard Lewis on lead guitar and Grant Gillingham on drums. Just to note here that Grant Gillingham later became politically active with the Labour Party and was the mayor of Milton Keynes for a while.

The Dancing Counterparts were obviously happy with my contribution to the couple of songs they recorded and duly asked if I would produce their first album. I accepted their invitation and suggested they try the Stable Studios where I had worked with Fictitious. I had really got to know my way around the Studio and it almost became a second home. When co-owner Phil decided to quit the studio, Steve asked me if I would get involved and help him on some forthcoming sessions. This was great experience and Steve made me feel very comfortable. I treated it like it was my own studio. Ironically though, I never found time to record my own album there which was my intention at some point. Steve had renamed the studio White Trax and we recorded quite a lot of mainly local artistes there.

Back to The Dancing Counterparts, these were really good sessions. I could feel that they were letting me have a free hand in contributing to the music and studio ideas. Daft as it may seem, I wanted to be like one of my heroes, George Martin and make my production ideas count. Not be just the bloke who sits behind the desk making it sound pretty. We tried a few experimental ideas with the instrumentation and arrangements, and it really got our juices flowing and the finished album sounded great. I played it again recently and even after all these years it still has a certain something. A big feather in my cap was getting a couple of their songs played on John Peel's Radio 1 show.

I sent John, who I had known since the early Stray days, a cassette of the album. One evening I am sitting at home and my phone rang and to my surprise it was John Peel. He said he had received the album and had played it and loved it and if it was okay he would love to play a song or two on his show later that evening. He particularly loved a song called 'Jacob's Room' which happened to be a favourite of mine too. I speedily phoned the band up to tell them to sit by their radios because The Dancing Counterparts were going to be on The John Peel Show. That was a very proud moment.

I must tell you a story about dad and John Peel. Let me take you back to around 1970/71 and I was playing at either The Nags Head in Wollaston or The Blisworth Hotel where John was the DJ. These days the accessibility for music is so easy now we have the Internet. Back then there was just vinyl and reel to reel tape and you had to search really hard for old records. John and I got into a conversation about the music of the 1930s and 1940s which we both liked. I told him that dad had quite a large record collection and had a lot of records from that period.

John talked about a singer called Al Bowley who dad had a couple of records of, but the artists that John was interested in was a vocal harmony group called The Mills Brothers. I told John I was sure that dad had something by them and I would see him next week at the next gig. I asked dad if I could borrow his copy of The Mills Brothers record so that I could lend it to John Peel top BBC radio Disc Jockey. Dad was always quite precious about his records but when he heard that it was John Peel, that was a different story. I saw John the following week and he was really pleased that dad had lent it to him and as promised John returned it to me some weeks later.

I was about to write I wasn't sure who was the happiest, John or dad, but it was dad obviously. He was so proud lending John Peel one of his records and for many years after, he would recall "Ere son, do you remember when I lent John Peel my Mills Brothers record?". How could I forget. Dad certainly wouldn't have let me.

Back at White Trax Studios while on another session, Steve said he had a duo coming in to record a couple of songs. They were a country music female duo. They both sang and one played acoustic guitar. I said okay great, what about the band? What is the instrumentation. Steve looked at me and said, "Well they don't have a band. I wondered whether you would play all the instruments. You could be the band".

Coincidentally the duo called themselves The Rondells, so having Del in the name it seemed to make sense. So I listened to the songs and recorded the backing tracks on guitars, bass guitar, keyboards and drums, so when the girls came in, all they had to do was sing along to the backing track. Fortunately, they were really pleased with me, 'the band'. So they recorded the vocals, then Steve and I mixed the two songs. The Rondells took the recordings to their record label and to our joy one of the songs was included on a country music various artists album and their song was chosen as record of the week on BBC Radio Oxford.

My friend 'Wixsy' (Steve Witcomb) came to see me one day to say that drummer 'Bert' (Paul Herbert) and guitarist Don Hollis, all formerly with Teaza had a new band project and they wanted to go into the studio to record a couple of new songs. Wixsy had switched to playing bass guitar and they were going to call themselves Private Lives. They had found this young guitarist in Milton Keynes and they were bringing him along to play with the new band. The day of the recording came and I recognised this young guitarist straight away. Milton Keynes was a much smaller place then and I had seen this young guy quite often walking around town and he always seemed to have a guitar in a case strapped to his back.

His name was Michael McDonald. I think he was about eighteen at the time. He played a Fender Stratocaster and was one of the best guitarists I had heard for ages. They recorded a couple of songs, I don't know what happened exactly, but they never came back and properly mixed the songs although the rough mixes off of the desk sounded pretty good. A shame because I thought this new band had a lot of promise.

To his credit young Michael attended various auditions in London and consequently began to make his name as a session guitarist. Then in the 1990s Take That were seeking musicians to form their backing band. Another local musician, Mike Stevens had become their Musical Director and I believe recommended Michael as the guitarist in the band. Here's a funny story, when the rehearsals with Take That began, the lads asked Michael what his name was? They said "There's already someone called Michael McDonald, the fella who plays with The Doobie Brothers. Where are you from Mike?" "Milton Keynes" he replied "Okay then, from now on you will be called Milton McDonald" said Take That. Michael, or Milton has recently been on tour with Jeff Lynne as part of the new line up for ELO.

There is a good music venue in Wolverton, Milton Keynes called The Craufurd which these days hosts gigs almost every night of the week. I have played there myself and it is a great venue to play. Back in the 1980s it was a pub called The Craufurd Arms and even back then was a music pub. In brief, I along with my friends in the band Alibi on alternate weeks hosted musicians Jam nights which later transferred to The Cosgrove Lodge Hotel, not far from Wolverton.

It was around this time at The Craufurd, I first met Andy Viccars. He was a very good bass player and I had seen him play with a band called Rain. When Rain split up some other friends of mine had a band called Freeway Jam and they were looking for a bass player. I had become friends with guitarist Ben Bennion and drummer Mick Bullard. Mick had played with Bernie Marsden in one of his first bands, Skinny Cat. I suggested Andy would be ideal for the bass gig and I wasn't wrong because he was in the band for over thirty years.

Andy trained as a carpenter but as the years went by he became a well-known guitar luthier. I have been taking my guitars to him for as long as I have known him, for repairs or a little TLC every now and then. It must have been around 1989 that Andy asked me if I fancied going to a guitar exhibition in London. The Hamsters were doing a 'demo' that day and I think that was the first time I had met their guitarist Slim (Barry Martin). I think it was that day the subject of guitars came up in conversation (now there's a surprise). I mentioned that the night before I had seen a Lionel Richie concert on TV. I noticed his guitarist had a really nice Fender Telecaster in black with white binding around the edges and a maple neck. Back at The Cosgrove Lodge Hotel, I was hosting a musician's jam night and on one night in particular I noticed Andy eyeing up the two guitars I had brought with me. A Gibson Firebird and a Fender Stratocaster.

In retrospect I now realise that Andy was inspecting the guitars, particularly the necks to see how they felt. How wide and how fat the frets were. A few weeks later he telephoned me and said, "Hello mate, are you home now?" or something like that? I relied "Yes I'm home". Andy said okay then boy, I'll be 'round in about twenty minutes. Andy arrived at my house with a guitar case. "I want to show you something, have a look in the case," said Andy. Inside was a beautiful Telecaster, black with white binding and a maple neck. I was shocked. It was like the guitar I had seen on TV. It had two pickups. One neck pickup made by Kent Armstrong and the bridge pick up, an old genuine Fender Telecaster pick up which I believe dates back to 1963? I was totally shocked when I saw it! "Do you like it?" asked Andy. "Like it, I love it. It's gorgeous" I replied. "Well it's yours, I made it especially for you".

As it transpired a coincidence was that the date Andy made the guitar which is stamped on the back of the neck is 1st June 1989 which unknown to me was the day that my partner Annie gave birth to her first son Alex, who also happens to play guitar. Over the years I have had many people comment on this guitar. It is a bit special... as is Andy.

****

One person who I feel has really flown the flag for Milton Keynes is Lee Scriven. Although originally born in London, I believe he moved to Bletchley with his family in the early seventies. This was the start of what was known as the new towns slowly springing up around the UK, predominately in the South Midlands area. Lee is from a family of drummers. His dad was a jazz drummer and both his brothers Gary and Blair are drummers too. Blair is a very good drummer who I have had the pleasure to work with on many occasions over the years. I think I first met Lee when he was playing drums for Fictitious. He then went on to be a journalist working predominantly for the Citizen newspaper group covering music and the arts. He now works for The MK Dons football team. He often broadcasts on local radio and I have been a guest on his shows from time to time.

Lee is also a good photographer and filmmaker, and he took the photographs and produced and directed the promotional film for my song 'White Feather'.

Lee formed a successful band in the late eighties called The Blues Collective. Sometimes there appeared to be about twenty people on stage. Several vocalists and varying brass section guitars keyboards drums and percussion. It must have been a nightmare to transport that lot around, but they were a good band and a lot of fun and I had the pleasure to dep on guitar a couple of times with them.

When Lee decided it was time for a Blues Collective album, he wanted it to be an album of original songs rather than the soul band covers they were playing live. I gave him a few songs but he and producer 'Big' George Webley chose a song of mine titled 'If You've Ever Loved Somebody'. My version was originally an up tempo tune in the style of Otis Redding, but Lee wanted a ballad on the album. It was George's suggestion to slow it down and it really works that way and there is a brilliant vocal by Graham Dee, who these days you will find as the lead singer/songwriter for the successful Climax Blues Band.

The thing that has taken up most of Lee's time in the past few years and something I have been involved in has been his story of Fred Burrett. Lee being a David Bowie fan had heard stories of how this local Bletchley lad was a clothes designer for David Bowie and when he followed the stories up it turned to be true. Lee made a documentary in 2015 about Fred Burrett, titled *Starman – The Man Who Sewed The World*. Burrett was a young man living in Bletchley in the late sixties who had a real gift for making clothes. He was homosexual which particularly in a small town was frowned upon then, so consequently he always felt out of place. He loved nightclubs and dancing and eventually decided to move to London where he met David and Angie Bowie in a nightclub. They became friends and subsequently David asked Fred to design clothes for a new musical venture David had in mind, which became Ziggy Stardust.

David also renamed Fred. Apparently he told him that, "From now on you will be known as Freddie Burretti", which you must admit has a better ring to it. The rest is history as they say, but at the height of Freddie's success, he turned his back on it and moved to Israel of all places, but passed away in Paris on May 11th 2001.

I played guitar on the film documentary. It was well received and there were various offers to take it further but Lee was aware that people wanted to take it and change it too much so he turned down potentially good offers. However, that was not the end of it. Lee decided to write a musical based on the life of Freddie Burretti and *Burretti – The Man Who Sewed The World* was born.

He got together a fairly large cast of actors and musicians and another local actor and director Caz Tricks. Something I have discovered about Lee is that he has the ability to put combinations of people together who you might not necessarily consider would work but do. I think he has this infectious gift of inspiring people to try something, an idea he has had, and work with it. If 'Burretti' was anything to go by, then future productions or projects are going to be worth watching and partaking in, should he ask me of course.

The band for the musical was myself on guitar, another guitarist Sean Walmsley who played electro-acoustic 12 string (like Bowie), Steve Sciberras on bass, Phil Chamberlain on keyboards and harmonica, and Blair Scriven on drums. On paper you would not necessarily have put us together, but it ended up sounding really good. The show ran officially for only three nights — 16th, 17th and 18th May 2019 but we did a full show run through the night before the opening night for all of the staff and colleagues of The Chrysalis Theatre Milton Keynes. It was sold out and the shows were great, a totally new experience for me.

Finally, I remembered one thing that was quite funny. During one of the scenes, Lee gave me a solo and I moved to the centre of the stage and I ripped into a big lead guitar break. I changed my clothes for this scene into a white shirt and a long black velvet coat. On this particular night I hung the shirt and coat on a hanger and hung it on one of those clothes racks on wheels which was to the side of the stage near to where I was standing, so the plan was during the scene before my solo, I could nip to the side and do the clothes change.

The band and I were situated at the back of the stage all dressed in black so unless the lights were on us we kept quite inconspicuous. Each scene had a change of scenery etc and I was sitting waiting for an opportunity to change, when to my horror the hanger with my clothes on was pushed onto the stage. It was a scene set in a clothes shop and I didn't consider that the clothes hanger was one of the props! When the scene finished I did the fastest clothes change in the west and all went well after all.

After one of the performances, I was talking to some people when from the corner of my eye, I could see a chap making his way towards me and he seemed quite determined that he wanted to speak to me. As the people I had been speaking to departed, the chap came over and proceeded to shake my hand firmly and thanking me for my wonderful guitar playing, but more importantly, was the fact as it transpired he was an old friend of David Bowie's guitarist Mick Ronson. He said that when he closed his eyes it sounded like Mick playing the guitar and if Mick had been there he would have been really proud. His words that night meant a lot and a huge compliment after all the hard work which had gone into it.

# 29.
# Baron Rojo/The Red Baron

The 1980s was a busy time but a time of constant changes for me. Bringing up a family, earning a living and still keeping my foot in music — musically varied it certainly became.

Ritchie, Gary and Pete had been discussing getting the band back together again. I had a couple of conversations with Gary and he asked me if I would be interested in playing again, but I was already committed with Javelin, so I couldn't accept the invitation. Gary asked if I had any songs I would like to contribute to a new Stray line-up and also if I could recommend a guitarist to take my place. I immediately thought of Don Hollis. In brief Don accepted the invitation and joined Stray. Pete had not touched a guitar since the last show in 1977. I believe he became so disillusioned with the business; he just didn't have the inspiration to pick a guitar up.

Gary knew a guitarist named Tony Pow, so now Stray had two guitarists and Pete would just concentrate on lead vocals. I think it was Ritchie who organised the shows and they had a run of gigs up and down the country. Ritchie's wife Lyn's best friend was Sherry Squire sister of Yes's Chris Squire. Chris had a studio at his house and allowed the guys to record there. They recorded three songs 'This One's For You', 'Wide Eyed Girl' and my song 'Need Your Love'. I managed to get to see them play at one of their shows at The Civic Hall in St Albans and it was an odd feeling standing in the audience watching.

When the 5-piece line up with Don and Tony on guitars ended their run of gigs, Gary and Ritchie asked me again to re-join. I cannot remember the exact details but I think Ritchie was offered a Stray show on Sunday 29th November 1981 at The Ilford Palais. I think we had one rehearsal, basically to see if it worked, particularly as Pete was no longer playing guitar. When we had played together before we did some twin lead guitar parts. The rehearsal went well, but the more I thought about it, I suggested that we ask Stu Uren to join. He was also a very good guitarist and I knew he knew a lot of the songs. So the following week we rehearsed with Stu playing second guitar. I was pleased to say I was right and he fitted in well. It sounded good and everyone agreed he should do the Ilford show. I don't remember too much about the day to be honest, although what I do remember was that it all felt a bit chaotic and disorganised although it could have been the way I was feeling. I'm sure there was a band on before us and then Stray, followed by Atomic Rooster. The gear changeovers seemed frantic and there was no chance of a sound check, or even being able to check to see if the equipment was working okay. It was one of those walk on stage, plug in, play and hope for the best.

I don't have good memories about the performance. The sound on stage was awful and I felt sorry for Stu because he said he could not hear himself. Most of the time all he could hear was Gary's bass equipment right behind him. I don't recall receiving rapturous applause after the performance and if it sounded out the front like it sounded on stage I'm not surprised. However, my diary entry for the day reads 'went down well'.

I was mainly doing studio work at White Trax Studios during 1981/82. Various artists came through the doors and it was all very enjoyable. I do not remember a session that I didn't like participating in. I received a phone call from Ritchie saying that Stray had been offered a tour in Spain with a top Spanish Heavy Rock band called Baron Rojo. One of the top promoters in Spain had made contact and asked if the band could open the shows in March.

The promoter's name was Robert Mills, who had his own company RM Promotions. We had all known Robert from the seventies when as a fan of the band he often used to come along to the gigs. I was already booked for some studio sessions so the band drove over together in the van with roadies and equipment. I flew over and met them in Barcelona on 10th March. None of us at that time had any idea just how big Baron Rojo were. Most of the shows were in arenas. They seemed all nice guys, friendly and the bass player had an English wife who we met on the tour. Coincidentally she was from Ealing. They also had saxophonist Mel Collins as a guest on the tour. We did have some laughs with Mel. No disrespect to Baron Rojo, but I think Mel felt more comfortable being around the English guys even though by the time we had finished with him he might have regretted it!

What started it all was a Spanish journalist came backstage to interview us and Mel. On more than one occasion he called Mel, Phil (Phil Collins). Mel kept correcting him but he still called him Phil. Well that was it, we were giggling like schoolchildren and from that moment on, for the next three weeks we all kept calling him Phil.

The last night of tours can be dangerous if another act are intending to play a trick on you in one way or another. On this particular last night we went into the dressing room and saw Mel frantically stuffing, socks pants and any other material he could fit into the end of one of his saxophones!

What are you doing Phil? We asked.

"I'm stitching myself up before you buggers get to me" he replied.

He was safe from us that night.

Mel was a very nice guy and we had a lot of laughs... great saxophonist too.

****

Neither Stray or myself did much musically for the next few years with the exception of the *Live At The Marquee* album released on Gull Records. It was actually David Howell's idea when he mentioned that Stray had never released a live album which was quite surprising as the band were known primarily as a live band. So David got the wheels in motion. Our mutual friend Gordon Rowley was just back in the UK having worked for Rudy Records Recording Studios in LA (via Graham Nash), so he came along recorded and produced the album for us. This was a strange album for me because I didn't sing on it! Not even the songs I had recorded on the original albums as the band were basically carrying on from where they had left off with Pete no longer playing guitar.

We should have been playing shows to promote the album but alas without any representation that was not to be. To be honest, I never liked the album very much and I think I've only ever played it back once or twice! Apologies to anyone who really likes it.

I carried on working doing sessions at White Trax Studios, when one day Steve White announced that he and his family were emigrating to Canada so he was selling the studio.

I had spent all my time recording other people and I never got around to making my own album which was a shame because I had really made myself at home there.

With no likelihood of any paid music work in sight, music royalties dwindling and like most others, a family to support I had to find a job (again). I had lost count of the amount of phone calls I had made to music management companies, made even more frustrating with their promises of someone will call you back tomorrow but never did. I was collecting a large pile of rejection letters from record labels so musically, it all seemed quite hopeless. That reminds me... at this time I wrote a song titled 'Yesterday's News' which I never recorded. Perhaps I should?

Fortunately, at this time a couple of friends were refurbishing offices in Milton Keynes and the manager of this company asked them if they knew anyone looking for work. The company was Nina Ricci, a perfumery company whose head offices were in Paris but were setting up in the UK. One of my friends knew that for a while I had worked for a designer and printers and that I had done some marketing work for a couple of perfume/fashion houses, so the manager asked to meet me. I met Dennis Holmes and he offered me the job straight away. Although it wasn't the job I was expecting to get, it was warehouse based and pretty much like I did a few years before when I first moved to Bletchley at Hammond Organs. It was a small team and we all did a little bit of everything, although Dennis did give me most of the advertising material to sort out. Actually, as jobs go, particularly for a musician, it was okay. We were a small friendly team who overall got on quite well and the atmosphere was laid back. We played music all day and one thing I didn't miss was the hassle you get from trying to organise gigs and dealing with the Music Biz over the phone. I was getting really disenchanted with the whole business. Not only that, but I was also getting paid regularly and I didn't have to fight for everything.

# 30.
# New Life

The decade of the eighties gave us some good times. Zoe and Jodie were going to school and both doing very well. We made good friends with our neighbours and often had little get-togethers such as barbecues in our gardens. I had one neighbour, Jim who lived two doors along who used to brew his own beer and other things alcoholic. Sundays was the male neighbours washing cars or doing minor repairs day. We must have saved ourselves plenty of money on repairs because we were all such good friends and neighbours. If someone was out doing a car repair, there was always someone who would come over and help to fix it, or if you didn't have the right tool for the job, someone would have one in their garages, which were like a collection of Pandoras boxes. No wonder car boot sales became so popular, if all the garages were like ours, then there was always something for someone in them.

One day Jim invited me along to his garage to sample his latest homebrew. Like most of his homebrews, I could tell it was going to be a strong one. He had metal racking that stood with the various nectars he had brewed. We both had a pint in our hand while having a chat, when there was a loud bang from behind us, followed by another bang! A couple of bottles of beer who had got a bit lively while waiting to be opened. They couldn't wait any longer so they had decided to open themselves.

Jim's wife was Eileen and they had two sons Scott and Gary who were the same ages as Zoe and Jodie. When they all got to be teenagers and started staying out late at the clubs it was good to know they all looked after each other and many times if either Jodie or Zoe found themselves on their own at the end of the night, Scott and Gary would escort them home.

Both our families shared some good times together. We even went on holiday to Menorca where we rented a villa for a couple of weeks and had a great time there, even without the home brew!

I have always considered myself lucky that all through my childhood mum and dad took me on holiday, always to a seaside resort and when I had children I wanted to do the same. So I am proud to say, whatever the financial situation was, I always managed to take the family away for a summer holiday. The last holiday we had in the UK, we went up to Scarborough. Although it was in the summer, the weather was awful. It felt like we were literally dragging the children from one amusement arcade to a café and then another arcade just to find things to do. All we wanted to do was to take them on the beach and play in the sea sand and sunshine. We must have spent a fortune and I think we may have even cut the holiday short and come home. After that holiday, I vowed I would never take the children on holiday in the UK again.

The first time we took the children abroad was to Spain and we had a couple of weeks' in a hotel in Santa Susanna. What a difference. The weather was beautiful and we spent most of our time on the beach and in the swimming pool. This was the holiday where I was determined to learn to swim. I had watched my children in the pool and I felt inadequate that I could not enjoy it with them. When we got home me and the kids went swimming every week and I conquered my fear of the water and learned to swim.

In the years that followed we always had holidays abroad in the sun. We went to Florida two years running, mainly for Disneyworld and all the other resorts locally. We stayed in Clearwater which was a little over an hour's drive from Disney, but the drive was not a problem and seemed all part of the adventure. I could write another book on those holidays in Florida, they were great fun. I must admit, I fell in love with the USA all over again and saw a couple of houses I considered buying, but decided against emigrating mainly because of Zoe and Jodie and their schooling which was going well for them at home.

I had not been playing live for some time, when Bill Gammond told me he had met a guy called Robin Mathews who was a good singer and played a bit of guitar. Robin was the singer in the seventies band The Radio Stars. Bill also introduced me to Martin Hartup, a singer and guitarist who I had seen play with a band Madrigal — one of the first bands I went out to see when I first moved to Bletchley back in 1978.

I must admit to not being too bothered either way about forming another band, but I wasn't doing much else musically at that time so I just went along with the flow as the saying goes. Who was going to play drums? I remembered that I had been to a local gig where there were a couple of bands playing and there was one band in particular called Jump. They had a great drummer and I spent most of the time watching him because there was something about his style. He had a great groove going on whatever song he played along with. We arranged a rehearsal and it must have gone well because after a couple of rehearsals we were off and running and playing at clubs and airbases and company dances etc.

His name was Lee Maloney and not only was he a great drummer but he could sing too which meant that we had five vocalists in the band. I was amazed at how much money a function band could earn, particularly playing corporate functions and airbases. More money than I was earning as a serious musician. We named the band Alibi and it was fun while it lasted. We played our own arrangements of other people's songs and I suppose it made us feel better that we weren't totally selling out as such. We earned a good reputation and many people were quite shocked when we announced we were going to call it a day only a couple of years after we started.

I remember playing one show at RAF Chicksands, an American air base. When we got there, because technically speaking we were on American soil so we had to change sterling into US Dollars for a start. It goes to show that looks can be deceiving because all the G.I.'s had shaved heads or very short haircuts. Some guys dropped by when we were setting up and they began to tell us what kind of music they liked and were looking forward to some live music. It was very apparent that despite their look they were rock fans and they wanted it loud and rocky. That presented a slight problem because as Alibi we had never been in this environment before, so I said prior to the show, we should pick certain songs and maybe improvise a few others and generally turn the volume up! I am pleased to say it worked and it went down a storm.

I suppose when you are all mates and are having fun, no-one really wants to be the person to say that you don't want to play in the band anymore. Without sounding too grand, we all were serious musicians who had been involved with serious bands and the novelty of playing in Alibi was clearly individually wearing off. Silly as this may sound, one night we were playing in a club and during a song I began to think of what wallpaper I was going to buy the next day to decorate my dining room. I knew then, it was time to call it a day.

Before I got a chance to hand in my notice so to speak, Lee said that he didn't want to play in the band anymore, which led to both Bill and me saying the same thing. We agreed to finish the shows we had booked in and that was going to be it. Bill and I talked about playing a few gigs in pubs as a three-piece rock and blues type band. We didn't play a lot of gigs as we couldn't find a regular drummer. We called ourselves Lock, Stock and Barrel. First we had a drummer called Lynsey who was good but musically he had other ideas. We then played some shows with Drew Murphy who was a great drummer. I remember on the first gig he played with us, he hit the snare drum so loud it made me jump six foot up in the air. Not since Ritchie Cole had a drummer done that to me! Drew moved back to London so it made continuing difficult, but Bill and I decided to continue but I thought we should change the name and maybe introduce some original songs in the set. I suggested the Killer B's as the band name. I had seen an article where the B sides of some singles were better than the A-sides. Also there were bands around who had quite unorthodox cool names like Fischer Z for example.

Once again the problem was, where do we find a drummer? Lee Maloney had not played for a while and through a chance conversation we asked him if he fancied doing something different. He came along and we played as a three piece and it sounded good. We began to play the more rock orientated clubs. It had a big sound for a three-piece band and we were going down really well and I began to notice some Stray fans were turning up at the gigs.

I am not going into details but there were some personal things going on behind the scenes which I was not happy with so I quit The Killer B's which came as a surprise to a lot of people. I needed to get away with my family, so I booked a last minute holiday and took Jackie, Zoe and Jodie to Crete. It was April and being typically English we packed our cases with summer clothes. Unfortunately, it was unusually cold for that time of year, so we had to go out and buy some warmer clothes. Nevertheless, we had a good time away and the weather did improve.

The holiday gave Jackie and I a bit of breathing space and a chance to think about our future. We had been experiencing a few personal problems and after a while we thought it would be a good idea to move house and have a fresh start.

# 31.
# Razorback

It's funny how in life of all the people you meet you will remember one person and if you are lucky they remain friends for the rest of your life. One such person is Gordon Rowley. Let me take you back to about 1967 when The Stray were playing The Romford Market Hall, Essex.

As I said in an earlier chapter, this was a kind of audition where an agent was putting on a several bands who all played for nothing in the hope that the aforementioned agent would sign you up and get you more work. I remember another band arriving and setting up opposite us on the floor in the hall. We looked really clean cut and young compared with this other band. They looked older and as mum would have said looked a bit rough and ready. They made us look like young kids, angels even! They had some equipment I had never seen before. Triumph amplification and their music sounded raw and uncompromising if that makes sense? I am sure they were called The Emotions, well whatever they were called, I was drawn towards the bass guitarist who was very visual. He moved around and had a way of holding and playing the bass guitar. His name was Gordon Rowley, but I didn't know that until some years later.

The incredible thing is and I often ask myself why out of all the bands I have played with, why do I remember that band but in particular Gordon? As it transpires when I got to know Gordon well, he told me virtually the same story but in reverse. He too remembered that venue in Romford and that I was one of the first guitarists he saw using a wah-wah pedal live. Like The Stray, Gordon and his band were attending the audition for the same reason as us, except they had driven all the way down from Liverpool in search of a deal.

It wasn't until some years later when Gordon's band Strife were on the same bill as Stray. Gordon had remembered our band name and after all those years reminded me of that evening in Romford. Stray and Strife played many shows together and were eventually with the same agency Outlaw Artistes. We all became good friends and always looked forward to meeting up with Strife: Gordon, John and Paul. Quite ironic really as both Stray and Strife had received a reputation for going down so well at gigs that many headline acts would not have either band on the same bill, for fear of being blown off stage.

That's not necessarily my opinion, but that is what has been written about both bands over the years. Like I said, we became good friends and I don't think it ever entered our heads about any rivalry. We enjoyed each other's company and the music, which is what it's all about at the end of the day. It must have been around 1979 that Gordon suffered a heart attack which led to the break-up of Strife.

He was too ill to tour so he worked as a studio engineer in the USA and eventually worked at Rudy Records Recording studios in Los Angeles. He decided to come back to the UK and was offered the job playing bass for Rainbow but turned it down in favour of forming his own band in 1982 known as Nightwing. They had a degree of success particularly in Europe.

I can only assume that after a few years Gordon wanted to try and bring something new to Nightwing and to my surprise he asked me if I would be interested in joining. A meeting was arranged and I travelled up to his home in Ellesmere Port to meet the rest of the band. To be honest and to be as tactful as I can be, I don't think some of the members of Nightwing shared Gordon's view that I would add anything to their band. Nothing was said as such but I could sense a slightly uncomfortable atmosphere. There may have been a train of thought as to when they already had a guitarist in the band, and they also had a couple of songwriters, why would they need me?

The next day I spoke to Gordon and said I really appreciated his offer and thanked him for thinking of me, but I would have to decline.

As it turned out, Nightwing had all but folded by 1987, but not to be put off, Gordon phoned me once more and we had a long conversation (that's nothing unusual for Gordon and me). He explained that he had always wanted to play with me and he said he could keep some of the shows in the UK that Nightwing were booked to play and he could perhaps get a few more. The feeling was mutual as I had always thought we could make a good noise together. So twenty years after our first meeting we found ourselves in a rehearsal studio.

Gordon had asked Nightwing drummer, Steve Bartley if he would like to play and the three of us set about putting a set together for some forthcoming shows. We didn't know for sure how this trio would sound, but the strange thing was, almost right away it was like we had always played together. It seemed so natural and Steve on drums and vocals was great to play with. It was all really weird how it came together so easily. We learnt a couple of Stray songs, a couple of Strife songs and a few covers, one cover being the Tim Rose song 'Morning Dew' which Gordon wanted to play with me because this is the song he remembered me using the wah-wah pedal in, all those years before in Romford.

We wanted a powerful sounding name and I don't know where it came from but I suggested the name Razorback, which Gordon liked immediately. I can remember him saying that a Razorback was a disgusting looking creature and would be an ideal name for us. I know what he meant, we were no boy band although I was thinking more of the sound of the name rather than what we looked like, but I get his point.

There is some live footage on YouTube of a couple of songs from the set we played at The Mardi Gras in Nottingham on Saturday 26th March 1988.

After a few good gigs we decided that we should record an album. So on Monday 3rd October 1988 we started recording the first Razorback album which was to be called *First Bite* at Studio One in Saughall near Chester. I think the optimism in the title suggested that this album would be the first of many. We recorded from the Monday to the Friday, including playing a show on the Thursday evening at The Tivoli Ballroom, Buckley. We worked hard and completed everything by the Friday early evening. We recorded the Alex Harvey song 'Faith Healer' as a tribute to Alex as Gordon was a friend of his and was with him on the night he died. We also recorded a song written by Steve titled 'Mercenary Man'. I wrote six more songs. 'Give 'Em Enough Rope', which was a song I wrote after Gordon and I had a long discussion over dinner about the state of music and predominately the charts which at that time seemed to be dominated by The Stock Aitken and Waterman synth and drum machine pop music. Other songs were 'Here I Go Again' (my song not the Whitesnake song of the same name), 'The Game', 'Good To Be Alive', 'Angel Love' and 'The Book'.

Gordon took the tapes to Rudy Studios in Los Angeles and mixed it there. On his return he reported that he had had some interest in the USA and in what was known as Yugoslavia, where Nightwing had a big following. There were also some possibilities of some forthcoming shows in Europe. It was a start which we intended to build on by contacting other label bosses, some we knew and some we didn't know. We were feeling very optimistic at this time.

Meanwhile back home I was about to play the last few gigs with Alibi also rehearsing a new set with the new side project Lock Stock and Barrel and putting my house up for sale and looking to buy a new one. I've never done anything by halves as they say!

Before we leave the year 1988, here's a couple of other significant things that happened. I was looking at an old diary and an entry for Monday 18th April, I have written about taking Zoe and Jodie swimming and that day I swam for the first time properly. Might not seem much for you swimmers out there, but having nearly drowned when I was a small child, it was a big moment and future holidays with the children would be much more fun.

Jackie and I took the children on holiday to Bugibba in Malta 29th June-13th July. Lovely holiday, spent a lot of time on the beach and in the pool. Also did some sightseeing on the island of Gozo where we visited the Cathedral. After we had a look around the Cathedral we went outside and it was a very hot day, so I walked along the street and found a small shop and went in to buy some bottles of water. The friendly shopkeeper asked where we had been and had we visited the Cathedral. I said yes, and that we were amazed by the way the Dome had been painted. He smiled and led me outside his shop and pointed back down the street to the Cathedral.

"Tell me, where is the Dome?" he said. Pointing towards the top of the Cathedral I gestured towards the rooftop.

"It's over er?" I could not see it!

The shopkeeper's smile became broader and said "There is no Dome. The painting inside is an optical illusion. Look it is a flat roof".

He was absolutely right of course. I urge you to visit the Cathedral if you ever get to visit Gozo. The Dome and all the other paintings therein are amazing.

Back to The Razorback project, by 1989 things had not gone quite to plan. Having a bit of bad luck is one thing but the series of events which took place are almost unbelievable. When Gordon returned from the USA, he stored the master tapes at the studio where we made the album. As it turned out they would have been safer in my garden shed. There was a fire at the studio and our master tapes were destroyed. All we had left was a cassette copy! Gordon then became very ill. First he got cancer and then he had a blood circulation problem which resulted in him having his right leg amputated! It put an end to any further plans we had as Razorback. Gordon has had health problems ever since but miraculously has fought off The Grim Reaper which is hardly surprising if you knew Gordon like I do.

It wasn't until 2015 after speaking to record company boss Peter Purnell that the Razorback album was finally released on Angel Air Records. However, even the release had its setbacks, for since we originally had the Razorback name back in 1987, another band in the USA had achieved success with the same name so we could not use the name after all. Peter and I knew that people would know the names Bromham and Rowley in the business so we made a compromise and the album was finally released as 'BRB' (Bromham, Rowley, Bartley) Razorback – 'First Bite'.

# 32.
# New Home And Leslie West

You would think that buying a new house and selling the old one would be quite a simple task. You want to sell something and I want to buy, the process sounds simple doesn't it? However, just like when we bought the previous house in Bletchley, we had a number of people let us down. Almost the same scenario as before where we found a house we liked. Agreed on the house price and then at the last moment the people we were buying from changed their minds, so by the time we found another house we had lost our buyer as they were impatient to move into our house (or any house I suppose?).

We eventually found a lovely house in a new area of Milton Keynes called Furzton. It was a white detached house, which I often referred to as The White House, although not at 1600 Pennsylvania Avenue. The house was set in a little cul de sac with about a half a dozen other new houses and we had parkland to the left of the house with a stream running down to Furzton Lake, which was opposite the now famous open air music venue The Milton Keynes Bowl. I can remember when standing in the garden, I could hear the sound checks of artists such as Bruce Springsteen, David Bowie, Genesis and Michael Jackson to name but a few. I went to quite a few concerts there which was very convenient as it was only a walk away.

Like our house in Bletchley we were fortunate to have good neighbours and over the years we had some good parties and get togethers at the house. We had a nice big conservatory at the back where I wrote quite a few songs and when it came to recording the Stray album *10*, John and Paul who were playing with me at the time rehearsed the songs for the album in my dining room. It wasn't mum and dad's old council house dining room, but it was comfortable and it did the job.

Zoe and Jodie were growing into young ladies and both learned to drive. On leaving school Zoe decided to go to University in Leicester and Jodie decided University was not for her so she got a job working for an estate agent. As children, Zoe and Jodie always got on well and their friendship continued into adulthood. We were very lucky as they never brought any trouble to our door and were wonderful children. I do miss those years particularly when they were youngsters. Zoe and Jodie were different in as much as Zoe was always studying. Even in later years, she enrolled on other courses and appeared to spend much of the rest of her life taking exams and am proud to say passing them all with flying colours.

Jodie on the other hand never appeared to put in the study time that Zoe did, so when she said she was leaving school and getting a job, it wasn't a complete surprise. The funny thing was, when Jackie and I went to one of the last school open evening where our children's education was discussed, we thought at first the teachers were talking about Zoe where in fact they were extolling the merits of

Jodie and her work! Jodie had her goals and knew what she wanted to do. She got a part time job when she was at school and said that as soon as she was old enough to drive, she would pass her test and buy a car, which she did. She said she would get a job and buy her own house and by the time she was twenty years old she had done that.

In 2004 while playing 'The Blues To Die For' tour. I invited Leslie West and former guitarist with Sheryl Crow, Todd Wolfe over to the house for the day for a drink and a bite to eat. Leslie took a fancy to my old Epiphone acoustic guitar and took it into the conservatory and played it for a while. I had to keep my eye on him and the guitar, just in case he took it home with him! It did occur to me that there would have been a lot of people who would never have thought that Leslie West was in my house in Milton Keynes, the 'rock 'n' roll' centre of the universe! As the afternoon wore on, our tour manager told us it was time to move on to the next show.

The tour was an idea by our tour manager Paul Newcomb. Paul had established a good rapport with Leslie West on the previous tour with Mountain. Paul would be the best person to explain the scenario, but in his absence this is my take on how the tour came to be.

Leslie was about to release his solo album coincidentally titled *Blues To Die For*. Paul suggested to him that he should come to Europe and tour the album. Leslie soon became excited and began telling him about all the big names he could bring over to play with him. I think Paul had to reign him in a bit because an idea like this would not have been financially viable. Paul suggested to Leslie that he should come over and play solo acoustic and tell some of his stories of life on the road and about the songs. Initially he didn't like the idea but Paul had got to know Leslie well enough to use his powers of persuasion. He told Leslie something to the effect of "I think it would really work. Your fans would love it and anyway, Del does this kind of show". I am not suggesting for a moment that my name being mentioned was the reason that Leslie eventually said yes to the tour, but there is an old saying about a red rag to a bull which springs to mind. Leslie's response to the idea was "Well if Del will do it, I'll do it as well" or something like that.

Of course I was up for doing the tour. I had my first solo blues album titled *The Devils Highway* and as I didn't have a band at that particular time, I was just getting into my acoustic solo stride by playing the songs and telling a few stories myself. The UK tour section went well and it was during this tour on Friday 23rd April that I first met Kate Moore, known in the music biz to some as 'Batttttty'. Kate was the web person for UFO and also sold their merchandise on tour. Although we hadn't met before, we talked for ages and it felt like we'd known each other for years. The following week Kate came to The Robin 2 in Bilston and I think it might have been this show where Kate offered to do my website for me. It certainly needed doing and the Stray site also.

I played a solo set then Leslie came on accompanied by Todd and then I joined them for a few songs. When the UK shows finished we arrived in Madrid on Monday 3rd May. We played a couple of shows in Spain and then on to Germany by 8th May until the 11th, on to Belgium then back to Germany and on to Zurich, Switzerland. After Zurich we went back to the UK, Scotland to be precise. Stayed for a couple of days then went to Norway 19th May and then to Sweden where we played Rockland in Sala then next day to catch the ferry in Stockholm to play The Silja Rock Cruise.

I was surprised and pleased to find that Kate was at Silja Rock. I think it was Paul Newcomb who had invited her along to help with the tour merchandise for Leslie and me and also on board was ex UFO keys player Danny Peyronel who was appearing with his new band. I had played the Silja Rock Cruise before with Stray and is a lot of fun a great atmosphere and strange as it may seem after a while you forget you are on board a ship. For me, this was a complete break, a complete get away from normal life. My marriage was now on shaky ground, dad had passed away the year before, mum had dementia and was still living at home with a part time carer and along with Aunt May and Norman we were trying our best to look after her as she needed 24 hour care!

I knew I had to make some important decisions but right now I had to get on with the job in hand and play the shows. Kate turned out to be a good listener as I probably bent her ear as well as getting it bent from Paul who was also having some personal problems himself at this time. What a pair we were, but Kate had time for both of us. We spoke for hours before and after the shows but little did I know that she was also having some problems too although she never let on and she appeared to have time for me. In fact, when the tour finished I had some solo shows in the UK and I was travelling completely alone and Kate turned up at a couple of shows to help with my merchandise. She is another one of those lovely people who I am pleased to call a friend.

Anyway back to the tour. I didn't realise until shortly before the first show abroad, if when I did my solo spot the audiences would know what I was talking about, because I was telling stories about the songs and anything else that would come into my head. I had to change my patter a little bit but all in all the European shows went very well.

I was pleasantly surprised at the reaction at some of the venues. I remember playing in Zurich and my set went very well indeed. Leslie played his set and the promoter of the club wanted him to play some more, but Leslie wasn't interested. So they asked Paul to ask me if I would play some more. Me being me, I did and the second set went down better than the first and the first went well. I made a few friends in Zurich that's for sure.

Another one which I remember was The Downtown Blues Club in Hamburg. Leslie got to a point where he wouldn't always turn up for a sound check in the afternoon and that day was no exception. So I sound checked my equipment and sound checked, as best I could, Leslie's equipment. When this was done I happened to be sitting on the front of the stage when a couple of guys arrived with cameras, equipment and microphones. One of the guys came up to me and said hello and said he was there to do an interview. We had a brief chat and then I said that I'm really sorry but Leslie wouldn't be at the venue until later, early evening maybe?

To my surprise he said that it was okay and that it was me they had come to interview! Well that was a surprise. I didn't expect that and in retrospect it was as well Leslie wasn't there because I doubt if he would have been impressed. Another thing happened at that show was some on stage shenanigans. By this part of the European dates, Todd had to go back to play some shows back home in the USA, so when it came to the second set I played most of it as a duo with Leslie. Leslie could be unpredictable at times. One moment he could be a real joy and then the next moment the devil would take over. Having now known Leslie for a few years I was quite used to these mood swings and I think I am probably one of the few people who have ever talked back at him or challenged him on something.

I will stand my ground if I don't necessarily agree with something. I probably got that off of my dad as well as other things. This particular evening was Les at his worst. I was playing guitar along with him and then one moment he would call out "Turn up, turn up", so I would turn up. Then it would be "Turn down, turn down". After a while I felt like I was going back and forth to the volume controls so often it was like my braces were caught on the amplifier. When we came off stage and into the dressing room, there was no shouting but Leslie started having a go at me about what I was doing on stage. I politely told him that he should make up his mind what he wanted from me. I can't be both too quiet and or too loud. If he had arrived for a sound check that would have been sorted. I could feel the tension rising in the room as was my temperature. I don't lose my temperature very often but when I do, I blow!

Sensing that my fuse was now burning short, I said something like "Look Les, I'm not going to stand here and talk to you anymore about this. I'm going out front and I'm going leave you alone for a while". I left the dressing room... closing the door firmly behind me! As it was the end of the show there were a lot of people queuing up at the merchandising desk and t-shirts and CDs were literally flying out of the door. Merchandise sales for me were very good that night. I think it may have been the club owner who passed comment to Paul and I that it was a good job Leslie didn't come out of the dressing room as he might have been even more pissed off with how well I was doing.

We played some shows in Scotland and at that time Paul owned a nice house in Stevenston not far from Saltcoats. We stayed over for a couple of days and one day Paul said go into the lounge, Les wants to have a word with you about a song. Les told him he had an idea for a song and couldn't finish it. Paul said, "Why don't you have a word with Del, he writes songs". So I went in and Les was sitting on the settee with a guitar on his lap. "Del" he said "I've had this idea for a song for ages and I'm really stuck, if I play you something... well anyway see what you think?"

Almost without any coaxing, he began to tell me what he wanted the song to be about. I was really struck on how he was letting me into a piece of his personal life. Probably telling me things he had never told anybody. For the first time he seemed quite sad and vulnerable and I still feel very honoured how he opened up and trusted me and wanted me to write a very special song with him. He told me about his life and how he got really addicted to drugs, cocaine and heroin. Despite the drugs and the fame and fortune, he felt he was looking for something but not exactly what. I am no psychologist, but the more the drugs get in the system it takes hold and the dependency just confuses the mind. He said it wasn't until he was off of the drugs and he became clean, that he could see things much clearer. Basically he was searching for something in life that he thought the drugs would help him find. I was really inspired by what he told me and although I have never really indulged in drug use personally, what he said really came home to me.

I was inspired and I started to write. I grabbed my guitar and as I wrote a line, I sang it back for his approval. Les became excited and his tone changed. I called out a line I had written and he'd shout "Yeh". I'd come up with another line and he shout "Yeh" and so on. I suggested a couple of chord changes here and there. He wanted this little break in the middle for a guitar solo and I suggested why don't you sing the line first and then repeat it with the guitar breaks? It seemed like the song was complete and written in no time at all. He had inspired me and I'd like to think that I had inspired him. With the song finished he called out "Paul, Paul listen to the new song". Paul came in from the kitchen and we played the song back. Leslie looked so happy and I think from that moment he saw me in a different light.

It was a few years before he actually recorded the song, but he did and it featured on his album *Unusual Subjects* and our song was 'To the Moon'. Also on the album were guests like Joe Bonamassa, Zakk Wilde, Billy Gibbons, Steve Lukather, Slash and some English songwriter called Del Bromham.

This was a very proud moment for me and if you would have told this young

18-year-old back in 1970 when I first heard Mountain that one day I would write a song for and with Leslie West, it would have only been a dream. Proof dreams can come true.

His album received some very good reviews and 'To The Moon' was singled out by a couple of journalists. One I recall wrote something to the effect of 'To The Moon' sounds like it could have been co-written by someone like Jack Bruce as it sounded quite British, different to the rest of the songs. That also was a compliment.

I had played a couple of tours with Leslie with Mountain and consequently I got to know the legendary drummer Corky Laing. A great drummer and a great showman also, sometimes to Leslie's annoyance as Corky did this trick where he fired a drumstick which rebounded off of the cymbal over the stage and into the audience. Except on more than one occasion the drumstick went low and almost hit Leslie on the back of the head. Standing side stage, even above the sound of the band you could hear Leslie's voice cry out to the drummer 'Cork!' Together they were a funny pair. They were always bickering about something like old women. Usually something with a financial connection, like the merchandise money as I remember them having words about backstage at a show in Sheffield. It shouldn't have been, but it was very funny watching and listening to them. "Ah, you're a Shmuck" said Corky to Leslie. "Ah, you're a Putz" replied Leslie and so on, hurling abuse at each other with words you don't hear in this country, only on old American New York based gangster movies. I have to point out though, that these two guys had known each other for literally a lifetime and despite how it looked on the surface I know they loved each other. Corky will tell you the same thing I know.

The last time they came over on tour I drove up to Leicester to see Mountain play. Annie came with me along with two friends John Lucas and Mark Proctor. Mark was a big fan of Mountain and Leslie West in particular, so I was looking forward to getting him to see his musical heroes. Speaking of heroes, while I was on tour solo with Leslie, we were sitting backstage one night at a venue in Swansea and we were talking about our musical heroes. It transpired we were both big fans of Steve Winwood and during the course of the conversation I started playing and singing the song Steve wrote in Blind Faith titled 'Can't Find My Way Home'. "Hey you sound just like Winwood" shouted Leslie, "We've gotta do that song, we are going to do it tonight" declared Leslie. "Tonight. You wanna do it tonight?" I said. "Yeh, we'll do it in my set. I'll tell you when" he said. So we played it later that evening and it stayed in the set for the rest of that tour.

Anyway back to the night in Leicester, to my surprise Leslie called me up on stage. Leslie didn't ask me, he told me (as only he did) I was going to play and sing 'Can't Find My Way Home' with Mountain. No-one has ever done that. A proud moment for me and probably for Annie, John and Mark. Since that tour I have occasionally included that song in my solo shows.

Back to Corky, he contacted me a few years ago and said that he wanted to go on tour and asked me if I would sing and play guitar for him. I didn't expect that! I mean this was Corky Laing for fuck's sake, asking me to form a band with him. A huge compliment, but I was busy touring with Stray and with my own solo shows so I had to say no. Some would say I was mad to turn that down but I've always believed that Stray comes first. Now if you would have told me all that years ago that... Ah well you know the rest.

When the tour with Leslie finished I played a few solo shows around the UK was expecting to continue touring solo in both the UK and Europe, but the agency I was with didn't come up with the shows as expected. Also Paul was having some personal problems of his own and had to deal with his own issues. Combined with my marital situation and the lack of income, this was one of the worst times of my life.

John Bootle and Paul Watson had decided that they no longer wanted to play with me in Stray. I put together a band line up of The Blues Devils with Karl Randall on drums, Dean Rees on Hammond organ and piano and not being able to find a bass player at that time, my friend and guitarist Tony Rolfe stepped in for a while. I was starting to smile again, but there was much more to come as this decade rolled on.

# 33.

# The Bedford Crew

**B**y 2005 Jackie and I had split up and quite honestly after much toing and froing on my part, I moved to Olney where Annie and her two sons Alex and Michael lived. It was (and is) a lovely little town which has plenty of history. William Cowper once lived in Olney and was famous for writing the lyrics of 'Amazing Grace'.

From my new base over the next few years the three-piece line-up of Stray which was Stu Uren, Karl Randall and myself, were playing a lot of shows up and down the country and without an agent or manager. I did manage to get the shows coming in and we had some busy fun times. Annie and Stu's partner Linny, used to come along with us on most gigs and started to become as well-known as the band, selling the merchandise. Annie and Linny became known as The Merch Maidens and I would imagine being a bloke myself it would have given someone the incentive to go over to the merch desk and buy something and have a chat.

Also around this time Peter Perks was often at the shows driving the bus, setting up my guitar gear or helping out with the merchandising. He was a big fella and an ex-wrestler, so I can't imagine anyone would want to muck around with him unless you carried a handbag with a brick in it! Back in the seventies during his wrestling, Peter reckoned that the women were more dangerous than his competitors. As he was leaving the ring, he would often get a clump from an irate female and quite often a slap with a handbag, hence my comment about a handbag with a brick in it.

For a while, when available, Dick Hammond came back as my guitar technician. I don't think Tony McPhee will mind me saying, but we played quite a few shows with Tony's Groundhogs and he seemed to be having persistent problems with his equipment. The guitar pedal board in particular and on more than one occasion Dick fixed his gear for him.

I remember arriving early to sound check for a show we were playing with The Groundhogs at The Robin. Tony was up on stage, clearly having a problem with his pedal board again. Before he even got a chance to say hello to me, he said "Where's Dick?" I replied "He's not with us now, he is working with The Baron Knights". "Oh fuck! I wanted him to repair my pedal board!" exclaimed Tony. I can't remember, if he managed to get it to work or if he borrowed my pedal board, but as they say in show business, the show must go on and it did.

About twenty minutes away from Olney, is the shire town of Bedford. I have made some good friends here and they have always made me feel very welcome and part of the family. They all love their music and there are some good musicians and bands in the area. Much of the musical fraternity is based around a club called Esquires, a great venue and quite unusual in that it has three different sized venues all under one roof.

There is the large concert hall upstairs, a smaller room known as Holy Molys (now called Stage 2 I believe), which has a club atmosphere and the ground floor bar area known as Danny's Bar. All three venues host live music which is quite an achievement in this day and age. What I find to be truly wonderful is the love of music in the area and how everyone, whether they be fans of music or musicians, are so supportive of each other and indeed other musicians who come to perform from out of the area. I feel blessed that I have made some good friends there and always feel welcome whether I perform there or just go to see other acts play. Pete Burridge of Esquires is a real supporter of live music and works very hard.

I'm sitting here writing and I am trying to remember exactly how and when I met many of these people I want to talk about, but am finding it difficult to do so as it feels like I have always known them, not for a few years but for a lifetime.

I can remember playing a show at The Boom Boom Club, in Sutton with Stray when Pete Feenstra, the promoter told me that he had booked an act from (as he put it) "from up my way in Bedford", a girl singer named Cherry Lee Mewis, with her band.

The load in door behind the stage was still open and following our sound check I wandered outside to get some fresh air. As I stood in the car park a couple of cars pulled up and out got Cherry and her band members. One guy looked familiar and it wasn't until he opened his mouth and said "Hello Del" that I realised it was my old friend from Alibi. It was Robbie Stewart-Mathews and he looked so different now compared to when I had last seen him. His head was now shaved and he had a little goatee type beard.

As it transpired where he was once the lead singer and played guitar, he was now the bass player in The Cherry Lee Mewis Band. It was good to see him again. We both had the same sense of humour and if felt like we had never lost touch. We seemed to pick up where we left off so to speak.

Cherry and the band played their set and I thought they were very good. All excellent accomplished musicians. She had a young guy on drums called Flo, who in a funny kind of way reminded me of Karl, or rather if Karl had a younger brother he might look like Flo. Nick Slater was playing mainly slide/bottleneck guitar, Max Milligan on lead guitar, Robbie on bass with Cherry on vocals.

As the weeks and months went by, I am pleased to say like many of who I call The Bedford Crew became friends and I went to see Cherry and her band play on many occasions. They were all great musicians and Cherry had a fantastic voice and great stage presence. With her band they played a kind of mix of blues and country blues, but the more I saw and heard Cherry sing I sensed there was a lot more she was capable of.

I began recording *Nine Yards* at Rock Hard Studios in Milton Keynes on Monday 25th June 2012. I had recorded a song titled 'What Goes Around'. Karl played drums on this song as he did on all the other songs on the album. Karl is a great drummer but he does prefer playing along with a click track. I don't know why because he is like a human metronome. For this song I insisted that we just play together in the studio. I wanted the sound to be raw and live sounding. So we just went for it and it came out as I wanted it. I added bass to it and that was it, the backing track (almost) done with guitar bass and drums.

I said to my engineer and co-producer Nigel Hart that contrary to how I had first envisaged the song I could now imagine it being a duet, like a kind of conversation. I just had a feeling that Cherry would be the other voice I needed. As Robbie had a good voice and could play harmonica, I invited both Cherry and Rob to the studios in the evening of Monday 9th July. There was another song called 'Walking Down

The Road' which I wanted some backing vocals for, so the three of us stood around the microphone and that song was completed within a couple of takes.

When it came to 'What Goes Around', and bearing in mind Cherry had never heard the song before, I got Nigel to play the backing track back while I sang and explained to Cherry my vocal idea. It didn't take Cherry long to nail it. She had a run through to get used to the song and the phrasing and another run through to get the balance right in her headphones. Then she went for another go and she wasn't aware that Nigel had pressed the red record button. When the track finished I just thought "Wow that sounded great... Wait 'til she goes for one". A voice from the control room, Nigel said something like "Yeh that's great, I've got it". I had asked Robbie if he could bring his harmonicas along with him, so having heard the song coming together I asked him to play some blues harp along with the track and I think he did that in one take as well. I think they arrived at about 8pm and left by about 9:30. Not bad eh?

The *Nine Yards* album was eventually finished and released on Angel Air Records a really good company run by Peter Purnell. He was good to work with and seemed to be sympathetic and understanding towards musicians who he had represented in the past but often in a legal capacity. When I was initially approached by Angel Air, my musical friend John McCoy, a well-known bass guitarist, recommended Peter and Angel Air very highly, so that was good enough for me. As time went on, I decided to put my first solo album *The Devil's Highway* with Angel Air as well as the Stray album *Valhalla*.

Around this time, things in the Stray camp had quietened down somewhat and I had been doing quite a few shows solo acoustic. I had already played some Blues Devils shows as a three-piece line-up. I really wanted to play some shows in the same vein or replicating live much of what I had recorded on the *Nine Yards* album. I had been offered a few good shows and I thought it would be great to put a big line-up together to perform some shows.

I had become good friends with the band Pearl Handled Revolver. I've been trying to remember how and when we first met as it seems like I have known them forever also. According to keyboard player, Simon Rinaldo, he first saw me playing with Stray when we were both on the same bill for a charity concert, and in his words 'I was a bit of a fan'. Following that gig, I appeared with them solo at a couple of their shows and I also guested a few times on electric guitar. They have become one of my favourite bands and the nicest guys you could ever wish to meet. I already had Karl Randall for the drum seat, so I asked my old buddy Robbie Mathews if he fancied playing bass. From Pearl Handled Revolver I asked Andy Paris on guitar, Simon Rinaldo on keys and Lee Vernon on harmonica. I wanted to include the duet that I did with Cherry Lee Mewis, so I asked her if she fancied coming out to play a few shows with me and she accepted the invitation.

We didn't have that many rehearsals, but I think that added to the magic of the sound we were making. It was quite loose a bit like The Stones or The Allman Bros. I think I realised after the first show that Cherry was just too good to sing one duet and some backing vocals with me, so the next shows I featured her more. These were good times and although it was primarily my project we all seemed to be on the same page musically. For example, I sensed that Cherry was potentially more of a rock chick than what she had been seen as with her solo performances. I thought at the time there was no-one around like Janis Joplin. I had seen Cherry sing 'Mercedes Benz' in her set so I suggested we include that. I was thinking of Janis Joplin's 'Move Over', when Cherry phoned me and said "How do you fancy playing 'Move Over'?" I said yes great and that I was thinking the same thing.

A couple of weeks later I was thinking of the Rolling Stones song 'Gimme Shelter' and in particular the live version featuring Lisa Fischer which I thought would suit Cherry down to the ground. What do you know? Cherry phoned me again and said she loved Lisa's voice and would I fancy playing 'Gimme Shelter'. It was a definite yes from me, and it turned out to be a real show stopper and my thoughts about Cherry were confirmed.

Peter Purnell had released a Mott The Hoople CD which coincided with Ian Hunter reforming the band for a tour. Peter phoned me to tell me that I had been offered the chance to open for them at The Birmingham Symphony Hall. It was too good an opportunity not to do and fortunately all of my band members were available. So off we went with our happy 7-piece band and 3-road crew. Nigel, Dick and Martyn on the crew did a great job and fortunately had the truck with a full PA system on board, not that we used it, but what they did was prepare a second set of microphones and stands and used them in conjunction with the equipment which Mott's crew had on stage so that when there was a gear change over their sound and our sound wasn't changed.

There was a huge mixing desk at the back of the auditorium so Nigel had that under control. So much so that it was noticed by quite a few, including Mott's management that our sound was better than theirs, which must be credited to Nigel with Dick and Martyn doing a ridiculously quick changeover in less than twenty minutes! I think it was Dick who assisted the Symphony Hall's crew doing lighting for my show. However, when Mott the Hoople went on stage, the lighting cut out and they performed with just the house lights on for about twenty minutes. I believe it was Dick who helped get the lighting rig up and running again.

Before the show, we were hanging out backstage when coming towards me in the corridor outside the dressing rooms was a familiar figure. It was none other than Joe Elliott from Def Leppard. He called out my name and gave me a huge hug and a handshake. "Quick, has anyone got a camera? I must have a photo taken with Del Bromham!" shouted Joe which rather tickled my entourage. Joe was keen to tell me what a big fan of Stray he was and said something like "I can't go for more than a few weeks without a bit of Stray on my radio show". He was referring to his show on Planet Rock where I was aware he had played our records, certainly on more than one occasion. His favourite Stray tune, by the way is 'One Night In Texas'. He was/is also a huge Mott and Ian Hunter fan, so that was the other reason he turned up in Birmingham.

Over the next couple of years, I did two shows at The Cambridge Rock Festival. By the time I played the second CRF Festival, Stu Uren was back on bass. I think my favourite show was The Rock and Blues Festival at Butlins, Skegness in January 2015. The venue, which I think was The Reds Stage, was jam packed with people and the show went down a storm! I have to give a shout out to our friends who I call the Bedford crew who often go to the Butlins Rock and Blues shows and gave us their support on the night.

It is expensive enough these days on the road, but a 7-piece band and three road crew etc can be mighty expensive as my bank account will testify. However, I have to say that all the Blues Devils and crew were very generous with their time and I didn't go bankrupt at that time. Well not yet!

I still believed there was some mileage with a band featuring Cherry and me together, but obviously I didn't want it to interfere with her solo project or with Stray. Although there appeared to be a rise in blues bands and female singers, I could hear no-one that was doing what I thought Cherry was capable of doing. I had this idea of a musical project, somewhat rockier than The Blues Devils. I remembered back in the 1970s playing shows with bands like Stone the Crows which featured Maggie Bell and Vinegar Joe which featured Elkie Brooks. Both bands had rock and soul and I was not aware of anyone who was playing a show like that at that time.

I spoke to Don McKay at Rhino and a few other promoters and although we all thought it had great possibilities, unfortunately nothing came of that project due to time and money. Cherry was offered some good session work and a couple of tours which she would have been mad to turn down. As they say, "Never say never". Who knows what tomorrow may bring?

Pearl Handled Revolver went on to record more albums and play their own shows as did Cherry Lee Mewis and her Blues Gems.

# 34.
# Influential Artists

Writing this has made me think of a few other artistes I have met, some of whom had a profound effect on me.

On the 29th November 2001, I played one of my first solo acoustic shows opening for Tim Rose at The Standard in Walthamstow, London. I had first heard Tim Rose with his recording of 'Morning Dew' which was included in an early Stray set as well as my later recording it with Razorback (BRB). He had also recorded a version of 'Hey Joe' which of course was made famous by The Jimi Hendrix Experience.

Back in 1968 I bought a sampler album called *The Rock Machine Turns You On* featuring various artists one of which was Tim Rose. On this particular album was a song called 'Come Away Melinda' which was a song Stray also featured in one of our early sets. Once again if you had told me when I was a fifteen or so, I would be sharing the stage with Tim Rose, it would have been unimaginable.

I got on stage to play my set opening the show and guess who was sitting right down the front to watch me… Tim Rose himself! Well I must have played okay because he sat through the set and told me how much he enjoyed my songs. Of course I had to tell him about playing his songs with my band.

Saturday 15th March 2014, I played a show with The Pretty Things at The Cheese and Grain, Frome. Once again as I wrote in an earlier chapter, when I was about fourteen, I would listen to The Pretty Things album at Alan Golding's house and once again one of their songs featured in an early Stray set.

I still get a buzz when I meet people like this and I hope I never lose that feeling. Being a fan is a great thing to be. The first Pretty Thing I met was the original guitarist Dick Taylor and what a nice chap he was. Very soon he was quick and keen to show me this really old guitar which he had been using for years. I was so blown away that he wanted to show me this so early in our meeting. I can't even remember the name or make of the guitar. Then I met Phil May, the lead singer. Amazing really that Phil and Dick had been performing since the early sixties and still sounding good. I stood side stage with Phil and told him that I was really pleased to meet him after all these years. He was really chuffed when I told him my band used to play one of their songs called 'Get The Picture'. I started to sing the chorus "I ain't gonna quit yer (you)"and Phil joined in with me on the line "get the picture". We both really laughed and then he was off to play his set on stage. It didn't matter that they didn't play "Get The Picture" because he had already sung it… with me! If I could go back in time and tell that fourteen-year-old Del Bromham, one day he'd meet The Pretty Things and sing along with Phil May, well you know the rest.

One of my favourite little venues to play in the early 2000s was Pam's Bar at Brentwood in Essex. The venue was run by two lovely people Pam and her husband

Mike. Pam's dad also lived with them and he was an ex-serviceman, probably about the same age as my dad was at the time and he reminded me a bit of dad. I could certainly imagine them being mates and telling a tale or two. He had a big, grey parrot and every time Pam's dad went out, Pam would go in and teach the parrot a swear word or three! Her dad couldn't understand why his parrot suddenly started swearing as her dad never swore in front of the parrot.

Our dressing room was in fact the kitchen next door to her dad's room. One evening when I was there I noticed the door was slightly open and the light was off, but not far from the door I could see the parrot's cage with a cloth draped over it. I crept towards the cage and put my head down so I was looking up at the cage under the cloth to see if I could see the parrot. As I looked up, the parrot appeared to be hanging upside down and the cheeky git told me to "fuck off!"

Anyway during this particular gig, I couldn't help but notice two big guys standing in the audience and one was wearing a cowboy hat. At the end of the show they came over to me. The guy in the hat introduced himself as Peter Barton who runs RAM (Rock Artists Management). He had heard good things about me and happened to be down near Essex and decided to come and check me out. He was very complimentary and told me that I was the closest thing he had seen to Jimi Hendrix for some time. He was managing Noel Redding the original bass player of The Jimi Hendrix Experience and he had been offered some really good money for a Noel Redding Experience to play in Japan and the USA and would I be interested in playing guitar with Noel? Well that was a daft question, but anyway he wanted to talk again later in the week but in the meantime he gave me Noel's telephone number and asked me to ring him.

"You want me to ring him" I said. "Yeh, he replied, I am having trouble trying to persuade him to do the shows and if you talk to him he might change his mind". Within a day or two I decided to ring his number and sure enough on the other end of the line was Mr Noel Redding. Here was another case of, blimey I'm actually talking to someone who was in The Jimi Hendrix Experience. I told him who I was and that Peter Barton had told me to call. He was chatting away for a while about nothing in particular. Very casual sort of chat like I'd known him for years. It was me who actually got around to talk to him about putting the band together to do these fantastic sounding shows Peter had told me about. I said I would really look forward to playing as I grew up on The Experience albums and I knew most of the songs. To my amazement his voice changed and he started coming out with statements like "I don't really want to play those old songs again. I want to do something new. I'm fed up with playing that stuff".

I couldn't believe it. He was in one of the biggest bands in the world for less than three years and he was fed up with playing that stuff! No wonder Peter Barton wanted me to talk to him. I would have thought Noel would have jumped at a chance to re-launch his career and earn excellent money in the process by doing these shows. He could have played a few audience pleasers and then introduced some new material if he'd had any sense. I was clearly getting no feedback from Noel at all. So reluctantly I said my goodbyes and told him he should have a chat with Peter and that you know where I am if you want to do something.

I telephoned Peter the next day and told him about the conversation I'd had with him and left it at that. It was probably a couple of years later that I crossed paths with Noel again, at Butlins Rock and Blues Festival, Skegness. There was Noel, Eric Bell (ex-Thin Lizzy) and John Coghlan (ex-Status Quo) were also on the bill. I popped backstage to the dressing room and said hello to Eric and John but Noel didn't say much at all, even less than he said on the phone to me. In fact, if I'm not mistaken it may well have been the amount of alcohol being consumed in the room that contributed to the speech impediment. It certainly seemed that way because when they went on stage it was a bit of a shambles. As the first song started, Noel turned around and knocked his microphone stand over. Quite clearly Eric and Noel had not tuned up together as Noel's bass was flat to Eric's guitar, so they stopped tuned up and started again. They played a couple of songs and I had to leave mid-way through their version of 'Stone Free'. I am sorry, but this was no way I wanted to remember my heroes. Not surprisingly, this band were not going to last and both John and Eric went off to form their own bands. Sadly, Noel died in 2003 with complications caused by cirrhosis of the liver. Clearly a man who had his problems.

I have been trying to remember the first time I saw Terry Reid or even how I heard about him in the first place. There were so many concerts and gigs in London around 1969/70. You could go into town any night of the week and if there wasn't a club, there was a college or university putting on music. Quite often there were varied bills, something which you don't get so much these days. You could go along perhaps to see one artist and find yourself discovering another who normally you might not necessarily have gone to see. Maybe that's how I discovered Terry Reid?

The Marquee Club became a favourite of mine to see artists and bands play. I found the Marquee had a great atmosphere, full of history and it seemed to bring out the best performances in people even though it was a comparatively small venue. I remember the carpet in the bar area was always sticky, almost as if your shoes had Velcro stuck to the bottom of them. I also remember the manager, Jack Barrie, who always sat on a stool at the end of the bar as you turned left into the dressing room. He was perched in such a way that you had to physically brush passed him. We were young guys and I know he particularly liked our singer Steve Gadd.

It's funny, most touring musicians will tell you that you can go anywhere in the world and fans will ask you if you ever played The Marquee in London. Doesn't matter if you'd played The Albert Hall or Madison Square Gardens, The Marquee seems to have the most kudos if you've played it.

It was at The Marquee Club I have the best memories of seeing Terry Reid play. He played a few alternate Tuesdays as some artistes did at that time. What was unusual was that Terry had no bass guitarist. He stood centre stage with his drummer Keith Webb to his left and on the right Pete Solley playing Hammond organ and bass keyboard and pedals. Apart from having an incredible voice it was his charisma on stage which really captured me. It felt like he was actually singing to me. I don't think I had ever seen anyone who had that effect on me live on stage. I think I played his album which was out at that, *Superlungs* until I had almost worn it out!

I was really excited to hear that Stray were going to play a show with Terry at The Lincoln Drill Hall. When we arrived I was hoping to meet Terry, but to be honest I never saw him or his band all the time we were there. It was if they had shut themselves away in the dressing room. The only time I saw them was when they walked on stage. He had a different band to when I had last seen him play a couple of years earlier. Gone were the drummer and the keyboard player, replaced by a drummer and a bass guitarist. Gone too were some of those great songs I had seen him play a couple of years before and the set he played was very loose and lots of spaces for just jamming along on a couple of chords. If you see a clip of him on YouTube from *The Old Grey Whistle Test*, that I believe is the Terry line up I saw at The Drill Hall. It was loose but I enjoyed it although I would have liked to have heard some of those old songs and I noticed that his stage presence had changed and was concentrating more on his band mates rather than looking out into the audience, which is where I got the personal connection back in those Marquee days. I think he had Lee Miles on bass guitar and Conrad Isadore on drums and they were funky!

While at the show I literally bumped into DJ and *Old Grey Whistle Test* presenter Bob Harris. It was great to meet him as he was quite a celebrity at the time and any possible endorsement from him in print would have been quite something. What was very weird was when I spoke to him, because he was the same person off screen as he was on screen, it felt like I was being interviewed on *The Old Grey Whistle Test*. Sadly, we never got to play *The Old Grey Whistle Test*, which was another bone of contention because we could see all the other bands on the scene at that time on there, but not Stray. Having only ever made one TV appearance on *Disco 2* it's even more disappointing that the tapes were wiped!

Terry Reid went on to live in the USA and has made some fine albums over the years. In May 2015 I somehow managed to be offered the UK tour dates with Terry Reid playing solo acoustic. I was really looking forward at last to meeting one of my musical heroes. I first met him at a venue called The Touchline, run by my friends Dave Kitteridge and his partner Trudy. A really lovely couple who were really dedicated to music and really looked after the acts they had at their venue.

Terry arrived dressed in a sailor's hat, collar and tie and looked like he'd just got off of his yacht, not out of a car. I think it was fair to say we hit it off right away and we had lots of laughs throughout the tour. When I spoke to him again on a few occasions he was still telling me the jokes I told him on that tour.

The highlight though was during his performance in a club up in Hebden Bridge. He had taken a fancy to one of my guitars, an old Aria acoustic. He asked if he could borrow it for a couple of days and when I got it back he had restrung it and set it up for me. He's not a bad guitar tech either! He decided to use my Aria for a couple of songs in his set. I was sitting in the audience with his wife Annette when I noticed halfway through one of his songs, his version of the Beach Boys song 'Don't Worry Baby', the guitar strap had slipped off and he was holding it up while playing it at the same time. That has happened to me on more than one occasion! Quite clearly no-one saw it, so I ran on to the stage trying to be as discreet as possible, slid along behind him and while he was playing secured the guitar strap back on.

As I am about to walk away, he turned and whispered, "Stay there". Moments later I found myself singing vocal harmony with him. I was his Graham Nash for the song, as I know he is friends with Graham and they have often sung together. Terry and I sang together again when we did a radio show up in Glasgow.

So if you had told me back in 1970 that one day that this 18-year-old would be singing with Terry Reid... well you know the rest!

Another thing is that when you speak to Terry, he has some great stories. He is not a name dropper but names like Graham Nash and Joni Mitchell crop up. Keith Richard and Joe Walsh often pop up in conversation. Which made me wonder if I had made that move to L.A. like I'd mentioned in an earlier chapter, how different my life might have been?

I mentioned earlier that one of the best live bands I had seen back in the late sixties was 'Spooky Tooth'. Their bass guitarist was Greg Ridley. A great player with a unique style and a pretty good vocalist too. As it transpired my soon to be drummer Karl Randall was playing in the Greg Ridley band along with another friend of my Dean Rees on Hammond organ. They had been playing shows when unfortunately, Greg developed pneumonia and subsequently passed away on the 19th November 2003.

In 2004 Dean put a band together and asked if I would sing and play guitar for a memorial show for Greg, which I did. There were a few other acts and friends of Greg who got up to play at The O2 in London. After I had played my set, I was in the small dressing room to the side of the stage, when the door burst open and two guys literally fell in to the room, when one of them said "Hi Del, nice set" and the other guy, sounding really excited said something like "Yeh, that was amazing. How did you learn to play guitar like that?".

To my amazement, I suddenly realised who was paying me this compliment. It was none other than the Mott The Hoople but more importantly for me Spooky Tooth, guitarist Luther Grosvenor (aka Ariel Bender). My immediate reply to his great compliment to me was, "Watching people like you". I loved his work in Spooky Tooth and to have your musical heroes appreciate your playing is a wonderful feeling. I am pleased to say since then Luther and I have kept in touch. Now if you had told me when I was seventeen... ah you know the rest by now!

****

While I was on tour in Europe in 2003 with Stray supporting Iron Maiden we played a big festival in Albecete, Spain. Also on the bill were Motörhead. Lemmy is synonymous with Motörhead. He was originally bassist with Hawkwind, although prior to Lemmy joining them, either 1969 or early 1970, Hawkwind opened for Stray at a club somewhere in London. I can't remember the venue, but I do remember that there were not many people in the audience.

However, by 1972 with Lemmy on board, they had the hit single 'Silver Machine' which Lemmy also sang. He was fired from Hawkwind in 1975 and formed Motörhead. He was also working for John Curd as the stage manager at The Roundhouse, which is where I got to know him.

Anyway, I was in the bar of the hotel when I met the other members of Motörhead Mikkey Dee (drummer) and Phil Campbell (guitar). They were sitting up at the bar and while we were having a chat more people began to gather and the talk got louder. Phil who looked over and said, "Oh it's Lemmy, he's here". Lemmy began to make his way through the small crowd which had assembled and I thought he looked a bit uncomfortable. It seemed to me as an observer, everyone wanted to get his attention and talk to him, which I suppose he was used to, but I'm sure all he wanted to do was come down and have a quiet drink before the show. I sensed that he was looking around to see if there was someone there he knew, maybe Mikkey or Phil. He saw me and pushed his way out of the little crowd and said in a loud voice "Del... fuck me I ain't seen you for years. What are you doing here?" I told him I was staying at the hotel and was playing the festival.

"Ah great, we'll have to try and meet up later" he said. Unfortunately, we didn't meet up later. Come Christmas 2015, I received a phone call that Lemmy had died on Christmas Eve. I had arranged with my friends Leslie and Nigel Moore to meet up with him. Nigel was in contact with Lemmy who was due to come over to the UK and we were to meet up with him in London in March 2016. Sadly, it wasn't to be.

Another project that wasn't to be happened! In 2004 I got a phone call out of the blue one evening from Dave Holland, drummer with Judas Priest and Trapeze. Trapeze were a great three-piece band who Stray once played on the same bill with at the famous Mothers Club in Birmingham. Trapeze were from the Birmingham area. Dave Holland on drums, Mel Galley on guitar and vocals and Glenn Hughes on bass and vocals (who also played with Deep Purple). Mel Galley telephoned me when I played a show at The Tackeroo, Cannock in 2008 near where he lived. He had planned to come along, but apologised as he was unwell. I didn't realise how unwell he was. Some weeks later he sadly passed away with oesophageal cancer!

Anyway back to 2004, Dave Holland told me that he was now living not too far from me in a village called Stoke Bruerne and told me that Trapeze had been offered some great deals and the opportunity to reform the band. Mel Galley had injured his hand in an accident and was unable to play the guitar so consequently they needed a guitarist. Was I interested? Of course I was. Trapeze were a great band and Glenn Hughes has an incredible voice and is a bit handy on the bass too! So I was now awaiting an update as to if and when this might happen. Then the totally unexpected happened. Dave phoned me and said that he was giving private drum tuition at his home and one student had accused him of a sexual assault. He told me in his words what had supposedly occurred and he thought that nothing would come of it as he stated he had done nothing wrong and the student was making a false accusation. How wrong he was. He was found guilty at Northampton Crown Court and was sentenced to eight years in prison! He served six years and moved to Spain where he died in 2018 from liver cancer.

Finally, I have to mention Gary Moore. If my memory serves me correctly, the first time I met Gary was on the 8th April 1971. We were playing at The Mayfair Ballroom, Newcastle Upon Tyne. I was looking forward to this show as usual as it was always a good venue to play and the audiences were always appreciative. I was also interested to see another act who were due to be on the bill, the duo Hardin and York. Pete York was the drummer of The Spencer Davis Group and Eddie Hardin was brought in to replace Stevie Winwood who had left to form Traffic. Hardin and York at this time were not with Spencer Davis and it was unusual to see a duo with just drums and Hammond Organ (no guitar or bass guitar), so I was fascinated to see and hear them. There was a third band on the bill that night and if I am not mistaken I think they were added quite late in the day because I don't think they were advertised much, prior to the show. They were called Skid Row, not to be mistaken for the American band of the same name who were formed some years later. This Skid Row were three guys from Ireland. Brush Shiels on bass, Noel Bridgeman on drums and Gary Moore on guitar.

My first sighting of Gary was when I was standing up on the balcony area looking down to see this young guy, long hair, wearing a white Indian shirt, carrying a 4 x 12 speaker cabinet on his own. I think there were just the three of them, no roadies to help. After a while when all the three acts equipment was its in place on the stage, I was in the dressing room, when the door opened and in walked Gary. He introduced himself and asked if he could have a go on my Gibson Firebird. If you have seen Gary play, then for want of a better description, he always looks very animated when he plays. Well I can tell you that this is not an act. He picked up my guitar and began to play it. It was not plugged in, he just tuned right into it and off he went! To be honest, momentarily I thought he was about to have a fit. He was no more than a couple of feet from me and the face was gurning, his head was flying back with his body motioning to every movement his hands were playing on the guitar. He scared me for a moment. When I had got over the initial shock, I could not believe how good this guy was on the guitar.

Judging by the date of the show we would have been nineteen. Being a few months younger than me, Gary would have had his nineteenth birthday about four days before this show. I was looking forward to seeing him and Skid Row play. They went on first and I watched their set. I was totally mesmerised by Gary. He was the best guitarist I had ever seen. How did he get that sound and how did he make it look so easy? The worst part was that I had to follow him. Although as I have said before, I was never that confident as the guitarist, but having to follow Gary on stage, particularly when you are that age, was quite something and I don't think the word competition had ever entered my head before.

Actually, there was no competition, he was a far better guitarist than me, but it's funny, once I had walked on stage and locked into my band, I just did what I do and the audience at The Mayfair loved every minute of it. I didn't see Gary for some time after that show and he went on to do great things both with Thin Lizzy and as a solo artist, but our paths did cross from time to time and I got to meet up with him a few times, mainly in London.

The last time I saw him was when I went to The Shepherd's Bush Empire on the 18th September 2010 to see Robin Trower. I decided to go upstairs to the bar area. First of all, I saw Eric Bell and standing with him was Gary. Gary was looking over the balcony so he didn't see me walk up to Eric and I didn't realise it was Gary standing next to him. He turned around, saw me with Eric and said in his lovely soft Irish accent "It's Del".

It was a few years since I had seen him at Morgan Studios with Chris Tsangarides and I'm pleased to say that fame had not gone to his head and he was still the same guy I had met first of all back in 1971. Sadly, as we know, Gary passed away six months later on the 6th February 2011, from a heart attack while in Spain.

Speaking of Chris Tsangarides, he also passed away, on 6th January 2018, he had worked with Gary and got to know him very well. While I was working on the *Valhalla* album back in 2009 we had talked about maybe one day Chris, Gary and I could have recorded something together at his studio in Deal in Kent.

Chris was heartbroken when Gary died and I was equally shocked when I heard of Chris's passing as I had only spoken to him on the phone a short while before and we were talking about making another album together. Sadly, none of this can ever happen. We have lost not only one of the best record producers but one of the best guitarists we are ever likely to have.

# 35.
# Maiden And Me

**A**nyone who knows me knows that I like a joke or two and fortunately most of my mates have the same sense of humour. One practical joke was to phone someone up with a silly voice pretending you were someone calling from some company or other.

One evening I was sitting at home, the phone rings and Jackie answered and then with her hand cupped over the mouth piece she said "There's a Steve Harris, from Iron Maiden on the phone and wonders if he could have a word with you?"

I thought to myself, yeh, of course it is. It's bound to be one of my mates mucking about! So I grabbed the phone and with a loud voice I said "Whaaat?".

"Hi Del, it's Steve Harris, how are you?" said the voice (or something like that). It certainly was Steve Harris and I apologised for my greeting.

Turned out he was a big fan of Stray and before Iron Maiden he often used to come and see the band play and had all the albums. Unfortunately, he wasn't asking me to join the band on guitar but wanted to know if it was okay for Iron Maiden to record 'All In Your Mind'. They were going to put it on the B-side of their next single 'Holy Smoke'. He sounded like a really nice guy on the phone not the usual rock star vibe from him at all, unlike some lesser known musicians there are around!

Having finished our conversation, I thought how good it was to have a conversation like that with someone from a band with such huge status. I tried not to think too much about it and kept it pretty much to myself because things don't always happen or go to plan in the music business and it's quite easy to say things and then they don't happen so you end up with egg on your face (or in the music business, probably custard pie).

Some months went by and then sure enough in September 1990, Iron Maiden released their single 'Holy Smoke' and on the B-side was 'All In Your Mind' and 'Kill Me, ce soir' a song originally by Golden Earring.

I later found out that both Stray and Golden Earring were two of Steve's favourite bands. Of course any Maiden fan will know that Steve's other favourite band is UFO and before every Maiden show they play 'Doctor Doctor' over the PA. to get the audience in the mood.

'Holy Smoke' went straight to number one in the singles charts and that was a proud moment for me and I knew some of the 'Maiden' fans would now want to know who this band Stray were and why they had chosen to record one of their songs when they must have had plenty of their own.

About a week after the release of 'Holy Smoke' they played a warm-up gig on September 19th at The Woughton Centre in Milton Keynes, billed as The Holy Smokers, but everyone knew who it really was. Steve phoned and invited me along to see the band and to meet him for the first time.

This was the first show that new guitarist Janick Gers had played and he was flying around like a wirling dervish on that stage which wasn't that big as their equipment had taken up a fair bit of room. As it turns out, Janick still leaps around like a man possessed but a great guitarist and showman nevertheless.

After their show I waited in the hospitality area put by and Steve came out on his own.

We shook hands and I said "I enjoyed the gig. How was it for you?"

"It was okay, but I felt a bit nervous" said Steve.

"I'm not surprised as it was your first gig with a new guitarist" I replied.

"No, I wasn't nervous about playing. I felt nervous because I knew you were in the audience," said Steve.

I didn't know what to say. It is a real compliment actually to be told something like that from someone like him. I think I am a pretty good judge of character and I sensed we could have a laugh given the opportunity.

"I thought your new guitarist, Janick did well tonight" I said.

"Yes he's good, working out well" replied Steve.

"I didn't know you were looking for a new guitarist. You could have asked me" said I (partly joking but partly serious).

"I would have done, but I didn't know how to get hold of you at the time" said Steve.

I think he got out of that one quite tactfully, bless him. Since that meeting we have kept in touch fairly regularly and I consider him to be a good friend.

A couple of years later I was going on holiday to Portugal and Steve said that he had a place there and was going to be there the same time as me and I should call him and we could visit him at his house in Santa Barbara de Nexe, where incidentally he also owned a place called Eddie's Bar.

When we got to Portugal, we arranged a day to visit Steve and his family. He suggested that we wait at a particular point in the nearby town, he would then show us to his place because he said we might not find it without directions.

My daughters were still very young and as we waited for Steve to meet us they were standing there guessing what expensive car our new rock star friend was going to meet us in?

"A Mercedes" said one, "A Porsche" said the other followed by a selection of the finest sports cars money can buy. It was around midday and the quiet was awoken by the sound of an old white single axle Transit rattling down the road into town. "There's Steve" I said.

The looks on Zoe and Jodie's faces were a picture. We arrived at the house and we met his then wife Lorraine, young daughter Lauren and baby son George. Also there was Ross Halfin the photographer, which was the first time we had met. We were all sitting around the pool when baby George cried out in pain. He had been stung by a bee!

Steve leapt up ran in doors and then moments later came running back out with a knife in his hands! I thought blimey he's not going to cut the baby's arm off is he? He held George's arm and with the flat edge of the knife blade, pushed the sting out. Well you learn something new every day.

Later, I happened to be looking down from the patio and pool area to a tennis court down on another level below. Steve came over and I commented how nice the court looked.

"Yes I've just had it finished" he said.

"I used to like playing tennis" I said.

"Oh, do you fancy a game?" asked Steve.

"Well, I haven't played for years" I replied "But okay then".

"Hang on, I'll be back in a minute" and off Steve trotted to the house.

Soon, Steve returned with new tennis rackets and wrist bands all still in their wrappers. I thought to myself, me and my big mouth, I'll probably make a right idiot of myself here. So we strolled down the steps to his tennis court.
When I got on the court, it looked bigger than I remembered.

When you get to know Steve he likes to do everything properly and I think he thought in his head he was on Centre Court Wimbledon. Whereas, I was on the tennis court in Wormholt Park opposite my old school in Shepherd Bush. He had a little spectators box to the side of the court near where an Umpire might sit, so friends and family were there to watch. I found I could barely hit a ball back at him because he was a seriously good player. Ross Halfin was sitting in the spectators' box and I called out to him to see if he fancied giving Steve a game. He said he would but he didn't really play Tennis but had played Squash, but he would give it a go. So I handed him my racket and to be honest he did much better than I did.

All was not lost though, our friends Brenda and Keith were with us with their two sons Chris and Simon. Chris as a teenager was having tennis coaching at his school and was pretty good. Just how good he was I never realised, not until I saw him give Steve a game. I think we were all surprised just how good he was playing against Steve. At least Steve got a decent game of tennis that day. When I was watching, I turned to Steve's wife Lorraine and said how embarrassed I felt hardly managing to get the ball back over the net and not being able to give Steve a proper game. To which she replied something to the effect of "Oh don't be silly, don't worry about it. He could have been a tennis player and anyway he normally plays with his two friends Pat Cash and John McEnroe" she explained. I think it made me feel a little better after that, not a lot, but a little.

I know Steve could have been a footballer too. He took up the bass and decided to play in a band instead. He'll never get anywhere playing in a band, if you ask me!

In the evening we all went out for a meal. There must have been at least 15 of us when we arrived at the restaurant on this lovely evening. The restaurant looked full and I could see no free tables and he hadn't booked. He knew the manager and as soon as we walked in, the manager came walking over waving, "Steve, Steve, lovely to see you. How many"? Steve pointed at our little entourage and the manager turned and walked towards this very long table which appeared to have a few local old boys sitting there drinking beer. He quite literally threw them off of the table to make way for Steve and his party. To see these old boys scatter, was quite a sight to behold.

Back home in the UK sometime later he invited Jackie and I to a party at his house. It was fancy dress. Jackie went in the Roman or Greek style toga and I, to compliment her dress, went as Hitler, but more in the style of Freddie Starr with long shorts and Wellington boots with Swastikas painted on the sides.

Steve, not surprisingly, looked immaculate in a Roman Centurions outfit and looked like he'd just come off of the set of Ben-Hur. I must admit I am ashamed to say I quite got into being Hitler for the night. It just got a bit complicated when I saw two other male guests dressed as Rabbi's and I had a replica Luger pistol in a holster which fired like a real gun, so you can imagine who my targets were. Politically incorrect but we all had a laugh and like it was some kind of Carry On film, actually more akin to a Mel Brooks script. Fortunately, no blood was spilled in the process.

****

Over the years Steve had often said in conversation it would be great if Stray could play a couple of shows with Iron Maiden. Obviously I thought that would be great and although I always hoped, I never truly believed that it would happen. Then one day, out of the blue, Steve phoned me. He said something to the effect of "Hi Del, I've got a couple of gigs for you. Have you got a pen and paper handy?" This sort of thing doesn't happen, does it?

So I grabbed a pen and paper and he said:

"Friday 23rd May, Coliseum Sports Palace Arena, La Coruna, Spain"

"Saturday 24th Gijon Sports Palace, Spain"

"Oh, great Steve, thank you" I said.

"Hang on, I haven't finished yet" said Steve.

"Monday 26th Le Zenith, Toulouse France"

"Tuesday 26th Le Zenith, Toulon France"

"I thought you said it was a couple of gigs" I asked.

"Well, there's a few more, okay?" said Steve.

"Okay, fire away" I said.

So Steve carried on.

"June 3 Spodek Stadium, Katowice, Poland

June 4 Kisstadion, Budapest, Hungary"

"Then July"

Wednesday 9th  Pavilhao Atlantico. Lisbon, Portugal

Friday 11th Esparrago Festival, Jerez, Spain

Saturday 12 Auditoria Municipal (Festival), Albacete, Spain".

I told Paul Newcomb of our good news but it was not definitely in the bag as it were, as we had to get a business plan together to present to Iron Maiden's office to prove and assure we would be able to do the tour without fear of us not being able to afford it midway through and pull out.

We had a date arranged at the offices of Sanctuary, Maiden's offices and met with Dickie Bell, who was their tour co-ordinator in Rod Smallwood's (Manager of Iron Maiden) office. Apologies to Dickie if that was not his official title. Paul had compiled a full business plan outlining our predicted expenditure in order to complete the selected tour dates.

After a general bit of chit chat with Dickie he asked if we thought we would definitely be able to afford the tour because they didn't want any band on their tours to drop out midway. Paul handed him the business plan file, which he had meticulously compiled.

Dickie took the file and proceeded to thumb through it. There was silence in the room. Every now and then Dickie would let out a noise like a "sigh" or an "oh!"

Dickie got up from the chair behind the large desk and wandered over to the door which led to the open plan office where a few of the others from Sanctuary Management were working at their desks. He opened the office door and called out to the staff, something like: "Here you should see this guys" along with some other complimentary remarks.

Dickie came back in and sat down at the desk, looked over at Paul and I and said, "I have to say, we have had some big bands in the past come along to try and get on an Iron Maiden tour, but this is the best tour plan I have ever seen. As far as I'm concerned you are on the tour".

Well as you can imagine Paul and I left the meeting feeling elated and I feeling very proud of the way Paul handled the business side of things. I think on the way to the train station we possibly or probably stopped off for a drink to celebrate. We then had to give the good news to the band and hope all of our plans and predictions would work.

The Stray line up for the tour, as it had been for the previous couple of years, was the three-piece line up with me John Bootle on Bass and vocals and Paul Watson on drums. Jay Stuart had been primarily Paul's drum tech for the past couple of years and I asked my good friend Tony Rolfe (who happens to be a very good guitarist) if he would come along and be my guitar tech.

I won't go into great detail about the tour but it turned out to be very successful and Paul and I managed to pay everyone as well as the expenses. We made sure we had plenty of merchandise with us and we were promoting the album *10* at this time. Paul and Tony did the driving and there was a lot of it.

Jay Stuart is a lovely guy and he always comes over as someone who is amazed or surprised by things that happen. If you remember the old television series *Mork and Mindy*, he is like Mork who has come to Earth and discovers things for the first time. He was a big Iron Maiden fan so to be able to be on tour with them, for him was unbelievable.

Not long after arriving at the first venue in La Coruna, Spain, we located the tour manager who coincidentally was named Steve Gadd also known as 'Gadsy'. He told me he often used to get asked if he was the singer with Stray. We met up with some of the crew and coincidentally one of the crew was a friend of Tony's.

Jay was already impressed to know that Steve Harris was a Stray fan and used to come and see me play many years before but then I think it was Adrian who came up and greeted me first. Jay was amazed when Adrian told us that he had band called Urchin who supported Stray back in the seventies. Jay's amazement continued when Janick Gers came out and shook my hand and said he had seen me play at The Rock Garden in Middlesborough. Nicko came out and had a long funny chat as only Nicko does and for most of the tour greeted me with the loud call of "Del Boy" any time he saw me or if he bowled into our dressing room.

We saw Bruce Dickinson who I hadn't spoken to since his days with the band Samson. Steve greeted us an asked if we were all okay. I don't recall seeing or speaking very much to Dave Murray much that day or throughout the tour in fact. I believe he is quite a private person and certainly is the quietest member of the band. We were sitting with their sound engineer Doug and Martin the lighting engineer when Doug said something like, "I reckon some of you guys have got friends in high places around here".

He went on to explain that as long as they had been working for Maiden they had never been instructed to let the opening act have use of the full the PA, sound system and lighting rig.

I was aware that Steve was probably taking a huge gamble getting Stray on these tour dates and I am pretty sure I am right in saying Rod Smallwood opposed the idea at first. I think, like I had said before, he was another person who thought that me/Stray was probably past it's sell by date.

Well here we go, the first stadium show in La Coruna Spain. The roar of the crowd as we walked on stage was quite something. I know that the Maiden fans are very loyal to their band and if they don't like the support act they are renown for making their opinions quite clear. Well we opened with 'Houdini' and got them rocking straight away. Their head of security who I think was called Wally, came running down the front and excitedly gave me a huge thumbs-up sign and actually told me after the show and following shows that he thought we went down the best of all the bands that had toured with Maiden. That was a huge accolade and for me a huge morale booster as you can have negative comments aimed at you so often that after a while you begin to believe them.

After the show had finished we all met up in the hospitality section and the first person I saw was Rod Smallwood. I had not seen Rod at any point so far and I didn't know what kind of reception I would get from him. To my surprise as I walked towards him, he stood up held out his hand to shake mine and said "Well done, good show Del". That meant a lot to me. Perhaps I wasn't passed the sell by date after all.

I have to say every show went very well indeed. I had one dilemma because at the end of the last song of the set 'All In Your mind' I had always done a bit of an act with the guitar. Laying it on top of the PA speakers or hanging it from the ceiling. The thing was I now find myself in stadiums, so what was I to do.

Bruce Dickinson has a walkway which formed a sort of figure 'C' above the equipment behind us, stretching from one side of the stage to the other where he could run around above the bands heads. When it came to the end of 'All In Your Mind', I had the guitar and I thought 'What am I going to do with it?' I noticed as the walkway came around to my side of the stage it was built using bolt on tubular metal crossbars. So I took my Stratocaster (nicknamed 'The Bat', by the way) and jammed it in one of the cross members so the volume of the guitar and the amplifier vibrated on the strings and it proceeded to feedback and make a sound of the guitar playing without me! It did the job.

Steve Harris used to come and watch us play from the side of the stage most evenings and on the second show he made sure he had Nicko there to show him what I was going to do with my guitar and Bruce's stage. There were some shows in Scandinavia which we didn't play and we re-joined them in Portugal on the 9th July.

What really surprised us was the greeting we received when we arrived. So many of the crew came over telling us how pleased they were to see us. We were told that they had a band The Murder Dolls playing some shows and they were a bit of a nightmare in as much as they didn't  go down at all well with the Maiden audiences and a couple of nights they didn't even play their full set. One techie told me the only good thing was that on one night The Murder Dolls had so many coins thrown at them, the crew went round afterwards picking up the loose change and went out for a drink with the proceeds.

The last show was a huge festival in Albecete Spain and there were around 100,000 people expected as far as I can remember. On this day there were other bands on like Dio and Baron Rojo. Maiden went on mid evening and naturally went down a storm. We were due to play the act after Maiden (can't remember who that was?) and it was running late so I don't think we got on stage until about 1am!

Now we knew Maidens crew had a long drive in their trucks and were due to get up early and set off in the morning, so they could have gone after Maidens set but to our absolute amazement they stayed to help us out. We got on so well they became our crew too. One of them said to me, "We had to say cos we had to put your backdrop up". Without them we would not have had the backdrop up. They secured it on scaffold poles and we very proudly went on stage with our name emblazoned across the back of the stage. Iron Maiden and their crew are like a big family and they welcomed us with open arms.

I get to see and speak to Steve whenever possible. He lives in the Bahamas now but is still passionate about touring. When Iron Maiden are not on tour he cannot sit still. So he goes out on tour with his other project British Lion, proof that he doesn't do it for the money. He does it because he is still as passionate about music as he was when he first started.

The following year, 2004, *The Citizen* newspaper held their annual award ceremony at The Woughton Centre in Milton Keynes. I had come to know Sammy Jones an excellent intelligent journalist. She appeared to be organising the event and invited me along to the ceremony. I didn't think a lot of it at the time, but in retrospect I should have found it odd that she phoned me on several occasions to make sure that I would definitely be attending. I think she may have suggested that I should be there as I might be presenting someone with an award.

On the night of the ceremony I took my seat at a table and watched various people, mainly local artistes and bands receiving their awards but I still hadn't seen Sammy for her to tell me when I should get up and to who should I give an award too.

Then a voice from the stage they said they were about to present a special 'Lifetime Achievement Award" to somebody. Ah that's interesting I thought. I wonder who that could be? As they were talking I began to think that certain things which were being said had an air of familiarity about them. Then all of a sudden the screen on the wall showed none other than Steve Harris from Iron Maiden paying tribute to me with some wonderful words. Quite emotional and totally unexpected. I went to the stage in a state of shock and tried to say a few words. I was truly humbled and got an amazing cheer and round of applause. How Sammy Jones pulled that off I'll never know.

While we are in this chapter I have a story which is nothing to do with Iron Maiden but does have a similarity relating to another awards ceremony I was invited to. Barry Middleton who was a well-known promoter particularly in the Blues music field telephoned me one day and asked if I would attend The Newark Blues Festival 2012 and present an award during the festival. He said it was to be held on Saturday 8th September and asked me if I would present an award to Tony McPhee. I checked my diary and told Barry I would love to be there and present the award to Tony who I have known since the 1970s and we have played many tours and shows together.

Much Like Sammy Jones in my last awards story, Barry telephoned me several times to check I was going to be there. I didn't think too much of it as I assumed he was checking with me if Tony was okay as he had recently had a stroke and because Barry knew that I knew Tony quite well, he was making sure we were both going to be there.

A few days before the festival a mutual friend or ours, a fantastic singer and lovely lady Maggie Ross passed away having fought cancer for a little while on September 2nd. Maggie was due to perform with her band on the festival and Roger asked if I could perhaps bring a guitar and do a short acoustic set in her place. The weather that day of the festival was beautiful, in the words of the song 'A bright sunshiny day'.

One of the last conversations Maggie and I had shortly before she died was our love of the old soul and Tamla Motown songs. I played about six songs, but I played one song titled 'Loving You Is Sweeter Than Ever' which was a favourite recorded by The Four Tops and written by Stevie Wonder. I dedicated this song to Maggie and I looked up at the sky and the sun seemed to shine even brighter. I must admit I choked up a bit at that point, but I got through it.

During the day I met up with the former Free bassist and songwriter Andy Fraser who I had not seen since the early seventies. He coincidentally went to St Clement Danes Grammar School where Ritchie Cole went. He had been living in the USA for some years but was back in the UK doing some promotional stuff.

When it came to the award ceremony, Barry ushered Tony and me to the side of the stage and Tony asked if I would say a few words on his behalf as the stroke had left him with little power of speech. There were various awards, best guitarist, best vocalist, best bands all the usual things you would expect and then they announced they were about to give out three special awards which were lifetime achievement awards under the title of Blues Greats.

Well it happened again. "The special awards to the Blues Greats go to Andy Fraser... Tony McPhee... Del Bromham! That was a huge surprise. I never expected to receive an award, particularly at a blues festival, because I never felt that I particularly fitted or was accepted even, in that genre of music. However, I accepted the award and said a few words for myself and on behalf of Tony. I'll never forget the grin on Barry's face, he well and truly stitched me up. Barry was a lovely guy and helped many acts on the music scene and I was very sad to hear that he had passed away a couple of years later on April 25th 2015.

# 36.
# Mistaken Identity

In recent years it seemed like I would arrive to play a show somewhere and someone at some point would say to me something like, "Here, you look just like the bass player in Wishbone Ash". It was something that was happening fairly regularly at that particular time. Wishbone Ash were touring regularly and so was I. I was playing a festival in Sweden and Wishbone Ash were on the bill. I was in the hotel bar when in walked Bob Skeat their bass player.

Although we hadn't met before I knew what he looked like as I was interested to see what my Doppelganger looked like and I have to admit there was a resemblance. It was funny because Bob had received similar comments about me also. Anyway we got chatting and I asked him where he was off to next to which he replied that he was going home. I asked him where home was and he said Ealing which I said I knew well. He asked where I lived now, which I told him but said that I was actually born and brought up in East Acton, London. He looked surprised and said "So did I. I lived in Bowes Road". I said "You are joking, I lived in Hilary Road". Bob lived literally on the other side of the road but the road was the busy A40 Western Avenue, so regarding schools, technically he was in a different catchment area so that's why we never met. We both agree there were similarities so I jokingly suggested that our mum's must have had the same milkman. We keep in touch and often refer to each other as Bruv.

A few years ago Simon Rinaldo and I played a show where we opened for the band called FM. After the show I got to have a chat with the drummer Pete Jupp. He said he had spoken to Bob Skeat who was an old friend of his and told him to send me 'his brother' regards. We both laughed and I began to tell Pete the story of how he and I refer to each other as brothers. Pete did see the likeness by the way.

Then he said, "I used to live in Bowes Road as well". That was almost unbelievable! East Acton was not a very big place and even though we had the same interests, we never all met. Just think, could have had a little band with guitar, bass and drums. I must point out that Bob plays bass guitar with Andy Powell's Wishbone Ash. I have also got to know the original bass guitarist Martin Turner, also a very nice fella.

Another story I have is not so much about a look alike as a sound alike. Over the years my name has been spelt incorrectly so many times I have lost count. I was doing a solo acoustic spot at The Borderline in London some years ago and early in the evening I was standing by the bar... I can't help but notice how many times in this book I just happened to be standing by the bar. Anyway, I was standing by the bar when this guy said to me looking up at the poster on the wall: "Del Bonham, does that happen to you often with your name being spelt wrong?" "Oh yes, too often" I replied. "I know what you mean, my name is Pete Bullick and I play guitar in Debbie Bonham's band" he said. Well that was it, we had a really good chat and exchanged contact details and as it transpired he also owns Sound Discs a company that presses CDs which has been a good thing for me because I have got Pete and his company to press CDs ever since.

Coincidentally soon after I played at a festival where Deb and her band were on the bill. We met up and immediately got on really well like we had known each other for years, so now I refer to her as my sister and I always look forward to meeting up with Debbie, Pete and their band.

A few years ago I went to see them play The Free Spirit tour, where Paul Rodgers was playing songs from the Free catalogue. Debbie went on first and did a solo spot which was good as always then Deb's band were backing Paul. I have to say that it was one of the, if not the best show I had seen for ages. Had Free ever recorded a bad song? I don't think so and Pete and the band sounded excellent. Free were a one-off kind of band and Pete and the boys did a wonderful job reproducing those great songs.

# 37.

# The Office Plus The Sitcom That Never Was!

I first got to know George Webley, also known as 'Big George' Webley around the time of working with the Blues Collective albeit as a composer and George was the producer. He was also known in the business as a bass guitarist and went on to compose title music for TV programmes such as *Have I Got News For You* and *Room 101*. He also worked as a programme presenter and DJ on television and radio.

George telephoned me one day early 2001 and asked if I could do a session for him and began to explain what it was for. George said that the BBC had signed a contract with a certain comedy artist and they had an agreement to make a sitcom which he had co-written and was to star in. However, this particular artist had recently had a chat show on Channel 4 and the ratings were not very good, but the BBC had a contract which they were obliged to fulfil so they didn't want to spend too much money on it.

They had asked George to arrange and record the title music which was to be the old sixties hit song titled 'Handbags and Gladrags'. Have any of you smart readers out there worked out where this is going? We were booked into a small studio in London. I'm not sure but it may have been Livingston Studios and if I'm right that was owned by Jerry Boys who was the young engineer on the first Stray album back in 1970.

George and I drove down to the studios together and met the rest of the band he had put together. I knew two of the musicians, Ben Hallett on drums and Fin Muir on vocals (Fin was the lead vocalist with Waysted formed by ex-UFO bassist Pete Way. On saxophone was Snake Davis and there was a young guy playing piano who I admit I didn't know and cannot remember his name. Not that I knew it anyway because he had a funny nickname like Wiggle or Tiggle. He was a great pianist and if he gets to read this, then I publicly apologise for not getting your name right. George completed the band line up on bass. Fin had a great voice, not unlike Rod Stewart which was ideal for this song as Rod had recorded a well-known version of this some years before. We changed the key to suit Fin's voice range and recorded the whole song in just a couple of run through takes.

In the control room while we were recording was the star and co-writer of this new show, a then relatively unknown Ricky Gervais along with the show producer Ash Atalla and a BBC producer who was in charge of the recording session. I never knew the name of the BBC producer but after we had recorded the whole song he said that they needed some incidental musical interlude breaks lasting only a few seconds per piece. So we recorded a couple of saxophone breaks and a couple of piano breaks and some little band sections.

This is where it gets pretty unbelievable. They were recording onto VHS Video cassette tape as some studios were doing around that time. Normally for inexpensive demo recordings which is not what you would expect from the BBC. Now consider this, he could have used another VHS tape. If I knew what was going on, I would have nipped down the road and bought one for no more than a fiver! The BBC producer said as we wouldn't need the whole song, he would just record over the last section of the song 'Handbags' and that would give him enough time to record the incidental music and have it all on one tape.

The show/series as you may have gathered by now was *The Office* and was first broadcast in July 2001. As you would be aware, the show became a huge success almost immediately. George telephoned me to say that the BBC wanted to release the full version of the title song we had recorded in the studio. Consequently, George had to explain to them that their BBC producer had wiped half of the track we had recorded in order to make room for the segways. George basically wanted to check my availability to go back into the studio and record the song again. I said I would make myself available, George would check the other musicians and get back to me. By the time the second episode aired on television 'Handbags and Gladrags' was in most people's heads, particularly if you had been watching the series.

Jools Holland had 'The Stereophonics' on his show and they, very astutely, performed a version of 'Handbags and Gladrags'. I have to admit it was a very good version and it was the song people wanted to hear at that time. Their performance of the song was so successful that their record company released their version and it was a hit record straight in at Number 1 in the singles charts.

You can only imagine our frustration, for the sake of the cost of a bloody VHS tape we could have had a number one record in the charts. So much for saving a few quid because Ricky Gervais or *The Office* will never be successful! Yeh right, nice one BBC.

Actually, since I am telling you about a sitcom, I must tell you of another one which I was almost involved in but never happened due to circumstances way beyond my control. I mentioned earlier about Rod Linton from 'Rupert's People' and my contact with John Sherry. He telephoned me one day to say that there was a new sitcom planned based on a story written by Roderick Brosse and adapted as a screenplay by Stuart Browne an established television writer.

In brief, here is the outline of the plot as explained to me by Roderick himself. "It involved a simple theme and very colourful characters, all extremes of their genre. A young hippy dude goes to Woodstock. Dude sees Hendrix, completely flips and stoned as can be decides to never leave Woodstock and learn to play guitar like Hendrix. Meanwhile, the son who was the result of his hippy free love night at the festival and a relationship that ended with the dudes partner leaving with son. Son becomes a top rock star. Woodstock has a revival. Dad is still there and he sounds more like Hendrix than Hendrix. Son's band are booked to play a Revival Woodstock Festival. Son discovers Dad and invites him to sit in with his band. Dad becomes the highlight of the festival and rockets to world fame overnight. Cue for countless humorous episodes of going from total obscurity to world fame, mega managers, stoned and coke and acid fuelled concerts, disasters, groupies, high life and low life etc, with characters coming and going. A mad *Spinal Tap* type crazy version of the then crazy overindulgent music business and zero to hero lives".

I was to play the dad and it would have been my acting debut as well as featuring music every week. I would have been the original real Del Boy. Unfortunately, the project was cancelled following the death of the writer Stuart Brown due to complications following an operation which he never fully recovered from!

# 38.
# Into The 1990s

I think possibly due to Iron Maiden recording 'All In Your Mind' and the fact that the early Stray albums had been re-released, there appeared to be renewed interest in the band once more. Gary, Steve and myself did actually speak to each other occasionally despite not actually playing in the same band anymore. Somehow we got to discussing playing together again, primarily because a couple of agents had enquired asking what the chances of Stray playing a reunion show. So to cut a long story short we agreed to play a reunion show at The Riverside Theatre, Hammersmith London on August 28th 1993.

We rehearsed for a couple of days at React Rehearsal Studios in Buckingham. This was the first time that Gary and Ritchie had seen Steve since 1974! Despite the differences and the length of time, we played the first song 'All In Your Mind' and I remember that we played the entire song through without any mistakes, as if we had only played it literally a week before. Following the last note of the song, we all looked at each other in amazement. The music had still brought us together. Every song we tried for the set, we appeared to play with ease. So within a couple of days we had a set list together and we were looking forward to the first show. I say the first show because once The Riverside show had been booked I had spoken to a couple of promoters and put together several more dates up and down the country. The show at The Riverside was a double bill with Man. It was pretty well attended and I seem to recall feeling quite encouraged by the performance and the audience reaction.

As the shows rolled on I could sense some of the old bad feelings and animosity had not healed and to be honest by the time the last show finished I think we were all pleased it was ending. Once again we went our separate ways and carried on with our lives. The few shows we played had raised some interest once again in the Stray name and I had various promoters offering shows again, but I didn't, nor did the other band members have any interest in revisiting it again.

I attempted a few variations of playing Stray songs with other musicians, one line-up was playing with Stuart Uren and drummer Andy Beirne. The latter who I had known since I was a teenager and played with Dirty Tricks as well as Grand Prix and Lionheart. Andy, Stu and I made a great little trio but, I don't know why, maybe we had other individual interests but we only played a couple of shows.

It must have been around 1995 that I was contacted by Don McKay of Rhino Agency. It transpired that he was a bit of a Stray fan in the 1970s and was at The Riverside show. He asked the inevitable question was there any chance of putting the original line-up of the band back together again, to which I had to reply "no". His other suggestion was I could maybe play the shows billed as 'Del Bromham's Stray', then at least people would be aware that it was not necessarily the original line-up, but fans of the band would hear the old songs performed by one of the original members and the main songwriter.

I had met a young drummer when I used to co-host a jam night at the Cosgrove Lodge Hotel in a little village just outside Milton Keynes. His name was Phil McKee. I had also seen him play with ex-Whitesnake guitarists Bernie Marsden and Micky Moody. He was (and still is) a great drummer and can sing too, which is handy. So I asked him if he would be interested in getting together and playing to see how it felt? I also asked Stu again as he knew most of my songs back to front, so that made learning songs much easier all round. After a few rehearsals the new little trio was sounding good and ready to play some shows. I told Don at Rhino Agency and he began to book some shows for 'Del Bromham's Stray'.

Following a meeting with Don, it became apparent that Stu and I had a difference of opinion on how business wise, things should proceed, so consequently I now found myself without a bass player for the forthcoming gigs! Phil said he had spoken to a mutual friend of ours, Dusty Miller who might be able to help us out until we found a permanent replacement. I had known Dusty for many years but as a guitarist rather than a bass player. He was also a knowledgeable engineer at Yamaha Musical Instruments in Milton Keynes.

Dusty agreed to play a few shows and I gave him the songs to learn for the first show at The Fairfield Halls in Croydon. I was really impressed how he easily transferred from guitar to bass and also sang backing vocals and vocal harmonies. We played the first show and it went really well and Don was pleased too, which is handy if the bloke getting the gigs is liking it.

Funny how you remember the almost insignificant things at times. I remember going into the dressing room on that first show and there was a nice buffet laid out for us. Dusty saying something like "Ooh, this is nice. I could get used to this". Well, get used to it he did although not every show supplied such generous backstage hospitality. He really enjoyed playing and offered to play more shows. The three of us got on really well and we had plenty of laughs along the way. For many of the shows we were joined by my road manager Dick Hammond.

Don Mckay had formed a record label called Mystic Records with his business partner Robert Barrs-James. With Dusty and Phil I recorded two albums for Mystic Records. The first studio album *New Dawn* was recorded at Liscombe Park Studios, Buckinghamshire and the second was a live album titled *Alive and Giggin'* recorded at The Robin, Brierley Hill.

I was really getting the Stray name and my face back on the music circuit around the country. After a couple of years Dusty found it difficult to juggle doing his day job and playing in the band so regrettably he left the band, as did Phil, which was a blow as I had to find replacements very quickly as Don was continuing to get more shows in.

I began working for a company aptly named Rockwell. For a while I must admit I quite enjoyed the work I was doing there and was getting used to not having to worry about everything that goes along with putting a band on the road. So much so that from time to time I even considered it might be better to pack the music business in and concentrate on a career with Rockwell. As time went on I got a taste of what it was like working in the corporate world and it opened my eyes and disappointed me. New younger management were brought in and some of the older employees were being replaced by younger ones, generally it seemed, if you were friends with the management you were in the club. The way some people were being treated left a bad taste in my mouth and life was made very uncomfortable for some who subsequently handed in their notice. This was very convenient for the new regime as they didn't have to pay redundancy packages or make up excuses to fire them.

After a while it was pretty obvious I was one of the few who as mum used to say "Your face doesn't fit" and I was certainly not in the new boys club. One manager actually told me I was "too vocal". By that they clearly wanted a bunch of yes men, and a yes man I am not. At this time, I was having a number of personal problems and this was another problem which I didn't need, so I handed my notice in and left to be a musician again. Easier said than done though.

Before I left Rockwell, I had found a drummer working there named Paul Watson. I went to see him play and although he was very different from the drummers I had played with in the past, there was something about his style which I liked and on top of that he was a very nice guy too. Around the same time, I met a bass player named John Bootle who was recommended to me by Dusty Miller.

Unlike people I had played with in the past, John Paul and I were not close friends to start with, so we had to get to know each other and break down the usual barriers. Very soon this new trio as Stray rehearsed and were ready and playing gigs up and down the country and in Europe. Dick Hammond had left to work for the Baron Knights. We were joined at this time by Jay Stuart a friend of Paul's and an excellent drum tech. During the UK and European Mountain dates, Jay had been setting Corky's drum kit up. Jay didn't have to, but he loves drums so much he wanted to make sure the kit was just right every night. Jay is very conscientious like that.

We went on to record two albums for Mystic Records. A studio album *10*, once again recorded at Liscombe Park and a live album *Live In Yer Face* recorded at The Robin 2, Dudley.

It was around the time of *10* in 2001 that Paul Newcomb began to be involved with me again. With Paul's help we increased the amount of merchandise at shows which had become a necessity in order to finance the band on the road and also liaising with business people on my behalf (who wants to talk to the guitarist after all?) Once again we felt things were going up another level with gigs around the country and in Europe including a UK tour with Uriah Heep, Nazareth and Stray which was a great package.

By 2003 not long after we finished that tour with Maiden to my complete surprise, John told me he was going to leave the band followed by a further surprise for when I went to discuss John leaving, Paul told me he was leaving too. They both had their own reasons for leaving and I respect them for that. I have learned that the band obviously means more to me than anyone else because I guess it has been my baby on and off since I was fifteen.

# 39.
# The Millennium

It seemed like the whole world were expecting disasters as the clock struck midnight on the 31st December 1999, because apparently the computers which were controlling most things wouldn't be able to cope with the transition to the year 2000. I know various companies were spending money putting their staff on training courses and companies were attempting to put other contingency plans in place in the event of a disaster! Well they were all wrong and there were no disasters and midnight came and went and everything was as normal as normal could be at that time.

For me, the new millennium would see a radical change of many things in my life for many years to come. Firstly, before I get too far into the new year, I have to mention a sad event which started in some ways the start of changes in my life. In 1999, Jackie and I had been on holiday in Cyprus and we arrived back home early morning of Thursday 17th June. A few hours later my phone rang. It was Paul Herbert, known to everyone as Bert. He gave me the shocking news that Don Hollis had passed away the previous Monday from a brain haemorrhage. Don as you may remember was not only the guitarist with Teaza, but also the guitarist who joined Stray on my recommendation when I was already on tour with my own band.

This was such an unexpected shock, he was a genuinely lovely man and loved by many which was very apparent by the amount of people who attended his funeral. A few friends got together and planned a celebration of his life which took place at Zaks in Wolverton, Milton Keynes. We put a band together for the night. Billy Gammond on bass and vocals, Paul Herbert on drums, Andy Lewis on keyboards and also Eddie 'Mac' McErlane on vocals and harmonica and me on guitar and vocals.

There was a touching moment during the bands performance when a string broke on my guitar. It seemed as if from nowhere his young son Nick approached the stage and offered me Don's old black Gibson Les Paul to play. My friend Geordie was quite emotional and said to me afterwards that it seemed like divine intervention, as if Don had somehow got me to use his guitar for the performance in his absence. I'll never forget that moment when Nick handed me the guitar, very moving.

I was already playing shows with what had become Del Bromham's Stray. However, it was fun to play with these guys. Bill and I had not played together for a while but decided to put aside what problems we had before and put a little side band together. So Bill, myself and Andy the keys player got together with our old friend, drummer, Phil McKee. Bert who played drums at the memorial for Don was now playing saxophone and gigging quite regularly. We called the band Curly which was the name we used at Don's memorial show, because Don often used to call or greet certain friends regardless of their names as Curly.

Bill and I thought it would be a nice touch. We quickly rehearsed mainly cover versions of well-known, primarily rock songs and a few originals and we started to play at various pubs in the area, I think it sounded good and was fun, which is what it's all about at the end of the day.

It was at Don's funeral I met his sister Anne again. I had not seen her for many years as she married had two sons and went to live in the North East of England as her husband worked at the Nissan plant. They had recently moved back to Milton Keynes but unfortunately Anne and her husband had divorced and she was now on her own with the two boys, Alex and Michael.

Anne if you remember, in an earlier chapter was the young lady who worked in the estate agent office in Bletchley when I went to buy a house. Anne was now going out with Andy. Anne often used to come along to the gigs we played. Now the funny thing is that when I started talking to her again I instinctively referred to her as Annie? I don't know why, but it transpired that Don called her Annie (and not Anne). She was okay with that and we used to have lots of chats at the gigs and plenty of laughs.

I hope she won't mind me saying this but it was like she was one of the boys and she got my sense of humour. The more we talked we realised we had a lot in common. We seemed to like the same music and could relate to listening to different albums at certain times in our past. Annie is nearly nine years younger than me, but Don and I were about the same age so she used to listen to his albums too. She says that I reminded her of Don particularly with our humour and music.

Life at home had become very difficult. There are two sides to every story and I am not going in to details but Jackie and I were not seeing eye to eye on very much at this time. We had different friends and she would often go out to visit certain friends on her own and despite her knowing me since I was fifteen, she didn't seem interested in my musical career. It seemed like we would argue about nothing in particular, but that's as far as I am going with explanations.

It seemed that I just had a small circle of friends who predominately revolved around my music. I loved seeing Annie. One could argue, was it that female conversation I really missed? However, neither of us thought of our chats at gigs were nothing more than two friends talking and enjoying being each other's company as friends do. Besides she was in a relationship with Andy, I was married to Jackie and anyway, this was Don's sister, someone I first met back in 1977!

As time went on, I was getting less interested in playing with Curly. I suppose one could say that the novelty was wearing off, much like I felt many years before when I was playing with Alibi and things were starting to pick up again with Stray. Andy and Annie had decided to part company and it was at this point when Annie came along to a gig following their split that she told me that she wouldn't and couldn't come to any more gigs because of her relationship or rather non relationship now with Andy.

It was on hearing what she had just said which really hit home, because I didn't, not want to see her again. My feelings were becoming stronger than being just friends. As she was about to leave what would be her last gig coming to see us, I caught up with her and asked if I could have as I put it, a little chat later.

On my way home from the gig, Annie and I met up for my chat and as it turned out she also really wanted to see me again, but how we could we possibly meet as it would only be seen by others as having an affair. We wanted to remain friends but how could we possibly meet up in public without the tongues wagging and people jumping to conclusions. The only time I went out now was when I was playing a gig, so having a night out would be unusual and result in telling lies which I wasn't used to.

Annie was now living back at her dad's home due to the disastrous result of her divorce, so it seemed impossible that we could ever meet up again. I dropped by her dad's house on a couple of occasions, staying no longer than twenty minutes or so, just to innocently to say "Hello how are you?" A few minutes were better than no minutes at all, so my dropping by became quite often and I'm sure her dad, who I had known for some years, must have been suspicious of my visits as he knew me and knew that I was a married man. As a dad myself, I would have been concerned if one of my daughters began seeing a married man.

Around this time, I was in the process of buying a property in Spain. I had never really had anything like a pension or any investments so I felt that buying a property to rent out would be a good business plan. Jackie and I flew over to Alicante and with the assistance of a Property Management company, we bought a property close to an area known as Villa Martin on the Costa Blanca. We had to go over a few times to sort out the details like finally signing all the paperwork and everything that goes with buying a property in Spain which without the right help can be a tricky process.

Fortunately, we had good legal team working on our behalf. This was something which should have been a joyous experience but unfortunately with our relationship as it was, these trips over to Spain could be very uncomfortable to say the least. Things between Jackie and I were not good and I had two friends who had also bought a place in La Marina, I think partly based on the fact that I had just bought in Spain they decided to do the same. Jackie and I had to go to Spain in order to get what they call an NIE number which is like a tax code if you have property in Spain, so I thought we could tie it in with a visit to our friends in La Marina, Geoff and Jeanette.

They had a lovely property which had separate one-bedroom apartment which they invited Jackie and I to stay in overnight rather than us driving back down to Villa Martin. We had a nice day with them at La Marina and then in the evening Geoff and Jeanette drove us to the coast to a place called Guardamar, where we had dinner at a restaurant. After dinner we walked around the town when my phone rang. It was my brother Norman on the line from the UK giving me the bad news that dad had just passed away. This was the 6th of July 2003. The news certainly made me put my immediate problems to one side for the time being.

Dad had been unwell for the past couple of years but not seriously ill. His problems really began when mum started to develop dementia. Dad kept this secret for some time. Sundays and Christmas time were times where the family used to go for dinner at mum and dad's house. Like I said before, we had quite a big family and it was nothing for them to prepare a dinner (and tea) for as many as fourteen people. I remember one time when mum had brought everybody's Sunday dinner plates out, dad came in from the kitchen and enquired if anyone wanted anymore gravy? That was nothing unusual, but on this occasion he was holding a large yellow plastic Duckhams oil jug. "Anyone want any gravy?" asked Dad. Seeing him standing there with a Duckhams oil can, we all burst out laughing. "Where did you get that?" asked Alan. Dad didn't have a car, but he always liked a bargain. A Homebase DIY store on the site where the old Western Pub used to be had opened, so with either something he bought or had spent over so much money, he got a free gift. He chose the Duckhams oil jug because he thought it would come in handy. He wasn't wrong was he?

On occasions when visiting mum and dad, some of us had noticed that mum didn't always appear to be herself. She would be prone to looking a bit distant when you spoke to her at times and when she was preparing food it didn't look very hygienic. One of the last times we had tea with them she dished up food which was frozen, fresh out of the freezer! It transpired that mum was literally escaping from the house at all times of the day and night, insisting that she had to go home. The more that dad tried to prevent her from leaving, she would become angry and aggressive which was not at all like her.

It was Friday 24th January 2003 when my sister-in-law Audrey telephoned to tell me that mum had gone missing! They thought she had her handbag and bus pass with her. She had ventured out and been on buses before. Norman telephoned the police and reported her missing! Later that day my niece Karen phoned to tell me mum had been found and was at Central Middlesex Hospital in Park Royal, London. I drove down to London and she looked in a sorry state. She had stitches and a plaster over her nose. A plaster on her forehead and two black eyes. I found it incredible that the hospital could give us no information as to what might have happened to her or exactly where she was found. We never knew if she'd had a fall or been mugged? Mum surprisingly seemed okay and had no recollection whatsoever as to what had happened?

We had to get home help when dad became unwell and too weak to cope. We had a lovely carer called Jackie Carey, who came in to help and she noticed mum's odd behaviour. Dad had to spend a bit of time in a convalescent home and we were lucky that the social services allowed Jackie to stay on and look after mum as well, because by now she was unable to look after herself. Norman, our Aunt May and me took turns in staying overnight with mum as she needed 24-hour attention. Dad did come home but soon went into hospital where he passed away on 6th July 2003 at the age of 92.

I must tell you this story about dad. It was probably six months or so before he died, we received a phone call from the hospital advising us that the family should come to the hospital as they didn't think he would last the day! So we all met at our old house in Hilary Road and walked up The Du Cane Road to Hammersmith Hospital. There were quite a few of us and they only allowed two or three people at a time to sit by his bedside.

He was laying there looking very peaceful, when he looked over at me and then looked back towards the corridor where he could see all the family members gathered and then he said to me "What day is it?". "Tuesday" I replied. He looked back down towards the family and said to me "Why aren't you lot at work?" I explained that we had come to visit him in hospital. Well dad was never the sort of bloke, as he would say "You can't pull the wool over my eyes son", and I am sure he realised what was going on.

After a while he looked like he was getting weaker, it was around midday, so we decided to take mum back to the house and get some lunch and we would pop back later, although we fully expected him to be gone by then. When we arrived back at the hospital, as we approached the ward, I was amazed to see dad sitting up in bed and at about the same time, the Consultant came rushing over to see us. He said something to the effect of "I cannot understand it. I've never seen anything like this. After you left earlier he sprang back to life, sat up in bed and had some dinner. I can't explain it, but you can go and see him now".

Norman and I went over to his bedside and there he was almost like there was nothing wrong with him. Not only that, he came out of hospital, stayed for a little while in a nursing home and lived for about another six months or so. Furthermore, I thought he was going to get really annoyed about being sent to a convalescent home, so I was dreading my first visit, but I need not have worried. There he was sitting in a chair telling me what a good time he was having, apparently it was just like staying in a hotel on one of his holidays. Telling me in his words, "You get a good bit of grub here son", and every time a nurse came by he would call them by their names and like a real rogue, it was almost like he was flirting with them and to be honest I think the nurses returned the compliment. I could tell they were very fond of him and he was a funny bloke.

A few things I should mention about dad was that he always said, "I don't want to go into hospital because the only way I will come out is in a box!" He was also stubborn so it made sense that he wasn't going to come out of that hospital in a box, he was going to have a bit of a holiday first. He probably realised that he couldn't go back home with mum the way she was.

This time was stressful for all of us and I would tend to go at weekends or when I could to spend time with mum. A typical scenario would be for me to have played a show somewhere, drive home, get in about 3am, get a couple of hours sleep then get up and make the drive down to London to stay a couple of days with mum. Trying to keep her occupied and getting her to eat a meal had its problems. In her mind she was much younger and it was not her house she was living in. In her mind she was popping in to visit the old man (my dad) who lived there. She always said she had to get home to do John's dinner. If I dished her up a dinner she would always say she couldn't eat it as she had just had her dinner or she had to go home to get John's dinner.

One funny memory I have is that one day I drove down in my band tour bus. I asked her if she would like to go out for drive with me? She didn't recognise me as her son 'D' because she would point and say, "Don't be stupid, you're not 'D'". 'D' is only that big (pointing to the height of about three feet) and anyway he can't drive". I took her out in the tour bus and from that moment on, if I asked her if she wanted to go out for a drive she would giggle and say "Ooh, are we going in 'The Passion Wagon?"

A most memorable drive we had out was when I took her to the place she grew up and went to school which was an area called Strand on the Green, right on the Thames near Kew Bridge. She probably hadn't been there for over seventy years but she recognised everything and was clearly transported back in time. She showed me the house, she lived in as a child which was still there right on the banks of the Thames and pointed to where her brother Sid had drowned in a boat accident when he was only thirteen. I found a paper cutting of the accident from a newspaper when clearing the house out.

We walked a little way where we came across a school, the kind of building typical of many schools of that era and beyond. In fact, my primary school in the 1950s looked no different overall to the one mum had gone to around 1920. Mum and I stood outside the school gates and she said, "This is my old school". Pointing through the bars into the playground she said, "I think that was my classroom over there". I found this amazing! She was taking me with her back in time and I so wanted to imagine what it would have been like for her. We carried on walking along a street away from the school and she really came alive, strangely recognising where she was although she had not been here for nearly seventy years, although where she now lived in East Acton, she didn't really know where she was. The mind can play such cruel tricks on you.

As we walked along she said that they (her family) lived further along this street. We kept walking, past a row of old Victorian houses which finished and there were what looked like a small block of maisonettes, built much later, most probably post war. She pointed at theses newish houses and said, "That's where we used to live, right there, but the house was bombed during the war". Consequently, that is why the new builds were there. It's funny to think that all those years ago people wanted to better themselves and move out of the area. These days property in the same area is worth a small fortune!

As time went on, mum's condition worsened and it was difficult to keep an eye on her all of the time. For example, one day she went out to the kitchen and decided she was going to make John some porridge. Of course John had died some time before, which she would not accept. She told us not to be ridiculous because he was out at work. Aunt May often had little arguments with mum about this, but arguing with mum was futile as in her mind what she knew was reality. Aunt May found it difficult to accept this. Mum made the porridge and proceeded to pour it from the saucepan into a bowl, but missed the bowl and poured scalding hot porridge over her forearm. One thing about mum, she did have a huge pain threshold. Obviously it would have been painful, but she rarely showed pain if she had injured herself.

A few times over the following couple of weeks a male nurse used to come in and check and change the dressing on the burn. He made an interesting comment about mum's dementia. He said that he had a few patients he had to visit in the area, all old age pensioners who had lived in the area for a long time and he said they all appeared to suffer from varying forms of dementia. He was sure it was down to the traffic pollution as all of these people lived either side of the busy A40 Western Avenue. Mum had lived in Hilary Road since about 1941 so that was a long time to be breathing in air pollution. He might have had a point.

It became apparent that we as a family were not able to look after mum to our best ability and for her safety. We had to make the almost agonising decision to put her into a Home to receive proper care. I looked at several homes and we felt the best one was Chaston House Residential Care Home in Acton. As it turned out we feel we made the right choice because the people who looked after her there were very good and surprisingly mum appeared to adapt almost immediately. You cannot underestimate the experience these people have who work in these places.

I used to visit every weekend, either a Saturday or Sunday and actually it could be quite entertaining as apart from mum there were some real characters there. Mum eventually passed away on April 2nd 2008. She was not ill as such, she just passed away peacefully in her sleep at the age of 96.

Now I have said earlier that when I was growing up there was always music going on in the house, what with dad and brothers' records and my brother's groups, but recently, thinking back, mum was going around the house doing the housework and she would often be singing away. She was also very funny, a wicked sense of humour and often as I realise more these days, coming out with sayings some of which would have originated on some of the early BBC Radio shows.

****

Now with the passing of both mum and dad we had to empty and clear out the family home in Hilary Road. I found this a very emotional time. I was born in this house and for many years it was The Hub of so many family visits and events. If those walls could speak, what tales they could tell (a line from a song I have yet to record). It is not a good feeling going through someone's personal possessions, but it has to be done. Clothing and paperwork and furniture, everything which they had gathered in that house since 1941. I had a look up in the loft but on this occasion there was no sign of Russian dignitaries or the sound of violins. I only realised recently that I must have left the metal stand from my first Vox AC30 amplifier which I put up there in about 1968. Funny how you remember things like that.

I had said to Annie that when it was to be my last visit to 56 Hilary Road, I would have to leave as quickly as possibly because closing the door for the last time was going to be very emotional. As I walked down the hallway approaching the front door for the last time, I happened to look back and saw dad's hat hanging on the hallway coat hangers in the corner. I went back grabbed the hat and put it on my head.

I vaguely remember dad buying that hat around 1970. He bought it in somewhere like Dunnes in Shepherd's Bush, along with his blue Crombie overcoat (which I have) he thought he was the bees' knees, Frank Sinatra or Frankie Sinatra as a certain gentleman from New York once referred to him as.

I began wearing that hat at various shows and it was slightly too big for me (I know some of you might think "you've got a big head, it must have fitted"), so I used to wear it back to front. Now I don't wish to claim to be a fashion icon but that hat started to get as popular as me and often if I did a gig somewhere and I didn't wear the hat, I would get people shouting out things like "Oi Del, where's your dad's hat?" Not only that I couldn't help noticing a lot of people (guitarists in particular) started wearing hats back to front or hats similar to dad's. Dad still got some kind of attention even when he wasn't there, bless him.

With Annie and I living together in Olney and with all that had been happening for the past couple of years I thought we could get back to some kind of normality and spend some weekends together, something I had been unable to do due to constantly being with mum.

At dad's funeral, I didn't get up and say a few words at the service because I didn't think I could handle it. Odd really as I spend most of my life performing in front of audiences, but this was different, I felt it would be too emotional. On the day of his funeral, I was surprised at how composed I was and in a strange way happy for dad that he had now found some peace.

When it came to mum's funeral, I felt I had to make up for what I had not done at dad's funeral and do something for her. All of my family would remember that when we were all babies and when mum had grandchildren she would hold them in her arms and sing the old musical song 'Daisy, Daisy'. I still have the first guitar, the Hofner Congress, which they bought for me in 1965. So I took the guitar to mum's funeral and I got up, said a few words and sang and played:

'Daisy, Daisy give me your answer do.
I'm half crazy, all for the love of you.
It won't be a stylish marriage
I can't afford a carriage,
But you'll look sweet, upon the seat
Of a bicycle made for two'.

Strange as it may seem, it was lovely, all the family in the congregation joined in and sang with me. The only time we have all sung together. The Vicar conducting the service thought it was wonderful and said if I ever fancied singing at any funerals to let him know. You mean dying could be a living?

After the service we congregated outside, said our goodbyes and I began to walk with Aunt May towards the car, when completely unexpectedly she collapsed! Myself and a couple of others helped her up. After a while she seemed okay and couldn't understand what had happened. We thought maybe it was the emotion of the moment, so didn't think too much of it.

Aunt May only had one child, a daughter who died not long after she was born. I always felt quite close to her and I think she felt the same about me because I would have been about the same age as her daughter. I jokingly called her my second mum.

I had spoken to May during the week to see if she was okay but she said she was feeling very weak and was running short of food and needed to pay some bills but didn't feel strong enough to get on a bus. So once again I drove to London at the weekend, did her shopping and cooked her a dinner. As the weeks went by she was not getting any better and she had a small blister which would not go away on her forehead. I kept telling her to call a doctor, which initially she kept putting off, but eventually she had tests and they revealed that she had Leukaemia!

By December 2008, less than nine months after mum had died, May was taken into hospital. To be honest I thought she would only be in for a while. I had bought her a mobile phone (new technology for her), so that she could keep in touch. While she was asleep someone had obviously seen her phone on her bedside cabinet, sneaked in and stole it! There are some rotten people in this world.

Aunt May spent Christmas in hospital, but took a turn for the worse and passed away on the 29th December 2008.

I guess she got her final wish. She told me she had had enough and just wanted to rest and have a long sleep.

# 40.
# The Millennium Continues

**W**ell eight years into the millennium and I've lost dad, mum, Aunt May, my marriage and my house, what else could possibly go wrong. It didn't get any better, read on my friends.

Aunt May had just passed away when I received a shock telephone call from my daughter Zoe in Australia. Let me tell you about Zoe. When she went to University her intention was to study law and at one time I remember she was thinking about training as a Barrister's Advocate. However, after a while she had a change of direction and decided to study psychology, as well as law and this change would go on to lead her to great things.

After she graduated from University, she joined the Metropolitan Police Force to work in forensics. She was based in Sutton, Surrey and lived in nearby Wimbledon. While living there, she made a lot of new friends, some of which were Australians living in the UK. I always had the feeling she had a soft spot for the Australian way of life, since the 1980s when they started broadcasting *Neighbours* on TV. For a while she had a hair style not unlike the curly style worn by Kylie Minogue at the time. Seriously though, she decided to visit friends she had made when they returned home to Australia. She fell in love with the country and decided to pack up and emigrate there. I believe she had a couple of legal based jobs but went on to work for the Australian Department of Criminology building physiological profiles on prisoners, even to the extent that she would have to travel around Australia interviewing inmates in prisons. She received The Golden Key Award. Only 2-5% receive this, a worldwide recognition.

She met Jason Heron and they bought a house and moved in together. Life and the future was looking great for her, when only after about a year of Zoe and Jason being together, she was given the bad news that she had developed breast cancer. This was what she telephoned to tell me coming up to New Year's Eve 2008. To say she fought cancer would be an understatement. As well as the awful effects of chemotherapy and everything that goes with it, she had to have a mastectomy. I was not aware until sometime later she was actually diagnosed with cancer a year earlier, but typical of Zoe I am sure she didn't want to worry me.

Following the operation, she seemed to be getting better, but the cancer returned and some years later she ended up having a double mastectomy. Like I said, she fought this awful disease. She joined a team of ladies who were cancer survivors who called themselves Sassy Survivors. A group of some of the strongest ladies you will find anywhere. They raised money for cancer research and Zoe, who as a youngster, was always a pretty good athlete, ran many marathons and collected medals in the process. Even when she was unwell herself, she counselled others who were going through cancer.

When I think of Zoe, I can picture her beautiful eyes and beautiful smile and she had an infectious laugh. I cannot imagine the pain and suffering that she must have gone through but Jason told me that even through the times where she was receiving treatment and being more ill due to the side effects, she still retained her sense of humour and smiled through the darkest times. These were also difficult times for her mum Jackie, sister Jodie and myself purely due to the distance between us here in the UK and Zoe in Australia, but obviously nothing compared to what Zoe must have been going through. I realise now having had hours of conversations with Jason, Zoe had really underplayed her illness to her family in the UK and I know her selfless attitude did this so that we would not have to worry about her so much being so far away.

I spent quite a lot of time with Jason and he gave me some kind of idea what she went through, but even so, he said he never saw her complain, in fact she would always ask if he was okay. She always considered others above herself. I feel it is worth mentioning at this point that we probably do not appreciate what husbands, wives and partners go through in these times. The worry and personal turmoil must be immeasurable.

I could understand why Zoe loved her life in Australia, because apart from having a good career and a beautiful home she had Jason and some great friends, who I know in their own way, looked after her. She was much loved there.

The love was very evident on the day they got married. It was April 25th 2015, a beautiful sunny day as it always seems to be on the Gold Coast. The wedding venue and reception was beautiful, as was the bride. As soon as the music started at the reception, Zoe was up and dancing and she danced all night. I had never seen her look so happy. Actually happy would be an understatement. Euphoric would be a more descriptive adjective.

Zoe and Jay (Jason) had booked a good function band to play for them and the guests and during the evening Jay and some of the others kept asking me if I was going to get up and play with the band which I had not considered. I did notice Jono, the best man and Jay having a word with the band from time to time and as it turned out they were asking if the Father of the bride could get up and play? I felt quite sorry for the band, because being a musician myself I know what it can be like at weddings when a guest gets up to play at a wedding. There might be good intentions but is can often be an embarrassment not only for the guests but for the band too when all a band want to do is what they were hired for, to play music.

Well, sure enough and probably reluctantly, the band called me over and we had a quick chat about what songs we could play together. They were good musicians and had a wide repertoire, so I got up and played maybe half a dozen songs or so and I have to say that I think it went well and the band said they really enjoyed playing with me, but more importantly, Zoe said she was proud that I had played at her wedding so I hope her old dad, didn't embarrass her too much.

My youngest daughter Jodie was unable to attend the wedding as she was very pregnant with her second child, but along with other members of the UK family, she sent a video message over which was shown at the wedding reception.

Jodie had tied the knot to Darron on 31st August 2009 in a Civil Ceremony held at Horwood House in Buckinghamshire. Jodie said she would like a string quartet to play at the ceremony. I contacted Julian Pentz, a talented violinist and music arranger who I had met a few years before, when I think he was playing with a folk/rock band called Togmor.. As Jodie and I entered the room Julian and his quartet played and they sounded wonderful, exactly what Jodie had imagined. They also played a selection of music when everyone was leaving the room. Jodie looked beautiful and happy that day and Zoe had flown over from Australia to be with us all. Zoe was allowed to travel as she had finished her treatment for cancer, but she was very conscious of her short hair style which had started to grow again following the chemotherapy she had been undergoing. The short hair suited her and she too looked lovely and Jodie was so pleased that her big sister could make it for her wedding.

In January 2012 Jodie gave birth to their first baby boy who they named Liam, then in September 2015 they had another baby boy named Jaxon. Actually, it was Zoe who suggested the name.

Me a Grandad? Well, people had told me it is really special when you have grandchildren. Different from having your own children. I have to agree with them although originally I couldn't see it, but when you are lucky enough to have grandchildren they are indeed very special.

Coming up to Zoe's birthday on February 11th 2016, both sides of the family (Bromham and Collins), decided to make bits of video footage with messages to send to Australia. A great idea which I think was instigated by my nephew Lee Collins. My contribution was filming me with the band Stu and Karl, playing a rock version of 'Happy Birthday'. One of Zoe's friends sent us a video of Zoe watching the video messages and it was great to see her and hear her infectious laugh.

Although I never mentioned it to anybody, it was noticeable that she had lost a lot of weight and didn't look well. She looked so very different from the beautiful bride I had walked down the aisle with only months before!

Zoe had been attending the hospital on various occasions for ongoing treatment and I know a couple of times she'd had a problem with her lungs filling with fluid. On 25th March (Good Friday! There's an irony), Zoe text me to tell me she was in hospital and not to worry as she would speak to me next week.

A few days later, quite early in the morning, I think it was Tuesday 29th, I received a phone call from Zoe's husband Jay. He was very upset and told me, in no uncertain terms that Zoe was very ill and that she might not last until the weekend and I should try and fly over immediately! Jackie managed to organise flights for us and also Jodie and baby Jaxon. It was very important for Jodie to show Zoe her nephew Jaxon who she had named. Zoe was planning to get over to the UK to see him, but it was obvious now why she had not travelled as she had been too ill to make the journey.

I am finding it difficult to write this next piece, so I hope you will understand. Jackie managed to find flights for us and a day after she booked them we found ourselves at Heathrow Airport bound for Brisbane. This sounds awful and selfish I know, but the reality that Zoe would not have long to live and we had a 24-hour journey to Australia. We just hoped we could be with her before she passed away.

Zoe had two good friends Jono and Elisha and it was Jono who met us at the airport in Brisbane so that Jay could stay at the Hospital with Zoe. As this whole episode is a bit of a blur, I think we made it to The Gold Coast Private Hospital late Friday 1st April. It was a lovely hospital and the nurses there were very kind and caring. They all seem to know Zoe personally and one nurse in particular had been on Zoe's cancer journey almost from the beginning. Without going into details and not being too graphic, it was a shock which I don't think we were prepared for, seeing our beautiful Zoe laying peacefully in the bed! Most of the time she appeared to be sleeping although every now and then she would briefly open her eyes and on a couple of occasions she was clearly in some discomfort and a nurse had to give her something to ease the pain.

A wonderful moment in all this sadness was when we arrived and took Jaxon in to see Zoe. Jaxon was only about eight months old, but it was very moving to watch him crawl along the bed to Zoe and touch her face and arm at which point Zoe opened her eyes and smiled. This was the first time they had met.

One of their friends who I had met before was Dave but everyone called him Darth (Darth Vader). He had let me use his Jack Daniels acoustic guitar the last time I was over. Darth gave it to Jay to give to me as they thought it would be nice if I played some guitar to Zoe while she was in hospital. Zoe was in a private room and the hospital allowed us to stay with her as long as we wanted to. We stayed virtually all day and took it in turns to be with her a little bit at a time. It was hard leaving her at night because the fear of losing her while we were away. We wanted to be with her as long as we could. So each morning arriving at the hospital to find that she was still here with us gave us hope for another day. Each day, Saturday and the Sunday, the nurses warned us that she might not make it through the day, but she was still fighting in her own way and as each day passed she was still with us.

On the Monday, Zoe was quite peaceful. Once or twice she seemed to sigh or open her eyes slightly. We liked to think that she still knew we were there with her. When I was alone in the room with her, I just assumed although she was not moving that she might be able to hear every word I said, so as daft as this may seem and knowing she had the same sense of humour as me I started telling her jokes. I recollected memories from the past, all the happy times we had together. I sat next to her on the bed and sang her a few songs and it is odd how in this situation the words of a song can become so significant.

Her breathing became quite deep and the nurse who told us that it would not be long now! She was clearly very emotional, more than just a nurse/patient relationship. Nurses and Doctors worldwide are wonderful special people. Jackie, Jodie and I held Zoe's hand and she finally passed away peacefully just after 11pm Brisbane time. Jackie, Jodie and Jay left the room to speak to the nurses on duty. I stayed in the room with Zoe. Even now I didn't want her to be alone! I was surprised, for although this was the saddest moment of my life and although choked up, I didn't actually cry tears as such. I think it was perhaps something of a relief that Zoe was no longer in pain. All the suffering that she had endured for the past nine years or so had finally ceased. I have cried many tears since and writing this piece and reliving that time is difficult and I cannot deny the tears are falling as I write.

I am convinced she knew that she didn't have long to live. She's my daughter, I just know. She had chosen which funeral directors were going to do her funeral and we met them the next day to discuss the arrangements. They were an all women funeral directors called White Ladies, coincidentally based in Ashmore where Zoe lived. They came immediately and helped us with all the arrangements. The funeral was on the following Saturday 9th April. There was a bit of a blue theme to match Zoe's beautiful eyes and also butterflies which were on the white coffin. Strange as it may seem, Zoe did look beautiful as she lay there and this moment which was to be our last together was very tough indeed. Jay gave a moving speech about their life together as did Jackie and Jodie. To be honest, I wanted to say something but I just couldn't do it. The lady from Sassy Survivors, Deb Eccleston, stood up and gave a very moving speech about Zoe and what she did for others even when she was ill herself. This was echoed by several ladies who arrived at the funeral and they were keen to tell me what a wonderful human being Zoe was and how much she helped them in their darkest times.

Many of our family members and friends were unable to attend the funeral in Australia, so Jackie, Jodie and I decided to have memorial day or a celebration of Zoe's life so all the friends and family could come together. This was held in a little village hall in Eversholt, on the borders of Bedfordshire and Buckinghamshire on

Sunday 22nd May. The funeral directors in Australia, White Ladies, had filmed the funeral service and the speeches, so that enabled us to show it on the day everyone was together. All things considered, it was a lovely day. I got to meet up with family members on Jackie's side of the family who I had not seen for some time. Even on a sad occasion there were smiles and laughter which is what Zoe had brought to us. Her smile and laughter will never be forgotten.

Jackie's brother Peter had taken us to Heathrow Airport on our trip out to Australia and picked us up when we arrived back in the UK. We had only been home a few days when we heard the news that Peter had been to Heathrow Airport to collect some clients for a film studio. However, it seems that he must have been feeling unwell and decided to get out of the driver's seat and sit in the back passenger seat while he was waiting for his clients to arrive. We can only assume that he might have had a headache or felt unwell so that is why he was in the back seat of the cab. It transpired he'd had some kind of brain aneurism and was found unconscious. He was taken to hospital but never fully recovered and sadly passed away on Thursday 25th April. None of us could take it in. Like Zoe, he was a happy fun loving person, who always appeared healthy. He didn't smoke and used to go jogging quite regularly. To lose both Zoe and Peter within a couple of weeks of each other was really difficult to comprehend for family and friends alike. The year had not got off to a good start with my sister in law, Audrey, passing away suddenly on December 14th 2015. These were certainly testing times.

It was around this time that I wrote a song titled 'Wicked Man'. I suppose you could say I was feeling sorry for myself, but like a lot of things writing words and music has always been the best way for me to channel my feelings and emotions. The basis of the song is basically that I must have been a wicked man in a former life for so many things seemingly happening to me.

Despite having had various unexplained things happen to me when I was younger, my sensible head never really could believe in what might be known as The Afterlife and I never had any experiences as such not since I was a kid as I wrote in the earlier chapters. There were however some strange and significant things which happened after Zoe passed away.

The night after Zoe died, Jay and I had been sitting up talking and I decided to go to bed and left Jay watching the television. It was a very hot evening. Jay told me the next morning that something very strange happened while he was watching television. He said that the room went very cold and Zoe's two cats jumped up and stood almost frozen still for ages looking from the front room down the hallway towards the bedroom? After a while the cats ran off towards the bedroom and everything in the house felt normal again.

Zoe and Jay's house was divided into two sections, the downstairs area had the garage and a large communal area complete with television, pool table bar area and swimming pool. Upstairs was the large lounge opening up to the kitchen with the hallway leading to three bedrooms. The next day, about late afternoon, Jodie was standing at the kitchen sink and baby Jaxon was sitting on the floor directly behind her. She sensed something behind her and when she turned around, she could see Jaxon sat on the floor facing the doorway into the hallway with his arms outstretched and looking up, as if he was about to be or asking in his own way to be picked up by someone, but there was no-one there!

A few days later Jay decided it would be nice to have a drive out to visit their very good friends Dave and Sunelle. They lived on a lovely small holding. A bungalow with lots of land surrounding it. Jay and I drove up to the gates and I got out of the car to be greeted by Sunelle and we gave each other a big hug. It did feel very emotional. As we stood holding each other, Sunelle must have looked over my shoulder and noticed a white feather which had fallen from the sky. Here we are standing in wide open spaces with not a bird in sight and there was a white feather almost appearing from nowhere. Sunelle bent down picked up the feather and handed it to me and said something like "Here you are Del, it's for you from Zoe".

Another time Jay and I had been sitting up late one evening having a drink a chat about almost everything as we used to do. When something quite odd happened. It was a very still warm peaceful evening. Actually, it was possibly the early hours of the morning as our chats could go into marathon status. Anyway, I think it was Zoe's friends Alesha and Jono who had bought Zoe a large wicker chair which was suspended on a rope or a chain by the pool and was where Zoe often sat to relax particularly when she was unwell. There was no wind around and as we were sitting talking we were aware that the chair had begun to swing back and forth, side to side, very slowly. Once again, something we could not explain.

When I arrived back in the UK, about the first time I set foot outside the house, I was walking along the street, when a white feather came fluttering down in front of me. I looked up and there was not a bird to be seen anywhere.

The following year 2017, I went over to visit Jay in Australia to see how he was getting on. We spent a lot of time talking and really getting to know one another. I wanted to know he was okay because I don't think many people realised how his life had been affected by Zoe's illness. I think the physiological trauma the carer can go through during these times is often overlooked. I learned a lot about him and like all of us he has had his demons and a fair share of life changing events.

One evening, we were sitting out at the table at the bar in his pool area with our friends Darth and Troy. Jay said he'd prepared some food earlier and asked if we would like some? So there we were, all four us sitting around the table, eating and chatting away. I think Zoe had come up in conversation, when all of a sudden, my drink in a chunky glass filled with Jack Daniels ice and coke slid about a foot across the table on its own. Darth, who was sitting opposite me, leapt up off of his bar stool and shouted something like "Jeez, did you just see that?" Well I did of course and I'm glad Darth saw it too. It was unbelievable and we looked at the glass and looked at the table but could not understand how this could have happened. The table was dry, the table was level and the glass was quite heavy! It would have to have been pushed. "Is that you mucking around Zoe?" a voice was heard to ask.

I will tell you just one more story before the men in white coats come to take me away. It was 28th September 2018 and I was about to leave the house to go to Echo Studios in Buckingham where I had recorded my album *White Feather*. I was due to meet Lee Scriven, who was going to do a video shoot to accompany the title track, which I would assume by now you might have some idea what the theme of the song is about.

Annie was about to leave the house before me, when as she opened the front door, she called back to me. "Del, look at this". I went to the front door and she pointed down at the doorstep and lying there quite still was a white feather! Lee had previously said that he wasn't sure if he was going to produce the film in colour or black and white and suggested that I might bring a change of clothes or a white shirt which would be good if any or part of the video happened to be black and white.

Before I left the house, I went to the bedroom and went to a chest of drawers. One drawer (or more) full of predominantly black (tour) t-shirts. A drawer of miscellaneous coloured shirts and a drawer of white ones. Without looking, I opened a drawer and grabbed the first white t-shirt that came to hand. About halfway through the session, Lee suggested the change of clothes would be a good idea now. Up until that point I had been wearing a dark blue shirt with white feathers printed on it. I also decided to wear dad's old hat with the white feather tucked in the hat band. So I took the shirt off and picked up the white t-shirt which I had brought with me. This wasn't just any old t-shirt and the chances of this happening is, well I couldn't think of a statistic, but the t-shirt was not plain white. I had picked up a t-shirt which had a photo of John Lennon wearing a hat with a white feather in it. Not only that, but there was a logo under Lennon's image which read 'Is it real?' A line in White Feather reads 'Is it really real?' The look on everyone's face in the studio when they noticed the t-shirt was quite something!

The guitar which can be seen on the White Feather video has a touching story. It was the 23rd December 2015 and I received a telephone call from my friend Ronnie who owns the music shop and rehearsal studio in Milton Keynes called Rock Hard Music. He was enquiring as to whether I would be popping in to the shop before Christmas. As it turned out he was on my list of people to go and visit that very day. So a couple of hours later I went to see Ronnie. He was a bit mysterious and gestured me into the shop showroom. I must explain his building is divided into a music store and a studio. He told me to pull up a stool and sit in front of a little stage area he has at the back of the shop. I had an amplification endorsement with Carlsbro Amplification. I had been speaking to them about a small combo amplifier and I noticed there was a small Carlsbro amplifier behind me where I was sitting. He had a small camera which he was setting up, so by now I was thinking it must be something to do with Carlsbro and a promotion. "Right" said Ronnie. The camera was now rolling. "I have been asked to give you this letter" said Ronnie. He passed me the envelope and I pulled out a letter, which read:

Dear Dad,
A little birdie told me that there was a something in the shop which you really liked.
Happy Christmas,
Love Zoe

At this point Ronnie handed me a large cardboard box and inside the box was a Telecaster guitar which I had been looking at and had tried out a couple of times before.

This was a very emotional moment. I knew I had some big tears in my eyes and when I looked over at Ronnie, so did he and also my friend and sound engineer Nigel Hart was now standing in front of me looking a bit glassy eyed. I hope they don't mind me mentioning it?

It transpired that Zoe had contacted Ronnie from Australia and said that she wanted to buy me something special for Christmas, so rather than pants and socks, was there something I had particularly liked in the shop?

The more I think about it, the more I am sure that she must have known that she didn't have a lot of time left on this earth and presumably this is why she wanted to give me a special present to remember her by. It's only a guess, but this would be typical Zoe.

# 41.
# Viva España

**A** couple of weeks after I returned from Zoe's funeral in Australia, I decided to spend a bit of time over at my place in Spain. Considering that when I first bought it back in 2001, I bought it not to stay in it much myself but as an investment and as the years have gone by it has become a very special place to retreat to. Annie and I have had many holidays there as have Jodie, Darron and my grandsons Liam and Jaxon, as well as a few friends. Although it has a large rooftop solarium where you can see the sea in the distance, my favourite place is the small balcony which leads out from the lounge. I've spent a lot of time on that balcony just sitting thinking and watching the world go by. The night time is particularly wonderful where the sky is full of diamonds. It's not just me, friends have told me that there is something about just sitting doing not much at all on that balcony.

On this occasion Karl Randall came with me. It was a really nice gesture of him and we had a good relaxing time lots of chat, lots of laughter and a few tears. Just a small statistic here: Karl has been playing drums with me for longer than any other drummer and musician I have played with. We have had this running joke which has been brought onto the stage, because Karl says his mum who sadly passed away some years ago was, shall we say, a free spirit back in the seventies and he is sure she would have seen Stray back then. From that assumption and conjuring up a possible scenario, he now calls me Dad and I call him Son. It's only a joke but there again he is only a month younger than Zoe. On stage I point out to the audience what an uncanny resemblance he has to me! That always gets a laugh that one.

While in Spain, I had been in touch with a friend I had made on Facebook. His name is Dave Wilkinson and he goes under the name of Dave the Hat. It's funny how Dave used to live not far from me in the UK and I know most of the local people he does, although we didn't know each other when he lived in the UK. Furthermore, my bass playing buddy Colin Kempster, played in a band with him! Anyway, Dave knew I was in Spain and he was running an afternoon musicians jam session and invited Karl and I over to get up and play something if we fancied it. Well, I'm not really one for jam sessions but Karl and I hadn't played for a few weeks and after recent events having a bit of a musical blow out was something that perhaps I needed. Sure enough we got up and played a few songs. I think it had been some while since a proper rock drummer like Karl had been around those parts and he found himself playing with a few other musicians that afternoon as well.

Spain has become my second home and I have made many friends there over the years. When I'm not in Spain, my two good friends Caz and Steve, who live opposite my place, keep a watchful eye on the place for me. We have had a lot of laughs together and am embarrassed to say that Steve (without the aid of *Jack Daniels*, would not have been possible) had managed to get me up and sing Karaoke with him! We called our deadly duo The Self-Righteous Brothers. Actually Steve

229

has a powerful voice and can really belt out a tune. Coincidentally, he used to run a pub in the West Midlands and his good friend was the late Mel Galley. He has shared many stories of crazy nights out with their friend, radio and TV presenter Chris Evans.

Another couple we met in Spain were from Manchester called Ged and Mick. When I first went to Spain they lived next door to me. The early days in Spain were particularly funny. Opposite my place is a bar called The Pitch and Pint. These days it is run by a couple, Lisa and Joe, but in the old days it was run by Rob and Dixie. Rob was funny. A typical scenario would be, I would get off of the aeroplane walk into the Pitch and Pint and order my drink and "One for yourself Rob". Every time Rob would reply "It's okay, I'll get these". I would reply, "No you won't" and he would say "No, it's my round". I would have to try and emphasise that I was the customer and he was running a business. Then the other scenario would be that I would be in his bar all night and at the end of the night I would ask for my bill. It was always Ten Euros! My God he could pour a JD and coke!

One time I took Cherry and Tony Rolfe over to Spain. Rob poured them a drink and I watched with amusement as the strength of the drinks made them look as if someone had just removed a bone from their vertebrae! Tony is an old friend of mine and a good guitarist singer/songwriter. He always reminded me of how Francis used to look in the early days of Status Quo (Frantic Four time). In fact, when they arrived at Alicante Airport I had a small banner which read "Welcome Rossi". I think Tony muttered something like "You bastard Bromham". It didn't stop there though. I had already primed a few friends including Rob at The Pitch and Pint so that when Tony was in their vision they all enquired "Er, excuse me... are you that bloke in Status Quo"? or "Excuse me, aren't you Francis Rossi from Status Quo?" I suppose you get the picture now? I don't think I'd ever been called a bastard so many times in my life, but we had a good few days away with Tony and Cherry.

Just a walk away from my place I am lucky enough to have an excellent selection of restaurants within a small centre called La Fuente which opened up. I cannot mention La Fuente without mentioning the bar called Fuegos which is owned by Hazel and her husband Sammy Starr. We have had some good nights in there and unusually I had been known to play Hazel's acoustic guitar once or twice. One night my friend Colin and I were in there with just Hazel and maybe one or two others. I had my head down playing away (as you do) then next minute I looked up and the bar was full of people! That's what you call an impromptu performance. I don't think Colin or I had to pay for a drink that night, to which I think my newly appointed road manager was quite pleased about. Since then, Colin has mentioned on more than one occasion "If you ever need a driver..."

Two people who have become very good friends in Spain and the UK are Pat and Colin. When Annie and I first started going over fairly regularly, on one of the first occasions we had noticed a couple who lived two doors down from me. I think we had only noticed them once or twice, just to pass the time of day as you do with little comments like "Hello... Alright... How are you?" that sort of thing. Then the next time we flew out we took a suitcase full of clothes and odds 'n sods. When we arrived at Luton Airport to check the suitcase in, who should walk up behind us but the couple we'd seen the time before. As we were standing there we introduced ourselves properly and met up later in the day and a few times during our stay in Spain. This was Pat and Colin. That was many years ago and we often meet up socially in Spain and in the UK. In fact, Colin and I have been over to Spain on a couple occasions with the very lame excuse of "we are going to do some painting".

April 2017 Dave The Hat messaged to tell me that if I fancied seeing a good band The Kings of The Blues were playing a venue called The Hens Teeth in Villa Martin Plaza which is not too far away from my place. Annie and I went there had a good meal and watched the band which were very good. I gathered from the on-stage banter and introductions that the band had been put together for a string of Spanish shows, but more about that in a while.

When we were leaving the restaurant I said to Annie that I was sure I knew the fella who was at the mixing desk, but I couldn't place from where I might have known him? A few days later, I noticed advertised on Facebook The Kings of the Blues were playing another venue in the area. I was back in the UK by now, but I put a comment on their posting saying that they were a good band and were a bit like having two guitarists, one like John Mayer and the other like Warren Haynes. My comments must have been appreciated because I got a message from their manager thanking me and would I mind if they used the comment in their publicity? That person was the fella standing at the mixing desk and sure enough I wasn't imagining it. I had met him some years before in the UK. We began to message each other back and forth and his name was Bryn Slack. I had played with Stray at his club in Sheffield, The Boardwalk and he had booked Stray with Mountain at various northern venues via my then agent Don McKay. The young guitarist who I think was seventeen at that time was Austin Slack, Bryn's son. The other guitarist I had recognised from UK gigs was Tom Killner, a young blues guitarist. The line-up was completed by Bobby Nikolov on drums and a bass player with the unusual name of Maiden Ct. He was called that because he was an Iron Maiden fan so I'm lead to believe.

Bryn had been promoting Austin with his band The Streeters. Both Austin and The Streeters had been making a good name for themselves particularly along the Costa Blanca and Murcia Region. As time went on I got to know Bryn and his family including his wife Lisa and daughter Mariella. They had decided to emigrate to Spain some years before when Austin was very young, Mariella had not even been born. They live in a picturesque town called Caravaca de la Cruz. Very Spanish and I think apart from Bryn and his family there is only one other English family in Caravaca.

A couple of times when I went out to Spain, I tried to meet up with them and go to see them play somewhere. I got up and played with them a couple of times and if felt good. Austin now had a really good rhythm section with The Streeters. Bobby Nikolov was still on drums and a new name to me, David Gordon on bass. David had not long been in Spain. Although British, David had spent some time playing in Australia and had played with artistes such as Julian Lennon and Shakira.

Bryn discussed the possibility of me playing a short Spanish tour. Some of my songs, some of Austin's songs and a few cover versions thrown in for good measure. I first went over and played a couple of shows in June 2018, but we went on to play a short tour in the September. These shows were a lot of fun to play and we managed to do a fair bit of sight-seeing. Bryn would make an excellent tour guide if he wanted to make another living. There were a couple of festivals and some good small club gigs. I thought the band sounded really tight considering we only had about two rehearsals. Bobby and Dave did really well, particularly covering a couple of Stray songs which had some tricky arrangements in them. I hadn't played proper rock gigs in Spain since 2003 when I toured with Iron Maiden and Y & T, but I was pleased to find I was not forgotten as there were Stray fans at some of the shows with CDs and albums for me to sign.

The club promoters were all really good to us. I still cannot work out how you can go and play in Spain and along with a fee you also get a meal as well as snacks and drinks in the dressing room and hotel accommodation. Also the roads seem to be much better than the roads in the UK. These days, certainly at club level in the

UK, you are lucky to get a fee that will cover the costs of a show, something in recent times I am very aware of, as is my ever-depleting bank account! Once upon a time you could plan travelling to a show and know how long it would take. These days, you have to allow yourself an extra couple of hours because our British roads are a mess. There are always traffic jams and I have lost count of the amount of times coming home in the early hours of the morning after playing a show, finding that a motorway or a road is closed, so you end up following some crazy diversions.

There was none of that in Spain. There was a lot of driving on the Spanish shows, but the roads were so good, getting to shows seemed no problem at all. In fact, Bryn who happens to be an excellent tour manager had an App on his phone which showed us which towns where we stopped off on, you could by a three-course meal including drinks for Ten Euros per person. Suffice to say, I ate very well in Spain, we were treated well by everybody we met and I had a great time hanging out with Austin, Bobby, David and Bryn. I hope we can do it again sometime.

2018 turned out to be a busy and varied year. I released a live Del Bromham's Blues Devils CD and also my solo *White Feather* was released on Esoteric Records. Also the early Stray albums were released in two compilation sets. So apart from going over to Spain a few times I was literally putting on a different hat for solo shows and Stray shows.

****

In 2014 and 2015 a friend Tony DeLaye had a musical project under the unlikely name of Long John Laundry. He asked if I would be interested in playing a few shows he had lined up. Tony or Long John, sang and played guitar and harmonica along with Jules Fly on bass guitar, Lee Morley on percussion and on drums was Vince Street. I must mention that Vince is the son of the professional wrestler Adrian Street and another coincidence is that Peter Perks was Adrian Street's tag wrestling partner back in the 1970s when wrestling on the UK TV was arguably at its most popular. Peter used to be known as The Blue Devil, which when you think about it, is not far from the name of my other musical project.

I have to mention, Vince's brother, like his father, called Adrian (who uses the surname Stranick) as he is a talented singer guitarist and actor and has a Rockabilly style band called the Silver Brazilians. I think of mum many years ago when the television would be on and commentator Kent Walton would present Professional Wrestling on ITV on a Saturday afternoon. Mum would be glued to the wrestling and it was almost impossible trying to have a conversation with her, for although she would insist she wasn't really interested in it, her face and her physical gyrations' did imply quite the contrary. I bet mum would have loved going to a wrestling match but she would never admit to liking or approving of it.

Back to Long John Laundry whose brand of music he called "Dirty Blues" and dirty it was. This was as raw as it gets. I admit it took me a little while to adjust, because on the face of it, it seemed very basic. Well maybe it was, but sometimes the simpler it sounds, the harder it can be to get right. The rehearsals were loud and loose and I wondered how this would go in a live gig situation. You need to play live in front of an audience to find out and sure enough after the first gig, I felt that I got it and understood what the band was about and what my part was to play. Tony just let fly and let me do what I wanted to do guitar wise with the songs. There was room for improvisation and I really enjoyed the freedom as I was more used to playing songs which were structured and I only had certain places and times to play. We played quite a few gigs in the UK and a couple of short tours of the Czech

Republic. We recorded a live set *Long John Laundry – Live in London*. We didn't set out to record a live album, but the house engineer, Vasilis Chatzis recorded the set and did a great job capturing the raw vitality of it.

While we were in the Czech Republic we played a few shows with a well-known band called Sunflower Caravan. They were a three-piece band, Andy, singer who played piano, with Michel on bass and Vit drums. Musically very different to Long John, but together it made a great show. I got on well with them and at one gig they invited me up to play guitar on a couple of songs. When Andy the singer got up, I jumped on and played his piano as well. I had watched them on the shows we played together so I became familiar with their music. Andy and his lady friend Mata invited me back to their apartment in Prague where we sat around talking for hours. Czech Republic and its people are lovely and I particularly like Prague.

Another friend who I have worked with a few times over the years is bass guitarist and promoter Derek White. His field is mainly with the Blues market. He had been playing with guitarist Larry Miller who I had also known for some years. Larry suffered a stroke and was unable to perform so Derek decided to put together a benefit concert on 15th January 2016, featuring various artistes such as Ollie Brown and Bernie Marsden to raise some money to help Larry and his family. The show was sold out and was great fun and was heart-warming to see so many fans and musicians getting together to help Larry.

On a personal level I was disappointed with my performance and to be honest I rarely feel nervous playing a show, but maybe it was because it wasn't for me but for Larry that it put extra responsibility on me which I never expected. I am sure Derek White must have felt the same. At this time Larry is slowly getting better and we are all hoping that before too long he will be back on stage again.

Later in 2017, Derek contacted me again and asked if I would be interested in playing some shows with blues singer/guitarist called Big Gilson who lived in Brazil. I was to be part of the band with Derek on bass and Chris Sharley on drums. We all met up at Derek's house and this meeting was almost a rehearsal but more sitting around the house suggesting songs and the keys they were to be in. I was going to open each show with an acoustic set and then join Gilson and the band for the rest of the show. The first show was on 15th November at The Musician in Leicester and it went really well. We all travelled in my tour bus and we had a good time throughout the couple of weeks. Chris and I found we had the same sense of humour and I felt like I'd known him for years. Gilson too had a great sense of humour and picked up on our English humour pretty quickly for someone with Polish parentage living in Rio De Janeiro.

I recently wrote two songs with Gilson which are to be featured on his new album. The songs are titled 'Winner' and 'Peace In Our Time'.

This was a busy time, apart from touring with Big Gilson there was *White Feather* and Blues Devils and Stray shows. "No peace for the wicked" as my old mum used to say.

# 42.
# Japan, Robbie, Blue Coupe

It was May 2012 and I received an email out of the blue from someone called Ken Matsunami of Captain Trip Records in Japan. He offered a good deal to play some shows and make a live album in Japan. Initially I was suspicious of such a good deal, suddenly appearing from someone I didn't know, but I followed it up and got into a conversation about the possibilities of doing it. It was mentioned that the band Leaf Hound had recently done the same deal in Japan and as luck would have it I knew the singer Pete French and coincidentally we were due to play some shows together in the UK. Pete is a great singer and front man and has been in the business a long time working with bands such as Cactus and Atomic Rooster, so I figured he would not do something like this if it was not legitimate or worthwhile. I spoke to Pete about the offer and he said that his experience with Captain Trip Records and Japan was very good and well worth doing. That was good enough for me, so I got back to Ken in Japan and set the wheels in motion as they say.

To my surprise Stu Uren didn't want to go to Japan, in fact I hadn't notice he didn't appear to be so keen on playing as he had done before. I respected his decision because if you have your own reasons for doing or not doing something then so be it. Who am I to question ones' reasons? The year went on and by November the Japanese deal was done, but with Stu not being available, who could I ask to play bass?

Robbie Stewart-Mathews who had been playing bass for Cherry Lee Mewis and who had sung and played harmonica on *Nine Yards* sprang to mind. The Stray songs were very different to what he had been used to playing, but I remember from Alibi he was very adaptable and versatile, so I spoke to him about it.

Robbie's answer was yes, so I set about putting a set together which was the first time I had done that in many years as Stu and I had played together for such a long time, Stray up until then had not really had a set list. If I fancied playing a song, I would introduce it and Stu and Karl on drums would just be able to play it. They knew me so well. So putting a set together from a selection of so many songs was quite difficult, but it had to be done.

I got together with Robbie at home and then we went into the rehearsal studio to tighten everything up. As it transpired it was not just some dates in Japan which were now on for February 2013 there were a few other shows as well in the UK. Having a couple of rehearsals and good shows to warm up for the Japanese trip was ideal. The first show with Robbie was at Hessle Town Hall, near Hull with Blue Coupe which featured Dennis Dunaway from Alice Cooper and Joe Beauchamp from Blue Öyster Cult. That was on Friday 25th January and the following week we flew over to the Jersey Opera House to play another show with them. In between on the 26th January we played at the Rock and Blues Festival at Butlins Skegness, so we had some good venues and audiences to play in front of before the Japan trip.

I have remembered something about Robbie, we do have the same sense of humour. He and I are similar in that respect to how Steve Gadd and I behaved or rather misbehaved! When we played the first show with Blue Coupe, once the sound checks were finished, we were all served a meal. We had only known our American friends for a couple of hours, when Robbie and I got the giggles which got worse when the waitress walked towards the table and said in a loud voice "Two soups". Well that was it for Rob and me, the visions of Julie Walters in the famous waitress sketch floored us. I'm sure our tears of laughter must have watered down the two soups we had ordered. Our new friends from the USA must have thought we were on some kind of strange acid trip!

We arrived in Tokyo on Wednesday 20th February. The first two shows were at Club Fever and I have to admit on the drive to the venue I was beginning to think how embarrassing it would be to have come this far and play to hardly anyone. There had been times back in the 1970s when I thought Stray would play in Japan but for one reason or another it never happened.

We arrived at the venue around 4;30pm to sound check our equipment which had been provided by Captain Trip Records. To my complete surprise there were already fans waiting outside the venue holding carrier bags with CDs and vinyl for us to sign. Ken Matsunami along with his two assistants Rie Miyazaki and Kyoko Hyashi from Co Co International were with us coordinating the trip. The shows here in Japan are staged early, normally open for 7pm and finish by 10pm. We were due on stage at approximately 8pm and the show was to be recorded. I was really apprehensive as to how the show would go. Ken introduced us on stage and as we walked on there was a tremendous roar and applause. The place was packed, it was like playing The Marquee in London and just as hot I should mention. What was different about this show though was as it was so early and a weekday, most of the fans had come straight from their place of work, so they all looked very smart, in suits!

The other thing that really surprised me was that they appeared to know the words of my songs. Most of my songs do have choruses in and you could hear them along with the racket we were making from the stage. I did have to smile while we were playing the song 'I Believe It' and I looked around at Karl and Robbie to see if they could hear the audience singing the chorus which was coming over as 'I berieve it!" We played the following night also only this time being a Saturday, the audience were dressed casually. They went crazy and they certainly know how to enjoy themselves. We noticed there was a small platform to the left of the stage in the audience area and wondered if they were going to put a support band on a smaller stage. We discovered later that this was a seated area for the local dignitaries, important people and Captain Trip Records financial backers. We were introduced to the big boss man, actually he wasn't that big but you could tell he was someone of great importance by the way everyone reacted to his presence. The Japanese are a very respectful people, that is one thing that in all their walks of life is very apparent.

This show was as good as the night before and like the night before we didn't or rather could not get out of the venue until after midnight as there were so many fans who wanted autographs and photographs taken. We managed to get in some sightseeing and was totally fascinated by their culture, their ancient buildings and wait for it, their underground train system. Like everything else in Japan, the stations, platforms and trains were immaculately clean. It was like we had just got onto a brand-new train. I asked Ken if he had ever been on an underground train in the UK. I told him that ours looked filthy by comparison. One could quite literally eat your dinner off of the floor of one of the Japanese trains, not that I would try it! To be honest I wasn't a big fan of Japanese food and when we were waiting to board the plane for our flight home it would appear that all three of us must have got food poisoning from the night before. I spent a bit of time in the airport toilets doing the technicolour yawn! Oh it was a dodgy trip home!

It was a couple of months after we returned home that I received the files of the recordings from Ken in Japan. They needed mixing but I cannot explain the technicalities of it, but they had been recorded in such a way that you needed a specific pack on the PC. to decipher the instrumentation to mix. I had got to know a guy called Chris Surgenor who lived in Bedford and had a small studio who fortunately had what was needed to remix the album.

It was now May so Karl and I worked with Chris and it took some days to finally be able to get to a point in order to mix the album for release. Chris worked hard and did a great job. I sent the mixed album to Ken who loved it and I managed to get a release in the UK from Angel Air Records, the results of which can be heard on *Live in Japan*.

# 43.
# The Reunion

The Borderline Club in London was a great place to play. Unfortunately, it closed on 31st August 2019, but fortunately I played there several years running both as a solo artist and with Stray. Some years before I wanted to get Stray to play there but the response I got from a couple of agents was that it was hard enough to get a good audience there and Stray wouldn't pull enough people in to make it viable. One agent in particular inferred that we were probably past our sell by date. I wasn't having that so I contacted the venue direct and I am pleased to say it sold out on the night. We played another show in 2015 and I invited Pearl Handled Revolver to open for us. By this time the promoter Jim Driver was organising the bookings for The Borderline. In my opinion he is one of the good guys in the business and we always got on well and have done many shows for him over the years.

We had another show booked for 2016 and I wanted it to be an evening of Stray music as we had so many songs to choose from. The previous year's attendances at the club showed there were fans who appeared to know all of the songs (probably some of them better than I did). By this time Stu Uren was back and when the show was first booked in, I phoned Stu, to talk about the show and I mentioned that it was fifty years since Stray was formed while we were kids in school. Stu said something like "It would be great if you could get the original line-up back together again to play". I said that I thought that there would be little chance of that, purely from the geography alone. I was up in Buckinghamshire, Steve in London, Gary in Scotland and Ritchie was travelling around Europe and we hadn't actually played together for about twenty-four years and the last get together was not the happiest of experiences.

Anyway the more I thought about it, the more I thought it might be worth trying to contact all the guys. Recently a couple of old videos of the band had appeared on YouTube, one in particular of us playing Lennon's 'Cold Turkey'. It appeared to bring up a lot of nostalgic comments from fans of the band.

I began making phone calls, a yes from Steve, a yes from Gary and a yes from Ritchie! Unbelievable, maybe it was meant to be this time. Ritchie said that the worst-case scenario was that wherever he was in the world he would get a flight back to the UK to play the show.

Various phone calls took place and we decided on about five songs and also the version of 'Cold Turkey' that had resurfaced. The day of the show arrived. It was Friday 18th November 2016 and all band members and crew began to arrive around 4pm. We had family members and a few guests with us while the equipment was being set up ready for the sound checks.

There were people milling around outside the venue already hours before the show. You could sense that there was a buzz in the air and a certain amount of anticipation for what was to come. This may sound unbelievable and slightly absurd, but the original line up, Steve, Gary, Ritchie and myself had not had the opportunity to rehearse for one reason or another and to be honest I don't think it occurred to any of us that it could mean impending disaster. Not only had we not played together for over two decades but Ritchie in particular had not touched the drums for almost the same length of time. So our rehearsal was our sound check in the afternoon which went astonishingly well.

The journalist Mark Taylor recorded an interview with us earlier in the evening and that is still available to see on YouTube. I left the interview shortly before it ended as I had to get ready to go on stage at 7:45pm. I played a couple of solo songs and then Stu, Karl Randall and Peter Dyer joined me on stage and throughout the evening we played a selection of Stray songs recorded over the years. The place was packed and hot. The atmosphere electric!

Then it was time to introduce Gary, Ritchie and Steve, but before I made the introductions I said a few words of thanks to the audience, some of who had travelled many miles to be there. Not only the UK but France, Germany, Italy, Canada and the USA. It also gave me the opportunity to mention that there were those in the music business who said we would never get enough people in the venue to do the show. The show actually sold out three months in advance!

Considering we had not played for so many years and had no rehearsals, I guess that magic intuition between us going back to when we were kids at school came back. Just like riding a bike. We remembered the songs and remembered the endings of the songs. It was a great night to remember.

The following year, Friday 20th October to be exact, Stray were due to play The Borderline Club again. It had become an annual event. To my surprise the originals Steve, Gary and Ritchie wanted to appear again only this time with a rehearsal at least. I had phoned all three of them and I timed it to take exactly ten minutes to get a "yes, we will do it again" out of them. I suggested that on this performance we should bring in Simon Rinaldo who had been playing with me in The Blues Devils. My thought was that we could play some of the songs that we had strings and brass and keys on which were on record but not live. So we played 'Dearest Eloise' and 'Around The World In Eighty Days', neither had we played before live on stage. If my memory serves me correctly we also played 'Come On Over', 'The Gambler', 'Pretty Thing', 'After The Storm', 'Our Song' and of course the finale 'All In Your Mind'.

It was another great night and just like before it was sold out, in fact unofficially I was told by a member of The Borderline staff, they let more than the house limit. Apparently the feeling was if they did let all these extra people in there may have been trouble! I was told we broke the house record. Not bad for a band who had supposedly passed its sell by date. If that was the last show for the original line-up, then it wasn't a bad one to go out on.

# 44.
# Finally 2022

**N**ever having written anything like this before, it was difficult to know exactly when to stop writing. Should I put it off for another day, another week, another month? I know I would think of many more things which had happened in the past. So I have decided to draw a line in the sand and consider it complete (well for the time being anyway). I make no apologies for it not being in chronological order. Like my writing, my life has been quite varied, so far.

Right now it looks like there is a light at the end of the tunnel regarding getting back to a near normal way of life once more. Paul Newcomb at Monstrous Child Management and myself are looking at booking shows both for Stray and me as a solo artist. The new Stray album looks like it may be titled *Survivor* which we started at the beginning of the lockdown is now finished.

Due to the Covid pandemic which began in 2020, it has been two years since our last tour but the current Stray line up of Pete Dyer, Karl Randall, Simon Rinaldo, Colin Kempster and me are really looking forward to performing again.

Following the 2019 performances *Burretti 'The Man Who Sewed The World* show, Lee decided he wanted to make a film of the show, which is what we did early this year, 2022, resulting in the film being premiered at Cineworld, Milton Keynes on the 16th October.

Another friend John Verity is a great singer/guitarist, who has some great stories and should write a book. He and I have been asked by Peter Barton of RAM (Rock Artist Management), to put a project together featuring songs by other artists who were around when we first began touring. So it's been a lot of fun just belting out some old favourites of ours which we don't often get the opportunity to play. So look out for The Verity Bromham Band.

Annie and I moved into a new home in 2020 in a lovely village in Northamptonshire. The house needed quite a bit doing to it, so at least that has kept me busy, which might have been tricky if I had been out on the road with the band.

As for the future, who knows? But a few years ago I was being interviewed by journalist Dave Ling. As the interview finished Dave said to me, "Del, I hope you don't mind me saying, but you appear to be in good condition for a gentleman of your years. I've seen younger guys with less energy than you on stage. Do you think you will ever retire?"

My reply: "Dave, I'll be the B.B. King of Buckinghamshire". I was living in Buckinghamshire at the time and B.B. died at the age of 89.

"Ha ha" laughed Dave. "Can I quote you?"

"Yes Dave of course".

THE END... Or is it?